Entrepreneurship Development

Abhishek Nirjar

Indian Institute of Management-Lucknow (IIM-L)
Noida Campus

CBS

CBS Publishers & Distributors Pvt Ltd

New Delhi • Bengaluru • Chennai • Kochi • Mumbai • Pune
Hyderabad • Kolkata • Nagpur • Patna • Vijayawada

**Entrepreneurship
Development**

ISBN: 978-81-239-2461-8

Copyright © Author and Publisher

CBS Reprint   2014
First Edition   2011

Published by Satish Kumar Jain for
CBS Publishers & Distributors Pvt Ltd
4819/XI Prahlad Street, 24 Ansari Road, Daryaganj, New Delhi 110 002, India.

Ph: 23289259, 23266861, 23266867   Fax: 011-23243014   Website: www.cbspd.com
e-mail: delhi@cbspd.com; cbspubs@airtelmail.in.
Corporate Office: 204 FIE, Industrial Area, Patparganj, Delhi 110 092
Ph: 4934 4934   Fax: 4934 4935   e-mail: publishing@cbspd.com; publicity@cbspd.com

Branches

- **Bengaluru:** Seema House 2975, 17th Cross, K.R. Road,
  Banasankari 2nd Stage, Bengaluru 560 070, Karnataka
  Ph: +91-80-26771678/79   Fax: +91-80-26771680   e-mail: bangalore@cbspd.com
- **Chennai:** 20, West Park Road, Shenoy Nagar, Chennai 600 030, Tamil Nadu
  Ph: +91-44-26260666. 26208620   Fax: +91-44-42032115   e-mail: chennai@cbspd.com
- **Kochi:** 36/14 Kalluvilakam, Lissie Hospital Road, Kochi 682 018, Kerala
  Ph: +91-484-4059061-65   Fax: +91-484-4059065   e-mail: kochi@cbspd.com
- **Mumbai:** 83-C, Dr E Moses Road, Worli, Mumbai-400018, Maharashtra
  Ph: +91-22-24902340/41   Fax: +91-22-24902342   e-mail: mumbai@cbspd.com
- **Pune:** Bhuruk Prestige, Sr. No. 52/12/2+1+3/2 Narhe, Haveli
  (Near Katraj-Dehu Road Bypass), Pune 411 041, Maharashtra
  Ph: +91-20-64704058. 64704059. 32392277 Fax: +91-20-24300160   e-mail: pune@cbspd.com

Representatives

- **Hyderabad**   0-9885175004   • **Kolkata**   0-9831437309, 0-9051152362
- **Nagpur**   0-9021734563   • **Patna**   0-9334159340   • **Vijayawada** 0-9000660880

Printed at Swastik Packagings 506, FIE, Industrial Area, Patparganj, Delhi 110 092

Preface

Entrepreneurship thrives on change. The economies world over are benefiting from the emergence of a new class of people who started from small outfits and have been able to build large organisations serving different needs of the consumer. Entrepreneurs profit by fostering and commercialising innovation and by seeking and pursuing competitive advantages. This book will help the readers understand the fundamentals of the relationship between Innovation and Entrepreneurship and to understand the practical issues related to the creation, assessment, development, and operation of new and emerging ventures. Integration of learning's from various functional and integration courses would be utilised for understanding the nuances of starting a new business venture. Entrepreneurship is not just another activity. It requires a lot of sustained effort from the individual/s involved. The current situation in India is such that more and more people desire to start a venture of their own. This is certainly going to be fruitful to the nation in many respects. The government sector has limited options for jobs. The opportunities are more in the corporate sector wherein the quantum is not so large although fields like Information technology, e-commerce and biotechnology are providing a large chunk of opportunity. The larger issue is that if all aspire for jobs where the job- providers would come from. This book is aimed at helping those who intend to do something of their own and become job-providers. The book will help the reader identify personal goals, values, and entrepreneurial competencies, learn to identify business opportunities consistent with personal profile and prepare a dependable and defensible business plan. The book has been structured so that with an easy read one can get hold of the various activities that one has to handle in order to start and manage a venture of his own.

Author

Contents

UNIT - V : Family and Non-Family Entrepreneurs

UNIT - VI : Venture Capital

Unit I
Entrepreneurship, Classification and Development

Chapter 1
The Entrepreneur

Introduction

Since times immemorial, the world of business has witnessed some people who stood apart and chose a specific path with a strong desire to provide the products and services that people needed. From the times of barter trade to the present times of internet, there have been people who embarked on fulfilling needs, wants and desires of people as a means of doing business and in return being paid for those in different ways. These were not the people who were born to do so but they made a conscious choice over a period of time. By fulfilling some deficiency in the lives of the common man, they were making small, conscious and incremental improvements in the lives of people. Such persons who decided and chose to 'undertake' opportunities and provide goods and services to people by creating an entity for the purpose are those who are known as **entrepreneurs.**

1.1 Meaning

The word 'entrepreneur' dates back to the 13th century French verb 'entreprendre', meaning 'to do something' or 'to undertake'. By 16th century, the word 'entrepreneur' had come to be referred to someone who undertook a business venture. The first academic usage of the term was by economist Richard Cantillon in the year 1730. For Cantillon, the bearing of risk— engaging in a business without an assurance of the profits that will be derived out of it— is the distinguishing feature of an entrepreneur.

The term 'entrepreneur' was further popularized by economist Jean Baptiste Say, who in the early 1800s, used the term to refer to individuals who create value in the economy by moving resources out of areas of low productivity and into the areas of higher productivity and greater yield. In 1848, economist John Stuart Mill used the term in his very popular book, **Principles of Political Economy.** To Mill, the distinguishing feature of entrepreneurs was that they assume both the risk and the management of a business.

Schumpeter defined an entrepreneur as the person who destroys the existing economic order by introducing new products and services, by creating new forms of organisation or by exploiting new raw materials. Such a person is most likely to accomplish this destruction by founding a new business but may also do it within an existing organisation. Some have used a broader definition to the one given by Schumpeter and seems more complete: An entrepreneur is someone *who perceives an opportunity and creates an organisation to pursue it.*

There are different ways in which we can look at entrepreneurs. There are those who find an idea that they want to pursue and proceed to launch their venture. There are those also who decide that they want to set up their own venture and then embark on looking for an opportunity. There is a further category of people for whom entrepreneurship becomes the only possibility. Many people in India who fail to get employment for one reason or the other land up looking at starting their own venture. It seems like a survival necessity so that it can feed them and their family while at the same time creating jobs for others as well. In India, there are specific states and communities that have demonstrated far more entrepreneurial initiative than the others. Of late with the way things have changed with globalisation and liberalisation of policies by the government, there is a lot more entrepreneurial activity emerging from all parts of the country. This is an interesting trend as it will significantly contribute to the growing economy.

1.2 Four Ps of Entrepreneurship

Economists Ma and Tan (2005) recommend that entrepreneurship comprises the following four Ps:

- **Pioneer:** innovator or champion for innovation
- **Perspective:** the entrepreneurial mindset
- **Practice:** the entrepreneurial activities
- **Performance:** the outcome of entrepreneurial actions and activities

Further to this, they state that *entrepreneurship is a particular type of mindset, a unique way of looking at the world, a creative kind of adventure, and the ultimate instrument toward self-realization and fulfillment. At the heart of entrepreneurship lies the desire to achieve, the passion to create, the yearning for freedom, the drive for independence, and the embodiment of entrepreneurial visions and dreams through tireless hard work, calculated risk-taking, continuous innovation, and undying perseverance. People who dare such dreams and commit their spirit, soul, and entire life's work to realize their dreams are the privileged bunch that we call entrepreneurs.*

1.3 Essential Qualities of a Successful Entrepreneur

There are a number of characteristics that must be possessed to become a successful entrepreneur. An entrepreneur is a confident person. *Confidence* develops an edge over the competitors. Confidence is always impressive and wins others. Entrepreneurial personality demands a high level of confidence. This confidence has to be the confidence in oneself. This would be reflected in the appearance, body language, communication, work style and relationships. This will translate into a better organised, systematic effort that one would demonstrate in his/her entrepreneurial journey.

Perception plays an important role in everybody's life. Perception has a make or break capacity. The making is associated with positive perception. The breaking is associated with negative perception. Perception is to understand, interpret, draw inferences and form an opinion. Usually, an individual is guided by his/her set of perceptions which are comprised of the knowledge, deep-rooted impressions and pieces of information which one acquires over the years. An entrepreneur cannot achieve a desired goal with a set perception. One has to develop one's perception about people, consumers, events, objects, relationships, etc. There are a lot of products which are the outcome of the strong developed perceptions of the entrepreneurs. Mobile phones, CDs, etc. are products that are the outcome of perceptions about the fast changing technology. An entrepreneur can think of new products, new raw materials, new designs, new packaging, new uses and applications with a developed perception. Developing a perception means to collect more details to analyse all relevant facts and to draw impractical inferences. A developed perception is always objective, impartial, positive and prompt. To become a successful entrepreneur, one will have to work towards developing his/her perception about things around him/her.

In a business, no other factor of production, except the entrepreneur, bears risk. When the behavioural pattern of a large number of people is considered, some people are identified as zero risk-takers. They do not take any risk and are afraid to accept any challenges. They select easily attainable goals. Some people are hundred percent risk takers. They are excited by the challenges and risks involved. They are neither bothered about the method used nor about the attainment of goals. They get charged up only by the risk. An entrepreneur is not a zero risk taker. He/she is, at the same time, not a cent-percent risk taker. He/she assumes a *calculated quantity of risk* by consciously assessing the risk that is there and acting upon it.

Team building capacity is a key entrepreneurial success element. An entrepreneur requires a variety of skills and services and help from a large number of people and organisations, such as suppliers of raw material, machinery, workers, utilities, such as power, fuel, water, etc. Therefore, an entrepreneur has to demonstrate an excellent ability in building a team. On a more specific note, the success or failure of a venture is largely dependent on the level of cohesiveness, competence complementarities and team spirit that they demonstrate. The responsibility of developing these three dimensions to a high intensity level rests with the founder/founding team. At the same time, the issue of roles, responsibilities to be handled by different people is dependent on how the founder addresses these concerns. Multiple tasks are to be handled by people while in an entrepreneurial set-up. Some of the things that an entrepreneur can engage in to develop a good team can be

- adopt a positive attitude that you are an excellent team builder
- know each and every member (including their strengths and weaknesses)
- arrange for opportunities for people to meet and interact and know each other
- define the goals to be achieved by each team
- explain the team goals to each and member of the team
- decide the time frame for the goals to be achieved
- assign the role, specific responsibilities and duties of each member of the team
- mobilise and allocate resources
- announce incentives for teams to complete task
- appreciate team members for success that they achieve
- tolerate failure with a constructive outlook and try to guide them towards solutions to the problems
- anticipate obstacles
- monitor progress and feedback

The other important quality that an entrepreneur must have or will have to learn it the hard way is the *consciousness about time*. Time management contributes to achievement planning. Many a times, it is said that one who does not keep track of time is bound to lose in the long run. An appreciation that activities that are performed at a specific time are going to provide more benefit to the venture as compared to if it is executed at some other time. Any delays in performing mission critical activities can lead to either the venture not doing well or totally failing in achieving its objectives. Some of the practices that one can adopt in order to effectively manage time are given in the following:

- Make a list of activities to be performed. Objectivity of task is essential for time planning.
- Understand the importance and purpose of the time planning for the activities being listed.
- This should not include routine, recurring activities that one has to perform.
- Keep provision for adjustments that you may have to make.

- Implement your activities as per the time plan.

- At the end of the day, check whether you have adhered to your time plan and to what extent.

In all spheres of life, on-time performance is the key to success. Same is the case with an entrepreneur and his/her role as an initiator of a new venture.

The significance of fostering *relationships and networks* is another key quality that an entrepreneur should possess. It has been seen that at all levels of the start-ups journey, the role played by both business people and the social relations that one has goes a long way in ensuring success. How does this happen is that in a situation of scarcity of resources when an entrepreneur embarks on starting his/her venture, he/she is able to build the initial momentum to the venture through his/her social and business networks that he/she has and who reciprocate what he/she may have done for them at some point in time. The next thing that one needs to clarify it shows an entrepreneur is different from a manager.

1.4 Entrepreneurs and Managers

If we compare the role of a manager with that of an entrepreneur, there are some very clear differences that exist between them. At the same time, the one major similarity is that they both need to plan, organise and control their activities. The terms, entrepreneur and manager, are considered one and the same. But the two terms have different meanings too (see Table 1.1). The following are some of the differences between a manager and an entrepreneur.

- The main reason for an entrepreneur to start a business enterprise is because he/she comprehends the venture for his/her individual satisfaction and has personal stake in it whereas a manager provides his/her services in an enterprise established by someone.

- An entrepreneur and a manager differ in their standing— an entrepreneur is the owner of the organisation and he/she bears all the risk and uncertainties involved in running an organisation whereas a manager is an employee and does not assume risk to the level that an entrepreneur does.

- An entrepreneur and a manager differ in their objectives. Entrepreneur's objective is to innovate and create and he/she acts as a change agent whereas a manager's objective is to supervise and create routines. He/she implements the entrepreneur's plans and ideas.

Table 1.1 Differences of Settings for Managers and Entrepreneurs

Dimension	Entrepreneur's Unit	Organisational Unit
Objectives	Survival, maximise profits	Growth, maximise market share
Management	Owner-led, group of founders/ partners	Professional
Ownership	Concentrated with single individual/small groups of persons	Widely dispersed through shareholdings
Organisation	Synonymous with the owner/group of owners	A business entity with an institutional character

- An entrepreneur is faced with more income uncertainties as his/her income is dependent on the performance of the firm whereas a manager's compensation is less dependent on the performance of the organisation.

- An entrepreneur is not induced to involve in fraudulent behaviour whereas a manager does. A manager may cheat by not working hard because his/her income is not tied up to the performance of the organisation.

- An entrepreneur is required to have certain qualifications and qualities, such as high accomplishment motive, innovative thinking, forethought, risk-bearing ability, etc. Conversely, it is mandatory for a manager to be educated in the fields of management theories and practices.

- An entrepreneur deals with faults and failures as a part of learning experience whereas a manager makes every effort to avoid mistakes and he/she postpones failure.

- "An entrepreneur could be a manager but a manager cannot be an entrepreneur". An entrepreneur is intensely dedicated to develop business through constant innovation. He/she may employ a manager in order to perform some of his/her functions, such as setting objectives, policies, rules, etc. A manager cannot replace an entrepreneur in spite of performing the allotted duties because a manager has to work as per the guidelines laid down by the entrepreneur.

- On the downside, a typical manager brings professionalism into the working of an organisation. They bring fresh perspectives, ideas and approach to troubleshooting which can be invaluable.

- Lately, there has been convergence of the entrepreneur and the manager in certain sectors, such as software. An employee is being given highly valuable stock options, which make a typical 'manager' a part owner.

If we look at the units where the two operate and try to differentiate on the basis of objectives, management, ownership and organisation, we can get a comparison as shown in Table 1.2. So this shows that the settings are different in which the entrepreneur and the managers operate. Based on the same matter, if we now compare what are the demands of tasks/activities in which an entrepreneur and a manager are engaged based on the goals, time frame of tasks and the arena, we get Table 1.2.

Table 1.2 Task Demands for Entrepreneurship and Managership

Task Demands	Entrepreneurship	Managership
Major Goals	Profits	Efficiency
Time Frame	Short and long run	Short run
Arena	Enterprises and Markets	Enterprises

Table 1.2 tells us that the time frame of an entrepreneur is both short and long run which signifies that he/she is more focussed on the strategic side than the operational side of the activities as it is evident for managers.

1.5 Entrepreneurship as an Event

Based on an interesting work on personal dispositions of entrepreneurs and managers suggested by Gopakumar, Balakrishna and Kanungo (1998), entrepreneurship has been defined as an event that occurs when the five dispositions mentioned in the following converge at high intensity.

(a) Personal resourcefulness: Belief in one's own capability for initiating action towards creation and growth of enterprises

(b) Achievement orientation: A set of cognitive and behavioural tendencies those are oriented towards ensuring that outcomes, such as enterprise creation, survival, growth are realised

(c) Strategic vision: Future-oriented goal setting based on environmental analysis for determining the content of enterprise creation

(d) Opportunity seeking: One's ability to see unmet needs, identifying markets or gaps for which product concepts are to be evolved.

(e) Innovativeness: Creation of new products, markets, product–market combinations, method of production with an aim to gain competitive advantage

From this work, we also get to see that the managers are usually low on visioning. This is further substantiated by Table 1.3 wherein the time frame is said to be short. Further, the major differentiator seems to emerge from innovativeness and visioning in favour of the entrepreneur.

Table1.3 Personal dispositions of Entrepreneurs and Managers

Personal Dispositions	Entrepreneurship	Managership
Resourcefulness	High	High
Achievement Orientation	High	High
Visioning	High	Low
Opportunity seeking	High	Medium
Innovativeness	High	Low

The manager, since is more concerned with the routine task assigned to him/her and are to be completed in a specific duration, is low on innovativeness. While at the same time, the entrepreneurs' success or failure is based on the level of innovativeness he/she brings in to the activities and outcome of the venture. All entrepreneurs are managers but not all managers are entrepreneurs. It would require a significant effort for a manager to work as an entrepreneur. This transition is easier when one moves out of an established organisations setting as he is freed of the task that he has been doing with a short-run time frame and low level of novelty involved in it. There are a number of factors that impact the choice of people to become entrepreneurs. These factors can be both internal to the individual in terms of locus of control and at the same time there may be factors in the external environment that can impact the decision to become entrepreneurs. These factors are presented in the next subsection.

1.6 Internal and External Factors

When it comes to people who turn to becoming entrepreneurs, it is hard to single out one reason that takes them in that direction. It is more often a build-up with factors that are both under his/her control as well as those that are not under his/her control. The internal factors are more to do with two dimensions— his/her circumstances in terms of job, how comfortable he/she is on the job, family size, whether he/she is the eldest in the family or the youngest, etc. The other dimension is more personal to the individual and is concerned with his/her aspirations about what he/she wants to do in life. A number of researchers have looked at this subject and have found that there are different ways to explain this phenomenon of people becoming entrepreneurs.

There are various situations in which his/her individual aspirations may dominate. Such situations can be wherein he/she is able to identify an opportunity and is desirous of pursuing it. The other can be wherein the individual has time and again demonstrated certain attributes of behaviour, such as risk taking, tolerance to ambiguity, ability to get things done and a desire to look at newness in whatever he/she does. Such individuals are likely to become entrepreneurs some day. The other possibility is that the individual may in possession of a specific skill set which can become the basis of a new venture. At the same time, it has been seen that the fact that the individual has a fall-back option in terms of a family/spouse who can support him/her in case he/she needs bread and better in the times that he/she is struggling to start, grow and build his/her venture can go a long way in his/her ability to do a new venture. There are, however, examples of the other type, where individuals did not have a fall-back up option and because of that were in a somewhat do or die situation and succeeded. On the whole, it is advisable that those who have a fall-back option or support or the family should be able to do well.

While looking at the individual and related factors that lead to entrepreneurial actions, it is also imperative to understand that it is important to look at external factors also that can be a cause of entrepreneurial actions. Government policies at times have led to an increase in entrepreneurial activity. This is when there is a substantial support offered to entrepreneurs in terms of starting a business and doing business. There are states in India which have tried to create an environment conducive to starting new businesses.

There are situations where due to certain environmental changes- political changes that have displaced people from their original place or tasks have led people to start their own ventures. Similar situations have arisen across the world when people got displaced from a job or place because of recession/economic slowdown that led them to start their own ventures. If the internal and external factors are considered together, we can, to a great extent, say with certainty that entrepreneurs will emerge as in a country of the size that India is all types of situations happen on a fairly regular basis. In earlier times, if someone started his/her own venture it was looked down upon as it related to the high probability of not getting a salaried job. It did reflect on the social status of an individual even though a salaried job may fetch him/her less money than his/her own venture. This trend has changed over the years and now if a young graduate announces his/her intention to start his/her own venture, he/she is encouraged and supported. Factors internal to an individual, external to an individual as well as a combination of both have been observed to influence entrepreneurial activity.

1.7 Functions of an Entrepreneur

In his/her quest to create, establish and build a new business, the entrepreneur has to perform various functions. These functions that an entrepreneur undertakes are focussed on different aspects of the task he/she undertakes for establishing a business venture.

(a) Job creator: A business venture will require people who can accomplish the various tasks that would lead to the success of the venture. So the entrepreneur is going to create jobs for many more people besides him/her.

(b) Risk taker: The entrepreneur bears the risk of the newness that he/she brings to a venture by committing time, effort, resources to see the success of the venture.

(c) Coordinator: He/she decided how the different factors of productions have to be put together to get the venture up and running.

(d) Promoter: When he/she seeks funds from others and also puts in his/her own funds, he/she is acting like a promoter of the venture so as to achieve above-average or superior returns for all those who invest in the venture.

(e) Value creator: He/she is a value creator as he/she is able to create a difference in the way value is created in an existing process by initiating some newness. His/her way to create value is all about this difference that he/she tries to create.

(f) Profit maximiser: As every venture has as intention to grow, for achieving growth, there is a need to earn returns and circulate the earnings repeatedly. For this purpose, an entrepreneur does play the role of a profit maximiser.

There are some more specific sequential functions that an entrepreneur executes while embarking on his/her entrepreneurial journey.

- Idea generation and screening
- Determination of business objectives
- Product analysis and market research
- Determination of forms of ownership
- Completion of promotional formalities
- Raising of funds
- Procuring required equipment, machinery
- Recruiting people
- Undertaking the business operations

□□□

At a Glance

1. Persons who decide and chose to 'undertake' opportunities and provide goods and services to people by creating an entity for the purpose are known as **entrepreneurs**. An entrepreneur is one who perceives an opportunity and creates an organisation to pursue it.

2. Four Ps of entrepreneurship as recommended by economists Ma and Tan are:
   Pioneer: innovator or champion for innovation
   Perspective: the entrepreneurial mindset
   Practice: the entrepreneurial activities
   Performance: the outcome of entrepreneurial actions and activities

3. To become a successful entrepreneur one must have these essential qualities:

- Must have confidence
- Must have perception of things
- Must have the ability to face risks
- Team building capacity
- Must be conscious time manager

4. Differences of Settings for Managers and Entrepreneurs

Dimension	Entrepreneur's Unit	Organisational Unit
Objectives	Survival, maximise profits	Growth, maximise market share
Management	Owner-led, group of founders/ partners	Professionals
Ownership	Concentrated with single individual/small groups of persons	Widely dispersed through shareholdings
Organisation	Synonymous with the owner/group of owners	A business entity with an institutional character

5. Task Demands for Entrepreneurship and Managership

Task Demands	Entrepreneurship	Managership
Major Goals	Profits	Efficiency
Time Frame	Short and long run	Short run
Arena	Enterprises and Markets	Enterprises

1. "An entrepreneur could be a manager but a manager cannot always be an entrepreneur." An entrepreneur is intensely dedicated to develop business through constant innovation. A manager cannot replace the entrepreneur in spite of performing the allotted duties because a manager has to work as per the guidelines laid down by the entrepreneur.

2. Sequential functions that an entrepreneur executes are:
   - Idea generating and screening
   - Raising of funds
   - Recruiting people
   - Determination of business objectives
   - Undertaking the business operations
   - Completion of promotional formalities
   - Determination of forms of ownership

Multiple Choice Questions

1. The first academic useage of the "ENTREPRENEUR" was done by economist:
    (a) Richard Cantillon
    (b) John Stuart Mill
    (c) Jean Baptiste Say
    (d) Schumpeter
2. Four Ps of entrepreneurship was coined by:
    (a) Economist Ma
    (b) Economists Ma and Tan
    (c) Economist Richard Cantillon
    (d) John Stuart Mill
3. A successful entrepreneur must:
    (a) Adopt a positive attitude that he is an excellent team builder
    (b) Adopt a negative attitude that he is a no nonsense team builder
    (c) One who cannot mobilize resources
    (d) Would not decide the time frame for the goals to be achieved
4. Team building capacity:
    (a) Is a key managerial success element
    (b) Is a key entrepreneurial success element
    (c) Should not foster relationship with other entrepreneur
    (d) In all spheres of life, dead time performance is the key to success
5. An entrepreneur and a manager differ in their standing:
    (a) An entrepreneur is not the owner of the business
    (b) A manager is not the employee and also assumes risk and uncertainties involved in running an organisation
    (c) An entrepreneur is the owner of organisation whereas a manger is an employee and does not assume risk to the level than entrepreneur does
    (d) Specific sequential functions are executed by an entrepreneur

---

Ans. 1. a, 2. b, 3. a, 4. b, 5. c

Review Questions

1. Enumerate functions that an Entrepreneur executes while embarking on his/her entrepreneurial journey.
2. Write in detail different external/internal factors that urges one to become an entrepreneur.
3. What are the differences of settings for Managers and Entrepreneurs?
4. List some of the practices that an entrepreneur adopts in order to effectively manage time.
5. Enlist some of the activities that an entrepreneur can engage in to develop a good team.

Chapter 2

Motivation and Barriers to Entrepreneurship

Introduction

The term 'motivation' has been derived from the word 'motive'. Motives may be defined as a state of our mind that directs our behaviour towards our goals. Motives are expressions of a person's goals or needs. They give direction to human to achieve goals or fulfil needs. Motivation can be defined as the process by which an individual is encouraged into action and further prompts him/her to continue the course of action for the achievements of goals. It is an ongoing process because human needs/goals are never completely satisfied. As per McFarland, *motivation refers to the way in which urges, drives, desires, striving, and aspiration or needs direct, control or explain the behaviour of human beings.* The basic elements of the process of motivation are motives, behaviours and goals. There are a number of motivation theories that explain this link of motives, behaviours and goals.

2.1 Motivation Theories

The importance of motivation to human life and work can be judged by the number of theories that have been propounded to explain people's behaviour. They explain human motivation through human needs and human nature. Prominent among these theories and particularly relevant to entrepreneurship are the following: McClelland's Acquired Needs Theory and Maslow's Need Hierarchy Theory.

(a) McClelland's Acquired Needs Theory

According to David McClelland, a person acquires three types of needs as a result of one's life experience. These three types of needs are in the following:

(i) Need for affiliation: This refers to an individual's need to establish and maintain friendly and warm relation with others. This is about how people want to relate to others.

(ii) Need for power: This means the desire to hold power and be able to dominate and influence others by using physical objects and actions.

(iii) Need for achievement: this refers to one's desire to accomplish something with one's own efforts. This implies one's will to excel in his/her efforts

McClelland also suggests that these three needs may simultaneously be acting on an individual. But, in case of an entrepreneur, the high need for achievement is found to be a dominating one. In his view, the people with high need for achievement are characterized by the following:

- They set moderate, realistic and attainable goals for them.

- They prefer to situation in which they can find solution for solving personal responsibility.

- They need concrete feedback on how well they are doing.

- They have need for achievement for attaining personal accomplishment.

- They look for challenging tasks.

(b) Maslow's Need Hierarchy Theory

Maslow's theory is based on the human needs. These needs are classified into a sequential priority from the lower to the higher. According to him, human needs are classified into the five need-clusters as shown in the following:

(i) Physiological needs: These needs are basic to human life and include food, clothing, shelter, air, water and other necessities of life. They exert tremendous influence on human behaviour. Entrepreneur, also being a human being, needs to meet his/her physiological needs for survival. Hence, he/she is motivated to work in the enterprise to have economic rewards to meet the basic needs.

(ii) Safety and security needs: after satisfying the physiological needs, the next need felt are called safety and security needs. These needs find expression in such desires as economic security and protection from physical dangers. Meeting these needs requires more money and, hence, the entrepreneur is prompted to work more in his/her enterprise. Like physiological needs, these become inactive once they are satisfied.

(iii) Social needs: Man are a social animal. These needs, therefore, refer to belongingness. All individuals want to be recognised and accepted by others. Likewise, an entrepreneur is motivated to interact with fellow entrepreneur, his/her employees and others.

(iv) Esteem needs: These needs refer to self-esteem and self-respect. They include such needs which indicate self-confidence, achievement, competence, knowledge and independence. In case of entrepreneur, the ownership and self control over

enterprise satisfies their esteem needs providing them status, respect, reputation and independence.

(v) Self-actualisation: The final step under the need hierarchy model is the need for self actualisation. This refers to self-fulfilment. The term 'self-actualisation' was coined by Kurt Goldstein; it means 'to become actualised in what one is potentially good at'. An entrepreneur may achieve self-actualisation in being a successful entrepreneur.

In Maslow's theory, needs are arranged in the lowest to the highest hierarchy. The second need does not dominate unless the first is reasonably satisfied, and the third need does not dominate until the first two needs have been reasonably satisfied. This process goes on till the last need. This is because man is never satisfied. If one need is satisfied, another need arises. Once a need is satisfied, it ceases to be a motivating factor. For entrepreneur, it is mainly social esteem and self-actualisation needs which motivate them to work more and more for satisfying them.

2.2 Entrepreneurial Motivation and Barriers

(a) Motivating factors

To address the larger question what factors motivate entrepreneurs to start an enterprise, several researchers have tried to answer this by conducting research studies to identify the factors that motivate people to start business enterprise. Here are the findings of some of these studies.

In his study, Sharma classified all the factors motivating the entrepreneurs into two types as follows:

(i) Internal factors: These include the following factors:

- Desire to do something new
- Educational background
- Occupational background or experience

(ii) External factors: These include the following factors:
- Government assistance and support
- Availability of labour and raw material
- Encouragement from big business houses
- Promising demand for the product

While studying entrepreneurial motivation, researchers have found various reasons for people to start their own enterprises. Some of these are listed in the following.
- There are people who believe that they can bring about a significant change to the lives of people and, therefore, pursue their own way of creating value for people.

- There are those who start with the ambition of becoming the next Dhirubahi Ambani or Karsan Bhai Patel or Narayanmurthy.
- There are those who do not want to be confined to a 9–5 schedule and earn just about enough to make ends meet
- There are those who have been compelled by their situations
- No job available, need to earn bread and butter for family so they do a 'start-up'
- Displaced from a place due to a natural calamity or political reasons, existential necessity is to do something on their own
- Lost a job recently, may lead to an entrepreneurial start-up
- Being his/her own boss
- Independence of doing things the way he/she wants to
- Desire to do something different that others have not tried to do till now

This reveals that one's previous experience gained in the same and/or related line has been the most motivating factor to plunge into industry. The next important factor that brought people to industry is the heavy demand for the particular product in the market. Many individuals are attracted by extrinsic factors as well, such as government assistance in one form or other. In fact, an overriding inclination with them may not be their strong desire to do something independent in life nor any kind of experience gained; rather it may be the availability of financial assistance from the institutional sources which can kindle their entrepreneurial spirit. There were some stray cases also induced by varied factors, such as 'advice of business friends', 'the fabulous profits earned by others in similar concern', 'contact with others', etc.

Now, it is crystal clear from the foregoing analysis that the majority of entrepreneurs are motivated to enter industry mainly because of four factors: First, they possessed technical knowledge or manufacturing experience in the same or related line. Second, there was heavy demand for the particular product. Third, the governmental and institutional assistance available facilitated individuals to enter industry. Fourth, they have enterprising attitude, what McClelland designated 'an achievement motive', to do something independent in life.

Our understanding about what motivates the entrepreneurs will be clearer by going through the source of entrepreneurial supply and motivation reported by some behavioural expert. In the process of aspiring to achieve the best, it is important to know where you want to go in life and what is it that you want to achieve. Expectations should be clear to an individual. It is suggested that one should spend a fair amount of time to clarify and make sure what the objective of one's life is and in the process decide the clear objective that would lead him/her there. Motivation development is an important attribute of any initiative to encourage entrepreneurship. It is based on the belief that people can acquire motives and develop through education and the newly aroused motives are more likely to influence future thoughts and actions. The complete exercise of entrepreneurial motivation training provides the prospective entrepreneurs experimental learning situations which help them to analyse and understand their own attitude and behavioural patterns towards entrepreneurship. Training efforts are based on psychodynamic theories of personality formation, development and acquisition of motives. A certain mechanism is involved in bringing a change in the personality through motivational training. The main constituents of this mechanism are: know yourself stage, know the destination stage and empowerment stage.

In the *know yourself stage*, the trainers describes an ideal personality of an achievement-oriented person. The qualities, values, attitudes, skills of an achievement oriented person are described with examples. The trainee participants thereafter are required to probe into themselves. They create their own picture. Self-analysis is supplemented by the comments and observation of other participants. The discrepancy of the gap between ideal image and self-image is identified and understood. Thereafter, the process of internal change begins.

In the part of *knowing the destination stage*, the facilitator helps the trainee participants close the gap between ideal and self-image. The aim is not to disturb the trainees by creating discontent but to set this process of motivation. Participants are encouraged to identify new ways of thinking about actions and resources to close the gap. The changed attitude and behavioural pattern is practised in the real life situation.

The stage of *empowerment*, the trainee participants are allowed to take their own decisions and formulate their own strategies for experimenting with this newly acquired quality. This is to strengthen their belief and conviction that they can change and they have changed.

2.3 Classification of Entrepreneurship

There are different ways in which we can classify entrepreneurship. This classification can be on the basis of the following:

(a) Contextual basis
- Entrepreneurship (standalone start-up)
- Corporate entrepreneurship (new ventures within large established organisations)
- Co-preneurship (a working professional starts a business and runs it alongside his/her job)
- Technology Entrepreneurship (start-ups with product and process which are technology-based)
- Service Entrepreneurship (start-ups in the services domain of activity)
- E-entrepreneurship (start-ups wherein business is on the internet platform)

(b) Novelty basis: Besides the above contextual basis, we can decide on the basis of quantum of newness, innovation that is there in the organisation.

- *Innovating entrepreneurship:* Innovating Entrepreneurship involves introduction of new goods, new methods of production, discovers new market and reorganises the enterprise. This is usually the case with technology companies but is not ruled out for other ventures also. It can also be called **Schumpeterian Entrepreneurship.**
- *Imitative entrepreneurship:* This is the type of entrepreneurship wherein the entrepreneur is poised to adopt successful innovations which are already in the market.

In this novelty-based entrepreneurship, the degree of newness decides whether it is an innovating entrepreneurship or imitative entrepreneurship.

(c) Intention basis: Another interesting basis of classifying entrepreneurship is the intentions of the entrepreneur in terms of growth of the venture.

- Build to Sell Entrepreneurship (Serial Entrepreneurship)
- Build to Last Entrepreneurship

To be able to comprehend the situation of established companies, today we need to utilise the standard strategic management concepts of assessing the internal and external environment. The external environment is concerned with everything outside the company that includes the economic, technological, regulatory, social, labour and supplier environments and a more specific competitive environment. Each of these domains has critical implication for how things are done inside the company (i.e., the internal environment). The internal environment of an organisation addressed the organisation structure, system and processes being used by the organisation and the culture that builds up the climate within which people perform their work for the company.

The external environment has become increasingly unstable today and change and uncertainty seem to be routine. This is not a radical or new revelation. This has been the situation mostly with the advent of technology into our lives and existing business models becoming saturated in providing adequate returns. It is a continuous change, with a never-ending stream of new challenges deriving from each domain of the external environment. It is a complex change, as developments in technology combine and or lead to developments in suppliers' way of doing things which further affects developments with customers. Companies who are not able to appropriately respond to the changes happening are bound to reach a situation of dwindling returns. And this, in turn, is the kind of change that threatens the very survival of the company. A closer look at some of the changes happening around leads us to the following:

- Accelerated development of new technologies; rapid product obsolescence; greater difficulty in protecting intellectual property.
- Unpredictability of prices, costs, exchange rates; interest rates, tax incentives, business cycles.
- Growing scarcity of skilled workers; employees more mobile and less loyal; higher employee benefit costs.
- Resource scarcity on the increase; resources becoming increasingly specialised; rapid resource obsolescence.
- Demanding and complex customers; market that are more fragmented and more narrowly segmented; emphasis on investing in and capturing a customer's lifetime value.
- Changing regulation; virtually unlimited product liability; growing emphasis on free and fair trade; Increasing environmental regulation and associated compliance costs.
- Real-time communication, production, and distribution virtually anywhere in the world; more sophisticated suppliers, customers and competitors located virtually anywhere in the world; competitive advantage through global outsourcing and international strategic alliances.

These changes have important implications for companies and how they are managed. Quite simply; the modern corporation finds it tormented as it struggles simply to survive, much less to achieve sustained growth. On an internal environment assessment, we may find an equally changed and changing picture of the activities and the way these activities are being performed. There is a need to re-invent business practices. Today, managers are facing shortened decision window and diminishing opportunity streams. This means that they must act quickly or find themselves missing out on opportunities. The constituents (e.g., customers, suppliers, distributors, alliance partners, regulators) with whom they interact are continually changing. This suggests the need to adopt new performance standards and expectations that must be met. As resources are becoming increasingly specialised, companies tend to make short-term commitments to a given resource and rely more heavily on the outsourcing, leasing and leveraging (rather than ownership) of resources. The technological changes and technology providing for a new channel of information, and distribution of goods and services, there is a need for companies to redefine their offerings to suit the changing consumer profile. The firm's resource and its products become obsolete much faster, changing the economic realities that surround decision regarding which resource to employ, which products to develop, and which markets to enter.

In totality, companies are experiencing a general lack of long-term control over their external environments today. Never before have the past experiences been worth so less. No longer does company size matter; being resource-rich is hardly a guarantee of marketplace performance. The riskiest strategy of all is simply to pursue business as usual. How are today's firm reacting to this challenge? The response has been dramatic. A veritable cornucopia of new strategic initiatives has preoccupied executive's time over the past decade. These include rightsizing, unbundling, focusing on core businesses while diverting others, business process reengineering, total quality management, flattening structures and decentralising decision making, outsourcing creating self-directed work teams, forming strategic alliances, and more. Meanwhile, major companies have found themselves eliminating millions of jobs, closing plants, moving operations to low-cost countries, and attempting to become 'lean and mean'. Yet they continue to struggle.

❏❏❏

At a Glance

1. According to David McClelland, a person acquired three types of needs as a result of one's life experience. These three types of needs are in the following:
   - Need for affiliation
   - Need for power
   - Need for achievement

2. Motivation theories explain human motivation through human needs and human nature. Motivation theories relevant to entrepreneurship are McClelland's Acquired Needs Theory and Maslow's Need Hierarchy Theory.

3. Motivation factors which motivate entrepreneurs to start an enterprise are:
   - Desire to do something new
   - Educational background
   - Experience
   - Promising demand for the product
   - There are people who believe that they can bring about a significant change to the lives of people and, therefore pursue their own way of creating value for people

4. Entrepreneurship may be classified on the following basis:
   - Contextual Basis
   - Intention Basis
   - Novelty Basis

Multiple Choice Questions

1. One reason for people to start their own enterprise:
   - (a) Job available, do not need to earn bread and butter for family
   - (b) Dependence of doing things the way he/she wants to
   - (c) Displaced from a place due to natural calamity or political reasons, existing necessity to do something on their own

    (d)   Government assistance and support

2.   In Maslow's theory, needs are arranged in the:
- (a)   Highest to the lowest hierarchy
- (b)   Highest to the middle hierchy
- (c)   Lowest to the highest hierarchy
- (d)   None of the above

3.   In MeClellands's vies, the people with high need for achievement are characterized by:
- (a)   Do not look for challenges
- (b)   Do not want feedback on how well they are doing
- (c)   Do not set to situation to find solution for personal responsibility
- (d)   The need for attaining personal accomplishment

4.   According to Mc Farland motivation refers to:
- (a)   Need for power
- (b)   Need for achievement
- (c)   The way in which urges, lives, desires, aspiration or needs direct the behaviour of human being
- (d)   Individuals need to establish and maintain friendly and warm relation with others

---

Ans. 1. c, 2. a, 3. d, 4. c

Review Questions

1.   Define Maslow's Need Hierarchy Theory with explanation.

2.   What are the entrepreneurial motivations and barriers?

3.   List those entrepreneurial reasons which motivate people to start their own enterprises.

4.   Classify entrepreneurship on the basis of following:
- (a)   Contextual basis
- (b)   Novelty basis
- (c)   Intention basis

5.   The external environment has become increasingly unstable today and change and uncertainty seem to be routine. These kind of changes threaten the very survival of the companies. List all these changes around you.

Chapter 3

Concept of Entrepreneurship

Introduction

The field of entrepreneurship as an academic discipline draws from various fields of study. It has been impacted by and by its sheer nature impacts the activities of people around. There have been continuous efforts to draw out entrepreneurship as a unique identifiable discipline. A number of reputed institutions across the globe have done a lot of work in this direction. Whether it is the US or Europe or Asia or Australia, there are significant efforts to see that the discipline has its own identity. Today, entrepreneurship as a discipline has gained one of the most important places in the business world. Nevertheless, it remains a place where models, processes and systems do not always seem to convert to expected outcomes. Therefore, there is a lot that can be done in terms of both researches leading to contribution to the knowledge pool of entrepreneurship and at the same time practical insights as to how entrepreneurs and start-ups can deliver more than what they have till now to national economies, in particular and the global business arena, in general.

3.1 Development of Entrepreneurship

The concept of entrepreneurship has been addressed from the angle of different disciplines. There are factors on the side of the individual, categorised as the entrepreneur, the context of the economy in which he/she initiates the venture and venture in itself as a factor. All three of these have contributed to the literature on entrepreneurship as a discipline. From these three, we are able to understand that entrepreneurship is a theory of evolution of economic activities (see Fig.3.1).

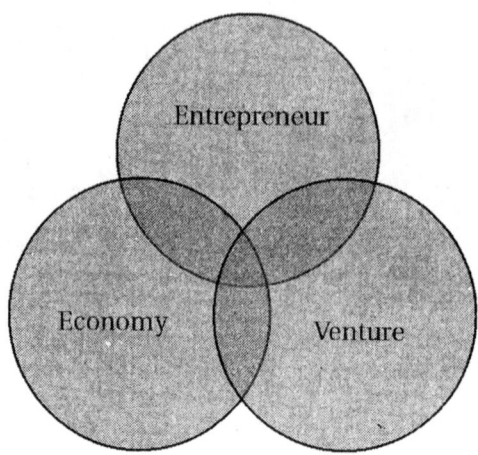

Fig.3.1 Key dimensions of entrepreneurship

The field of entrepreneurship has evolved in a very different way. Different researchers at different stages assigned different roles to the individual— the entrepreneur in the given set-up (the economy) to go ahead and create an entity (venture) with a purpose. The very first role that was assigned to an entrepreneur was that of a risk take. In the eighteenth century, economist Richard Cantillon (1730) coined the term 'entrepreneurship' by assigning the label of 'one who takes risk in business activities'. Further to this, some other proponents supported this view in the form of Mills (1848), Knight (1921). Knight suggested that entrepreneurs are a specialised group of people who bear risk and deal with uncertainty. Sinclair (1999) supported this view by stating that the owner manager of business who by risk and initiative, attempts to make profits are entrepreneurs.

J.B. Say, a French sociologist assigned the entrepreneur the crucial role of one who coordinates market activities, rationally combining, co-coordinating and supervising the various factors of production. Casson (1990) proposed that an entrepreneur is one who specialises in taking judgmental decisions about coordination of scarce resources. Further to this role, Marshall (1861) and Ronstadt (1984) and many others after that suggested that an entrepreneur also has the role of one who maximises profit. Karl Vesper (1982) stated that an entrepreneur is an economist who brings resources, labour, material and other assets into combinations that make their value greater than before, and also, who introduces changes and innovations. This view was further reinforced by Drucker (1983) who stated that an Entrepreneur shift resources from areas of low productivity and yield to areas of high productivity and yield.

One of the most significant explanations to entrepreneurship came from the famous economist Joseph Schumpeter (1934), who defined entrepreneurship as a catalyst that disrupts the stationary circular flow of the economy and thereby initiates and sustains the process of development. Embarking upon new combinations of factors of production: innovation which could be: introduction of a new good, new method of production, new market, new source of supply of raw materials, carrying out of a new organisation. This is based on his seminal work on creative destruction. Further to these explanations, researchers from different fields of study tried to find answers to questions that related to their field of study.

As per Fig.3.2, the different theories have endeavoured to explain the different dimensions of entrepreneurship. The psychological theorists addressed the personal traits, values, attitudes and expectations of the entrepreneur as well as the motivation and objectives for becoming an entrepreneur. They also tried to explain how the process of entrepreneurship develops in the light of skills, resources required to succeed.

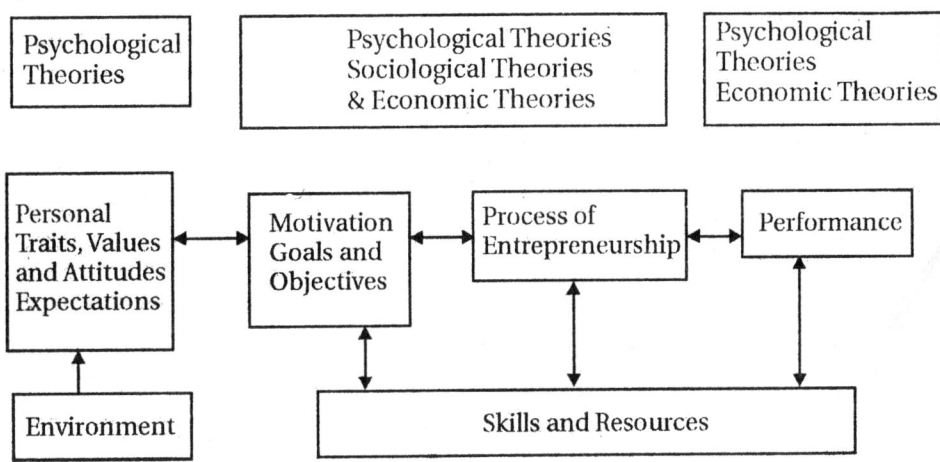

Fig. 3.2 Different theories and their efforts to explain entrepreneurship

Further to this, they also addressed the impact of the environment in building these factors. This is in line with the fact that was discussed in a recent article by Bargen, Freedman and Pages titled *The Rise of the Entrepreneurial Society*. This article talks about the role of public policy establishments in ensuring that the fundamental requirements of infrastructure, qualified people, systems for providing intellectual property protection, mature financial markets and providing access to markets as necessary for a nation to be able to foster entrepreneurship. In a similar manner, sociologists and economists have tried to find antecedents and consequences of entrepreneurial activities at different stages of venture creation and performance.

Another approach to view the concept of entrepreneurship was suggested by Kuratko and Hodgetts. They state that one can take a macro and a micro view to the study of entrepreneurship. The first of the macro view addresses the concerns of the external factors that affect the life of an entrepreneur (environmental school of thought). The next looks at the capital seeking process of ventures (financial school of thought), while the third and last one looks at the displacement of individuals and groups of individuals due to political reasons relating to regulations, absence of free enterprise. The other displacement is cultural relating to social groups and minorities (Chinese, Indians, east-Europeans in the US) and the last one being the economic displacement relating to economic variations of recession, job losses, capital shrinkage, bad times can create foundations for entrepreneurial pursuits as well as can effect venture development.

Proceeding to the micro view of research, the first school of thought is related to the traits of an entrepreneur, endeavouring to find one composite set of traits that can distinguish an entrepreneur from others. These relate to achievement, creativity and innovation, determination and technical knowledge. The next in the micro view is the venture opportunity school of thought which focuses on the opportunity aspect of venture development: Search for idea sources, development of concepts and the implementation of the opportunities into successful ventures. The strategic formulation school of thought wherein the main proponent is Ronstadt, views strategic formulation as a way to leveraging of unique resources that one may have. These elements may be 'unique markets': identifying major market segments as well as in-between markets; 'unique people: venture built around the skills of an individual or individuals; 'unique products': innovation encompassing new or existing markets and the last one being 'unique resources': ability to gather special resources over the long term. Further, innovation being an integral component of the definition of entrepreneurship makes the study of innovation as an integral part of the overall scenario of entrepreneurship research.

3.2 Entrepreneurial Culture and Stages in the Entrepreneurial Process

The consequence of an entrepreneurial thought process on the part of the founder(s) of a new venture is manifest in the form of the culture of the venture. The process through which an entrepreneur completes his/her journey has implications on what type of a culture would prevail in the venture. Timmons suggests that there are a number of questions that one needs to answer on his/her way to the final decision of starting a venture. After a brief description of these stages, we will get back to the issue of entrepreneurial culture of the venture. The stages in the entrepreneurial process as suggested by Timmons are as follows.

(a) Stage I: Entrepreneurial interest

This is the elementary stage where one is pondering over the thoughts of doing something on his own or continuing with the way life is progressing at any point in time. It is about evaluating your interests in life and what motivates you. There can be gaps between what one desires to achieve and what one is capable of. So, another question that needs to be evaluated is to assess what is that one is good at and then try to see that in the light of this does one really want to become an entrepreneur. If the answer to this question is 'yes', one should proceed to the next stage or else turn back and do what one is already doing.

(b) Stage II: Generate ideas for screening

Now that you are sure that you want to become an entrepreneur it is the time for you to look for that one elusive opportunity that can make you case stronger for you. Observation, trends of how things are changing, what do people like-dislike and past experiences can help one get closer to the fact that there are at least a few opportunities shortlisted from which one would like to choose. This would include a rough estimate of what one would do if a specific opportunity is pursued. So, effectively one would have an idea of what happens if opportunity 'A' or 'B' is pursued. An assessment of what would be required for each of these opportunities in terms of time, effort, resources, etc. needs to be addressed at this stage itself.

(c) Stage III: Venture screening

The venture screening stage is when we develop some mechanism or set of dimensions on which we would like to evaluate and screen opportunities. The outcome of this stage is the decision to pursue a specific opportunity.

(d) Stage IV: Develop and refine the concept

Now that we have decided on the opportunity comes the time when we need to collect information through both secondary sources as well as primary studies so as to refine our concept and give it the final shape in the light of some of the pertinent dimensions that would be studied in this stage, such as target customers, competition, organisational structures/forms, sales or distribution channels, start developing the business plan.

(e) Stage V: Determine resources required

Now that we have refined our business concept and offering we need to analyse what our requirements are concerning marketing and sales expertise, technical expertise, financing needs, distribution channels, supply, licenses, patents and legal protection. This stage would probably take a larger quantum of our time but less than what stages III and IV together would require.

(f) Stage VI: Acquiring necessary financials

At this stage as we know about our funding requirements, we look at the portfolio of sources of funds that can be utilised between the combinations of debt–equity. Precise requirements will have to be shaped during this stage.

(g) Stage VII: Developing the business plan

This is the time when we need to document each and every assessment based on which the requirements for being able to start the business are built. A detailed business plan should be prepared in this stage.

(h) Stage VIII: Implement and manage

At this stage, the venture is launched and the implementation of plan is underway. One needs to get into the monitoring and evaluation mode now so that the performance of the venture can be monitored, payback to resources providers can be started, matters relating to reinvestment of earnings and the achievement of predefined objectives should happen.

(i) Stage IX: Growth or exit

This is the stage whereby the venture has achieved the desired success and the entrepreneur is now in a position to take a decision about whether he/she would like to go for an initial public offering (IPO) (so as to grow the venture further), sell or merge the business to another business for a decent return or shit the venture and sell off its assets.

The issue of entrepreneurial culture in a new venture is such that it is shaped to a great extent during the stages I–VIII in the above mentioned stages given by Timmons. Further, Kuratko proposed that the stages through which an entrepreneurial venture emerges can be shown as in Fig.3.3. This figure shows that from the stages of innovation to growth, there are a number of environmental, organisational and individual factors that impact the decisions at these stages.

The triggering event is when one is inducted into launching a venture of his/her own. The personal value system of the lead entrepreneur and his/her founding team has a profound impact on the culture of the venture. The past experiences of working in different places have its shadow on the policies and practices of the new venture. This again has a significant impact in building the culture of the venture. Further, the investors and other stakeholders to the venture also have an influence on the type of culture that is being developed. The culture that emerges over a period of time when the venture is growing is also a reflection of the level of professionalism with which the venture is progressing and the chances that it will succeed in tomorrow's time. This is done by laying the groundwork culture as we have seen earlier can be said to be a balancing act between many elements of a company and requires careful execution at each level. This is especially true for entrepreneurial companies, where what is going on is the building of a business as well as a culture. Corporate culture must be led, nurtured, constantly monitored and adjusted.

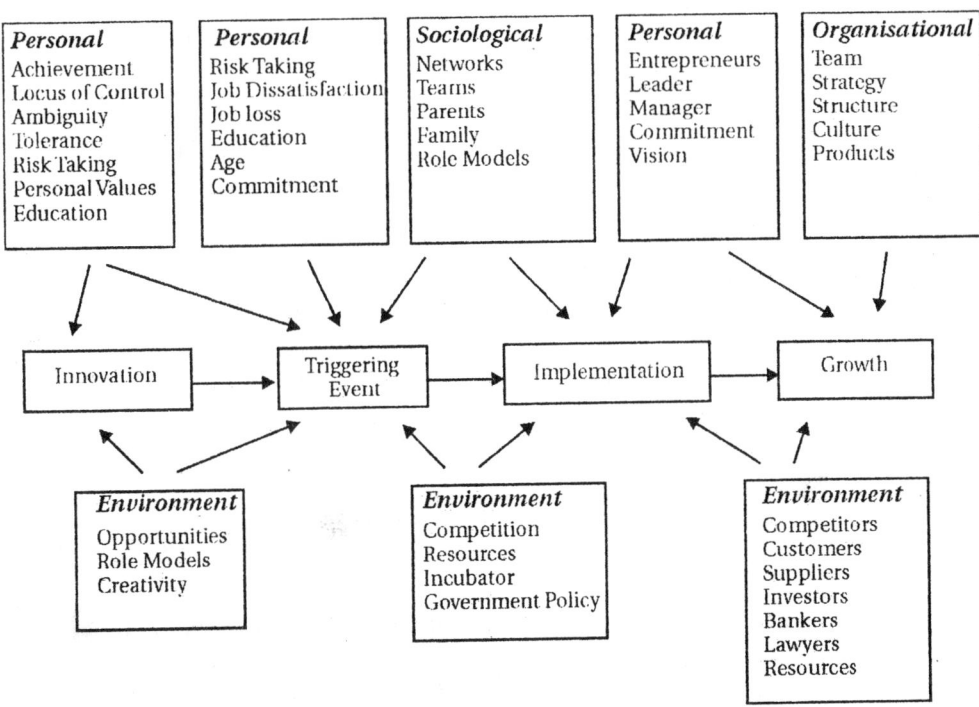

Fig.3.3 Factors influencing the entrepreneurial process

3.3 What Makes a Culture Entrepreneurial

As one of the employees of a start-up said, in an entrepreneurial culture, work is more than a job, it is a lifestyle. Employees are more like a team than in most companies, and in some cases, we are even like a family. In creating your own entrepreneurial culture, some of the things that may help are in the following:

(a) Treat people with respect: This is a very simple premise, which threads through each and every complicated issue that can arise within a company. Respect and trust provide the necessary base for a vibrant and sustainable corporate culture.

(b) Help employees stay healthy: When employees get sick, they miss work; so it makes sense to offer health insurance as a benefit. If an employee experiences an illness, he/she needs support. Usually people do not have the time for such things. It is advisable to work towards the overall health of employees and, thus, of the organisation.

(c) Open doors to communication: Create an environment where people can interact with each other, support each other and recognise each other's efforts and achievements. Provide positive rewards for positive behaviour. Share information, so that employees are aware of the direction of the company and are involved in it. Use all-hands meetings for financial and operational information, team building and social events. Offer incentive programmes to reward effort and improve quality of life.

(d) **Build camaraderie:** Make time for people to get to know each other and the company. We held an annual off-site meeting to build team spirit and discuss where the company was going. At such events, you can also distribute and share your business plan and discuss issues and ideas raised by your strategies.

3.4 Maintaining this Entrepreneurial Culture

Once you have healthy, trusted and informed employees, do not let the culture that is evolving just be. It needs to be watched so that it grows as you intended. The trick is standing back, but not too far back. In maintaining your culture, consider these rules.

(a) **Let the team build itself:** Within that safe, comfortable, open environment, let employees grow together without being made to.

(b) **Participate without controlling:** Let the culture thrive, without your either meddling with it or ignoring it.

(c) **Don't forget the little things:** Culture is made up of many small actions that, when put together, create something larger than the sum of the parts. There are many things a CEO can do to make employees feel a part of the company.

Treating employees with respect helps enable them to do their jobs to the best of their abilities. If you challenge people to raise their bars, provide fun activities, keep people informed and humanise your management, you get culture. From these basics, you will grow in your establishment a strong, healthy culture that will allow you, your company and your employees to flourish.

❏❏❏

At a Glance

1. J. B. Say, a French sociologist assigned the entrepreneur a crucial role of one who coordinates market activities rationally, combining, co-ordinating and supervising the various factors of production.

2. Kuratko and Hodgetts stated that one can take a macro and a micro view to the study of entrepreneurship. The first of the macro view addresses the concerns of the external factors that affect the life of an entrepreneur. The next looks at the capital seeking process of ventures, absence of free enterprise.

3. Entrepreneurial process as suggested by Timmons are entrepreneurial interest, generate ideas for screening, venture screening, develop and refine the concept, determine resources required, acquiring necessary financials, developing the business plan, implement and manage the growth or exit.

4. In creating your own entrepreneurial culture some of the things that may help are:
    - Treat people with respect
    - Open doors to communication
    - Build Camaraderie
    - Help employees stay healthy

5. Venture Screening is a stage where we develop some mechanism or set of dimensions on which we would like to evaluate and screen opportunities. The outcome of this stage is the decision to pursue a specific opportunity.

Multiple Choice Questions

1. What makes a culture Entrepreneurial?
    - (a) It is simple style
    - (b) It is lifestyle
    - (c) Both style and life style
    - (d) None of the above

2. Culture is made up of many small actions such as:
    - (a) Don't forget the little things
    - (b) Forget the bigger things
    - (c) Remember little things
    - (d) Do remember little as well bigger things

3. Entrepreneurial interest is a stage in the entrepreneurial process suggested by:
    - (a) Joseph Schumpeter
    - (b) Ronstadt
    - (c) Casson
    - (d) Timmons

Ans. 1. b, 2. a, 3. d

Review Questions

1. What makes a culture Entrepreneurial?

2. What are rules that you will consider while maintaining Entrepreneurial culture?

3. Give a brief description of the stages in the entrepreneurial process as susggested by Timmons.

4. Define what is entrepreneurship as suggested by:
    - (i) Richard Cantillon
    - (ii) J.B. Say
    - (iii) Karl Vesper
    - (iv) Joseph Schumpeter

Unit II

Creativity, Innovation and Entrepreneurial Planning

Chapter 4

Idea Generation and Creativity

Introduction

For initiating a new business, there is a need to have a specific business idea which has the potential to become a successful established growing business. For any prospective entrepreneur, it is important to have an idea. Ideas do not emerge from thin air; there has to be an effort to identify the opportunity in the market place that can be served. It is, therefore, pertinent to go for generating ideas from which one can select the ones that seem to have the requisite potential.

Where do ideas come from? Creativity is the ability of an individual to come up with something imaginative and novel. In other words, creativity is the ability to develop new ideas and to discover new ways of looking at problems and opportunities. Innovation, at the same time, is the ability to apply creative solutions to problems or opportunities to enhance or to enrich people's lives. It has been seen that while creativity can provide ideas for innovative products and services, what actually reaches the consumers or users is very different. It has been observed that for every 3,000 new product ideas, four make it to the development stage, two are actually launched, out of which only one becomes a success in the market.

The issue is that can we learn to be creative. The answer to this is 'yes' but it requires a significant amount of effort, as one has to overcome paradigms and suspend conventional thinking long enough to consider new and different alternatives. There is a need to challenge one's own mental models about things around us to be able to come up with novel ides about products and services that could gain acceptance in the future. Creative individuals are seen to be inquisitive and are always on the lookout for answers to questions, such as 'Is there a better way?' They have a tendency to challenge the routine and conventional things. They realise that there may be more than one 'right' answer to a problem and see mistakes as pit stops on the way to success.

Sources of ideas: Where do ideas emerge from? Ideas emerge from being able to comprehend an unfulfilled need of consumers or a situation wherein the need is currently latent but can be manifested by the presence of the product one intends to offer. To be able to comprehend such things, it is essential for one to be able to monitor, evaluate the environment in terms of changes happening and to identify the trends that can lead to identifying a gap or a latent need. These factors can be in the form of the current state of the economy, as in the globalisation and liberalisation has created a significant change in the overall condition of our economy. Factors, such as level of disposable income available to the people and patterns of consumer spending socio-cultural trends related to demographics and what people think is currently the 'in' thing. These trends can throw light on what are the changes that can offer an opportunity to create something that can be trendy and picked up consumers instantly. Technological progress in the recent times has seen the emergence of enormous opportunities for new businesses. On one hand, the usage of technology in different activities of our day to day life has changed our lives significantly with new products coming out, offering more or enhanced utility, contributing to easing our lives. On the other hand, technology is being used as a means to improve the efficiency and productivity of businesses. With the advent of the Internet, almost all businesses today seem to have a presence on the web also. All these technology matters are proving to be one of the biggest sources of opportunity. The e-platform has become very important in recent times.

Changes in the political and regulatory set-up sometimes lead to changes in the policies of the government. The recent enhanced focus on sustainability has seen an increased interest in environment, carbon credits and going green type of activities as the regulation dictates stringent levels for clearance of large scale infrastructure and industrial activity. Ventures, such as consulting for sustainability, indulging in green activities— plantation, maintenance of green belts in different places, etc. — are on the rise today.

In essence, ideas are about the notion that for every problem, there is an idea for a new business. Plenty of opportunity exists if one focuses attention on words, such as: reduce, improve, integrate, slow, increase, coarser, finer, quicker, longer life, additional applications, additional functions, waste reduction, cleaner, etc. These are all applicable to end products, components, raw materials, manufacturing process, by-products, environmental impact, etc. There are various techniques by which we can generate ideas which will then be screened and the one most feasible will be selected to be pursued further. The following section provides information about some of the most prevalent techniques for generating ideas.

4.1 Idea Generation Techniques

Idea generation is all about generating different options of what can one do in a specific context. Some of the commonly used techniques are presented in the following with details of how they need to be undertaken.

(a) Brainstorming

This is a group activity where with a group of individuals, we set out to generate ideas. The first step in this activity is to write the initial topic or problem on a whiteboard— clear and focused. Once it has been read and understood by all the participants, the ground rules have to make clear to all. The sequential steps for a brainstorming exercise are shown in the following:

- Present the problem.
- Check that everyone understands the problem or issue.
- Review the ground rules.
  - No criticism or judgement of ideas. All ideas are equally valid.
  - The more ideas generated, the better the solution.
  - Do not censor any ideas; keep the meeting flow going.
  - Listen to ideas and try to piggy-back on them to other ideas.
  - No discussion of ideas or questions in the brainstorming stage, as this stops the flow of ideas.
  - Choose one participant as facilitator to keep the ideas flowing and record them.
- Generate ideas— either in an unstructured way (anyone can voice an idea at any time) or structured (sequentially around the table, allowing people to pass if they have no new ideas).
- Clarify and conclude the session.
- Combine identical or very similar ideas and keep all the others. It is useful to get consensus on which ideas should be looked at further and where (and when) to go from here.

Brainstorming has been and is currently said to be one of the most common methods of generating ideas.

(b) Fishbone diagram

This technique is used to identify possible causes of a problem (see Fig. 4.1). The diagram encourages participants to develop an in-depth and objective representation and to keep on track. It discourages partial or premature solutions, and shows the relative importance and inter-relationships between different parts of a problem.

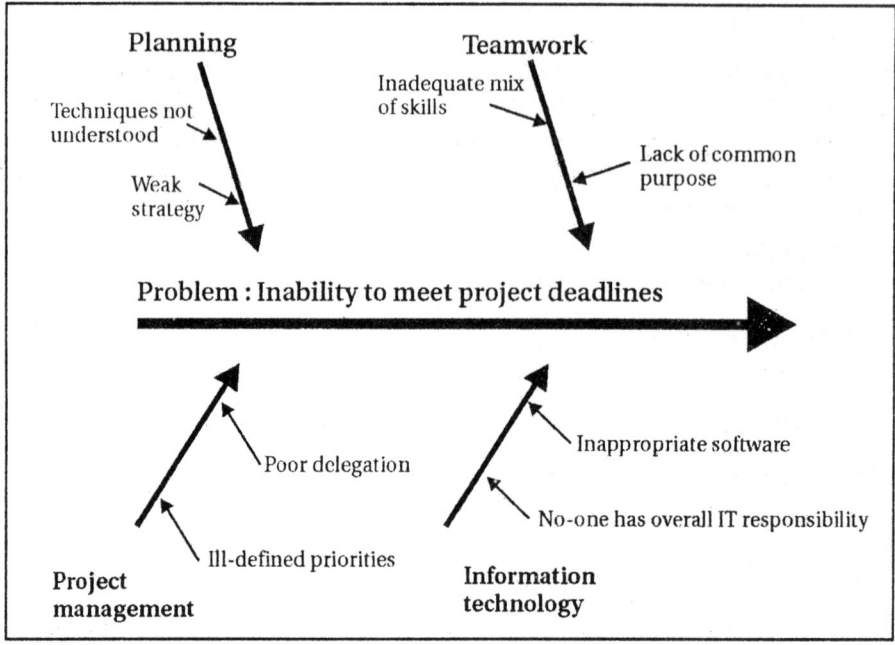

Fig.4.1 Fishbone diagram

(c) Free Association

Free association contains elements of several other idea-generating techniques and depends on a mental 'stream of consciousness' and network of associations of which there are two:

(i) Serial association: It starts with a trigger, record the flow of ideas that come to mind, each idea triggering the next, ultimately reaching a potentially useful one.

(ii) Centred association: It prompts you to generate multiple associations (which is close to classical brainstorming— see Fig.4.2) to the original trigger so that you 'delve' into a particular area of associations.

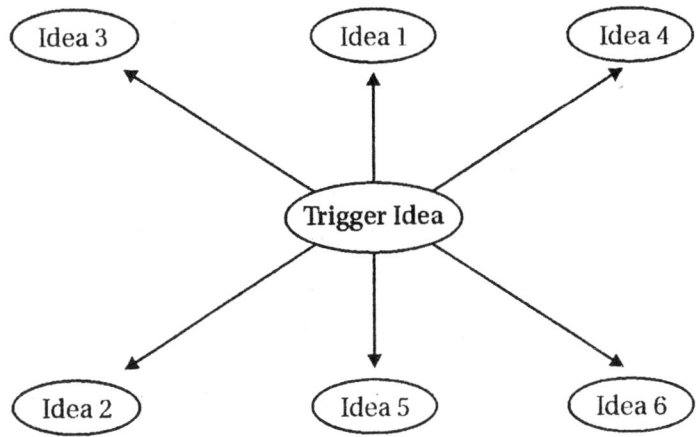

Fig.4.2 Centred association diagram

As a rule, the serial mode is used to 'travel' until you find an idea that you find of some interest; you then engage the centred mode to 'delve' more deeply around the interesting item. Once you have exhausted the centred investigation, you begin to 'travel' again, and so on.

(d) Mind mapping

Mind mapping represents ideas, notes, information, etc., in far-reaching tree diagrams. To draw a mind-map

- lay out a large sheet of paper in landscape format and write a concise heading for the overall theme in the centre of the page;
- for each major sub-topic or cluster of material, start a new major branch from the central theme and label it;
- each sub-topic or sub-cluster forms a subordinate branch to the appropriate main branch and
- carry on in this way in ever finer sub-branches

It has a lot of strength in finding links in problems. It may be appropriate to put an item in more than one place, cross-link it to several other items or show relationships between items on different branches. Coding the colour, type of writing, etc. can do this (see Fig.4.3).

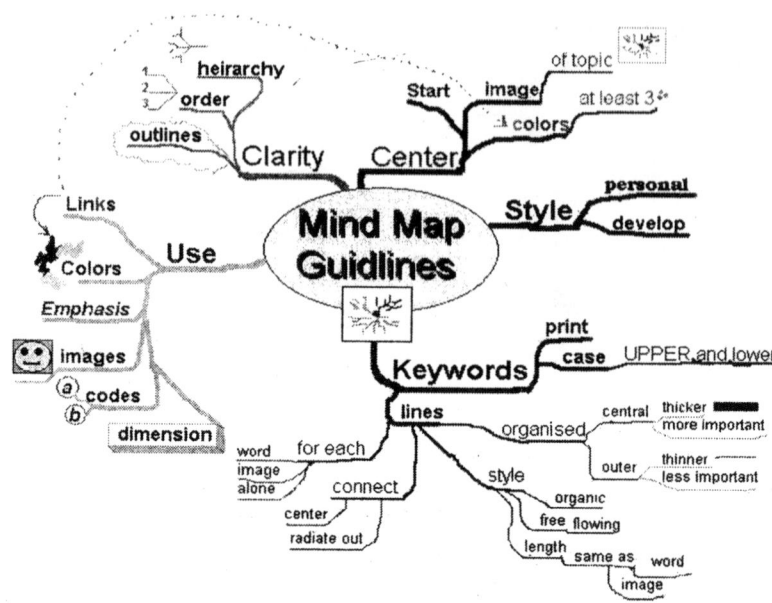

Fig.4.3 Mind mapping diagram

(e) Visual brainstorming

Visual brainstorming can be extremely useful for graphic conceptualisation problems.

(i) Idea generation phase: Set a high target. For example, to generate 20–30 basic idea-sketches on a specific problem in one hour. If participants are working in groups, they could begin with private sketches which are then pooled, perhaps in a round robin session. Quick, impulsive ideas put into sketches can help to avoid undeveloped 'lost' thoughts/ideas. Rapid response to an idea with an immediate sketch creates momentum, preventing any critical thought processes from intervening.

(ii) Evaluation phase: The collection of sketched ideas can now be evaluated.

- Each participant presents their idea-sketches, trying to observe them with as much openness as possible.

- The participants should think of themselves as critics, looking at the sketches from different perspectives.

- Rotate the sketches, place images on images, cover top or bottom half, for example. These varying tactics may inspire yet another idea.

(iii) Comparison phase: Clustering all the sketches together, place complex ones with simplistic ones, make comparisons, etc. More ideas could be generated at this stage.

(f) Alternative scenarios

Scenarios are qualitatively different descriptions of plausible futures. They can give you a deeper understanding of potential environments in which you might have to operate and what you may need to do in the present. Scenario analysis helps you to identify what environmental factors to monitor over time, so that when the environment shifts, you can recognise where it may be headed. To develop Alternative Factors Scenarios (AFS)

- state the specific decision that needs to be made;
- identify the major environmental factors (forces, drivers, trends, limits, etc.) that impact on the decision. For example, suppose you need to decide how to invest R & D funds in order to be positioned for opportunities that might emerge by the year 2010. The major environmental factors might include social values, economic growth world-wide and international trade access (tariffs, etc.).
- build four scenarios based on the principal factors. To do this, use information available to you to identify four (or more) plausible and qualitatively different possibilities for each force. Alternatively, identify the two most important and most uncertain factors that are outside the control of organisational strategy (e.g., high/low economic growth, good/bad weather, etc.) and develop a matrix of four outcomes based on the two factors. Assemble the alternatives for each factors outcome into internally consistent 'stories', with both a narrative and a table of key factors and scenarios. Build your scenarios around these factors.
- with the scenarios in hand, identify business opportunities and risk management strategies within each scenario.
- examine the links and synergies of opportunities and risk abatement across the range of scenarios. This would help you to formulate more realistic and robust strategy.

(g) Attribute listing

Attribute listing is a technique from the early 1930s which takes an existing product or system, then breaks it into parts. It then identifies various ways of achieving each part, and further, recombines these to identify new forms of the product or system. So to generate a new way of doing something, you could list all the key attributes of current approaches and try to improve on some of them. So

- identify the product or process you are dissatisfied with or wish to improve.

- list its attributes. For a simple physical object, such as a pen, this might include material, shape, target market, colours, textures, etc.

- choose, say, 7–8 of these attributes that seem particularly interesting or important.

- identify alternative ways to achieve each attribute (e.g., different shapes—cylindrical cubic, multi-faceted, etc.), either by conventional enquiry, or via any idea-generating technique.

- combine one or more of these alternative ways of achieving the required attributes, and see if you can come up with a new approach to the product or process you were working on.

(h) Card story boards

This technique (see Fig.4.4), although similarly named, differs from the Cartoon Story Board technique. It is an 'idea organising' method using tree logic. With card story boards, the facilitator can concentrate on idea generation of particular topics and sub-topics much more closely than typically possible in open-ended methods. Cards are arranged in a tabular format— a simple row of header cards (or possibly header and sub-header cards as in Fig.4.4), each with a column of idea cards below it, perhaps with added action or comment notes attached (index cards or Post-it slips could be used):

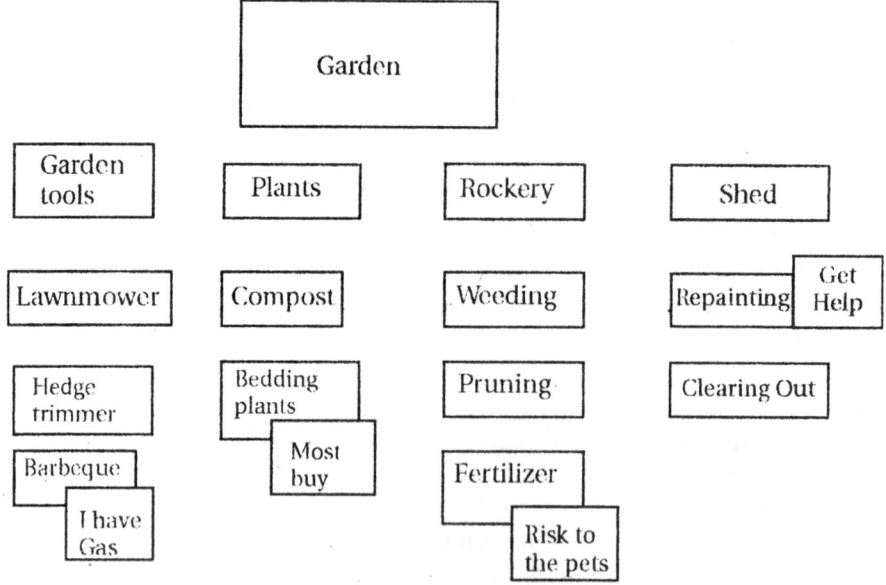

Fig.4.4 Card story board technique

Different-shaped or colour header cards look more striking. If you want to use non-sticky cards, you can make a re-stickable display area by spraying flip-chart paper with low-tack adhesive (available in spray cans). Then the cards can be positioned, rearranged or removed as you wish.

(i) Chunking

Chunking is a term used to describe the process of grouping items into larger or smaller groups (or 'chunks'). Chunking helps you to organise your thinking in order to better handle information. Chunking allows us to become more efficient at categorising information. Items can be classified into different groups moving from the general to the specific, and vice versa. When to use Chunking?

- When you are confronted with a task that seems daunting, chunk it down into smaller, more manageable mini-tasks.
- When you are overwhelmed by details, chunk up to find the overall meaning or purpose to 'get the big picture' or 'see the wood for the trees'.
- When you want to communicate more effectively, package the information in chunks that are the right size for your audience.
- When you want to find ways of reaching an agreement.

(j) False faces

This is a technique which proceeds by challenging the assumption and then recording different view points on it. Further, it works out to find how each different viewpoint can be accomplished. Some of the steps in false faces technique are presented as follows:

- State the problem.
- List the assumptions.
- Challenge the fundamental assumption.
- Reverse each assumption— write down the opposite for each one.
- Record differing viewpoints that might prove useful to you.
- Ask how to accomplish each reversal, listing as many viewpoints and ideas as possible.

(i) Problem reversal

This technique takes into consideration what is that should not be there or should not be done so as to identify new ideas to do better than before. It proceeds by

- making the statement negative, for example, if you are dealing with customer service issues, list all the ways you could make customer service bad. You will be surprised at some of the ideas you will be able to come up with.

- doing what everybody else does not. For example, Apple Computer did what IBM did not; Japan made small, fuel-efficient cars.

- the 'What-If Compass': The author has a list of pairs of opposing actions which can be applied to the problem. Just ask yourself 'What if I ....' and plug in each one of the opposites. A small sample:

  o Stretch it/Shrink it

  o Freeze it/Melt it

  o Personalise it/De-personalise it

  o Change the direction or location of your perspective— physical change of perspective, manage by walking around or doing something different.

  o Flip-flop results— If you want to increase sales, think about decreasing them. What would you have to do?

  o Turn defeat into victory or victory into defeat— If something turns out bad, think about the positive aspects of the situation. If I lost all of the files off this computer, what good would come out of it?

(l) SCAMPER

SCAMPER is the acronym for

S - Substitute— components, materials, people

C - Combine— mix, combine with other assemblies or services, integrate

A - Adapt— alter, change function, use part of another element

M - Modify— increase or reduce in scale, change shape, modify attributes (e.g., colour)

P - Put to another use

E - Eliminate— remove elements, simplify, reduce to core functionality

R - Reverse— turn inside out or upside down.

For instance, imagine that you are a producer of computers and printers, and you are looking for new products. SCAMPER would give you

Substitute— use of high tech materials for specific markets— use high-speed components.

Combine— integrate computer and printer, printer and scanner.

Adapt— put high quality ink in printer, use high quality paper.

Modify— produce different shape, size and design of printer and computer.

Put to another use— printers as photocopies or fax machines.

Eliminate— eliminate speakers, colour screens, colour ink, etc.

Reverse— make computer desks as well as computers and printers, or computer chairs, etc.

By using SCAMPER, in this instance, we have been able to identify possible new products. Many of the ideas may be unfeasible or may not suit the equipment used by the manufacturer, but some ideas could be good starting points for discussion of new products.

4.2 Idea Screening and Selection

Timmons suggested that in order to be able to assess the potential of an idea/opportunity for business, a number of questions need to be answered. These questions are listed in the following. To begin with, the first thing to be evaluated is the offering— the product/service that we intend to offer to the customer.

- *Product / Service*
    - o   Does your *product/service create or add significant value to customer* or end-user?Or, does it solve a significant problem/need for which the customer is willing to pay a premium
    - o   Customers are reachable and receptive
    - o   Product life is durable
    - o   Robust market in terms of potential revenues and margins
- The next concern relates to the *sources of advantage that exists as of now in our favour.*
    - o   'First mover' advantages
    - o   Control over prices or costs
    - o   Patents or trade secrets
    - o   Special know-how
    - o   Special relationships with customers or suppliers
    - o   Contractual advantages
- *Value creation and realisation of benefits out of it.*
    - o   Offers attractive returns for investors (ROI)
    - o.   Has low to moderate capitalisation needs that are fundable
    - o   Has a viable exit strategy
    - o   Risk/reward balance
- *Customer/Market*
    - o   Need/Problem
    - o   Customer Description/Identifiable and Reachable

- o   User Benefit
- o   Demand Durability
- o   Market Structure
- o   Market Size
- o   Market Growth
- o   Market Trends
- o   Market Capacity
- o   Market Share Attainable

- *Competitors' Competitive Advantage*
  - o   Competitor Assessment
  - o   Barriers to Entry
  - o   Competitive Lead Time
  - o   Competitive Advantage
  - o   Cost/Price
  - o   Channels
  - o   Proprietary Technology
  - o   Lead Time
  - o   Service
  - o   Contracts/Contacts
  - o   Key People

- *Management Team*
  - o   Entrepreneurial Skills
  - o   Industry and Technical
  - o   Integrity and Intellectual Honesty
  - o   Ability to Work Together
  - o   Balanced in Team Roles and Styles
  - o   Goal Alignment
  - o   Team Skills
  - o   Management Holes/Gaps

Subsequent to the above exercise of screening ideas, one can reaffirm that the selected idea for the project is appropriate by using the five characteristics that an idea must have to qualify as a potential business opportunity. This was suggested by Timmons.

- Creates *significant value for customers* by solving a significant problem or filling a significant unmet need for which they are willing to pay a premium

- Offers *significant profit potential* to the entrepreneur and investors-enough to meet their risk/reward expectations
- Represents a good *fit with the capabilities of the founder* and management team- experience and skills.
- Is *durable* in the sense that the opportunity for profits will persist over a reasonable length of time
- The opportunity is *amenable to financing.*

There are some other ways in which one can look at the overall suitability of an idea for business ventures (see Table 4.1). This is done by means of creating a table containing the requirements of the product/service concept and providing a weightage to the various dimensions in terms of the relative importance of the dimensions. Thereafter, one is to provide a score to the venture on the same dimensions. A multiplication of the relative weights with the venture scores provides us with the business venture score for each dimension. The total of the various dimensions becomes the overall score. This score can tell us if the venture is feasible or not.

Table 4.1 Idea evaluation

Product requirements dimension	Weightage	Venture score	Business venture rating
Unique product/service			
Favourable competitive situation			
Sales forecast justifies up front expenditure			
Technical feasibility of production and distribution			
Limited supplier power			
Limited buyer power			
High scalability of product/service			
High profit margins in industry			
Ease of raising capital			
Favourable time to market time			
Total			

□□□

At a Glance

1. Idea generation techniques include:
    - (a) Brain storming
    - (b) Fishbone Diagram
    - (c) Free association
    - (d) Mind mapping
    - (e) Visual brainstorming
    - (f) Attribute listing
    - (g) Card Story Board
    - (h) False faces
    - (i) Problem reversal

2. SCAMPER is the acronym for:
S	-	Substitute
C	-	Combine
A	-	Adopt
M	-	Modify
P	-	Put to another use
E	-	Eliminate
R	-	Reverse

3. In problem reversal "What-If-Compass" — The author has a list of pairs opposing actions which can be applied to the problem. Just ask yourself 'What if I_____ and plug in each one of the opposites. A small sample:
    - Stretch it/ Shrink it
    - Freeze it/ Melt it
    - Personalise it/ De- personalize it
    - Turn defeat into victory or victory into defeat

4. Some of the steps in false faces techniques are presented as follows:
    - State the problem
    - List the assumptions
    - Challenge the fundamental assumptions
    - Reverse each assumption- write down the opposite for each one
    - Record differing view points that might prove useful to you
    - Ask how is accomplish each reversal

Multiple Choice Questions

1. Timmons suggested that in order to be able to assess the potential of an idea/ opportunity for business a number of questions need to be answered. One question is:
    - (a) Why your customers are not reachable and non-receptive?

(b) Do you have any special know- how?

(c) Does your patent or trademark has secrets?

(d) Does your product/ service create or add significant value to customer or end user?

2. Create significant value for customers by:

(a) By solving insignificant problem

(b) Do not offer profit potential to the entrepreneur

(c) The opportunity is amenable to love making

(d) Is durable in the sense that the opportunity

3. Idea generation techniques include:

(a) Brain testing

(b) Brainstorming

(c) All of the above

(d) None of the above

Ans. 1. d, 2. d, 3. b

Review Questions

1. According to Timmons some questions need to be answered to assess the potential of an idea. Please form at least 15 questions under different heading.

2. What is chuncking & when to use chunking?

3. To generate a new way of doing something you could list all the key attributes of current approaches and try to improve some of them. Pleaes enlist them?

4. Briefly describe the idea generation Techiques as discussed in the chapter.

Chapter 5

Feasibility Analysis

Introduction

The feasibility analysis of a new venture is done with a determination of the likelihood that a proposed product or service concept will fulfil the objectives of the entrepreneur(s) and investor(s) in terms of returns. For this purpose, a significant number of activities need to be undertaken and placed in the form of a report. These activities constitute the components of the feasibility report and subsequently can be utilised by the entrepreneur by producing the feasible business ideas assessment in the form of the business plan for the venture. The activities are in the following:

- Economic Feasibility
- Market Feasibility
- Financial Feasibility
- Technical Feasibility

The above listed activities tell us that from the perspective of the economics of the business in terms whether it will be possible to command a price for the offerings, the possibility of having a sizeable market for our products and services and that the venture will be able to source and payback the fund requirement from the activities of the business. The various details that emerge from the feasibility analysis and contribute to a larger portion of the business plan are as follows:

- Executive Summary
- The Industry and the Firm
- Market Research and Analysis
- The Economics of the Business
- Marketing Plan
- Design and Development Plan
- Manufacturing and Operational Plan

- Management Team
- Overall Schedule
- Critical Risks, Problems and Assumptions
- Financial Plan
- Appendices

The details that go into these are discussed at the end of this chapter, wherein you would find that how do the various dimensions of feasibility contribute to the final successful business plan document.

5.1 Economic Feasibility

Economic analysis is used for evaluating the effectiveness of a proposed system. This method is also known as **cost/benefits analysis.** The procedure is to determine the benefits and savings that are expected from a proposed system and compare them with the costs. If the benefits outweigh the costs, then the decision is made to design and implement the proposed system.

The economic feasibility is addressed by studying what goes into the business model of the venture. The business model is typically about the summation of the core business decisions and trade-offs employed by a company to earn a profit. A business model is an ecosystem that determines three key variables and how they interact: price, cost and value.

So, essentially to assess economic feasibility, the starting point would be the business ecosystem in which we intend to operate to be followed by identifying the critical success factors for the venture (CSF). Questions related to the CSFs would be as follows:

- Which elements of a company's business model are most important to achieve its profits goals?
- Which of these elements are the most difficult to execute?
- Will they change over time?

One of the ways in which we can look at the economic feasibility of a venture is to address the questions provided herein.

- Value-cost-price
  - o Is every step in your process adding value?
  - o Is your product or service optimally designed?
  - o Are your costs as low as possible?
  - o Are your prices appropriate given the value, competition and costs involved
- Hidden Costs

- o   Have you identified any hidden costs?
- o   Have you quantified your hidden costs? (Made them visible)
- o   Have you eliminated them?
- Trade-offs
  - o   Have you identified your trade-off decisions involved?
  - o   Have you quantified the pain vs. gain in each case?
  - o   Can you justify your trade-off decisions?
  - o   Do you really face trade-offs? Can you avoid them?
  - Cost functions
  - o   Do you know how your costs are changing as output changes?
  - o   Do you know what are your marginal cost and your average costs?
  - o   What are your fixed costs and variable costs? Can this combination be modified?
- People/Knowledge and Machines
  - o   Are all resources being used cost effectively?
  - o   Do you have the right mix of people/knowledge and machines?
  - o   Can you substitute one for the other?
- Scale vs. Scope
  - o   Can you achieve cost savings by expanding your scale?
  - o   Can you achieve cost savings by expanding your scope?
  - o   Can you combine the two of them?
  - o   Can you mass customise your product?
- Market and Demand
  - o   Do you know how your product service creates value?
  - o   Do you manage in terms of the key forces of demand for your products and your competitions?
- Risks
  - o   Can you appropriately evaluate the risks involved?
  - o   Can you measure and quantify all the risks?
  - o   Can you avoid the pitfalls of managing probabilities?
  - o   Can you justify the risks involved in key business decisions?

The requirements for raw materials, level of capacity utilisation, anticipated sales, anticipated expenses and the probable profits emerge from the answers for the above mentioned set of questions. It will have to be calculated how much sales would be necessary to earn the targeted profit. Undoubtedly, demand for the product will be estimated for anticipating sales volume. Demand for the product needs to be carefully spelled out as it is. Further, the location of the enterprise decided after conserving a large number of points also needs to be mentioned in the project. Government policies that can have an impact on the business also need to be considered.

5.2 Marketing Feasibility

All feasibility studies should look at *how* things work, *if* they will work and identify potential problems. Feasibility studies are done on ideas, campaigns, products, processes and entire businesses.

Feasibility studies assess and analyse potential business scenarios. While a marketing plan maps out specific ideas, strategies and campaigns based on feasibility study investigations that are intended to be implemented. Think of market feasibility studies as a logistical study and a marketing plan as a specific, planned course of action to take. 'Things to Include' in a market feasibility study should include:

- Description of the Industry
- Current Market Analysis
- Competition
- Anticipated Future Market Potential
- Potential Buyers and Sources of Revenues
- Sales Projections

(a) Industry description

Give a brief one-to two-paragraph description of the industry your business is categorised as per the product-market fit that you are trying to establish. Determining your industry is important for receiving government support, attracting investors and for receiving grants (if you form as a non-profit).

At the same time, this will help to ascertain where the competition is going to be from.

(b) Analysing your current market

This section of market feasibility study describes the current market for your product or service. If you are offering something so unique that there is less or no information about the market then you can either use related industry information, or even conduct your own independent primary study. There are several ways to conduct your own research for new ideas include: polling Internet forums, questionnaires addressed to targeted consumer groups or the general population, or even customer surveys. Any 'proof' you have that there is a demand (or market) for your product or services will help you sell your idea. This is particularly important if you are marketing something unique, or within a very small, specialised market. You need to show that your ideas are novel because you have found a niche and not because there is no existing market for the idea. A good source for finding out what is selling (and what is not) is to have an in-depth study of the different industry reports of products and services related to your offering or same as your offerings. Industries showing employee growth is often a good indicator of an industry's overall stability. Massive layoffs or few employer or employees indicates fewer business opportunities. Where there is demand for something, there should be correlating growth in employment, the number of new companies being formed or in the industry's overall combined revenue.

If you are planning to serve only a local market, start by identifying every competitor within the vicinity of the place. This would mean at least looking at a few nearby cities. The fastest way to do this is using a telephone book or online business locator or one may do a survey of the cities if it is possible for them to spend that much. List each competitor by location and distance from you, and from each other. You should closely examine all competing businesses that are within a specific distance of your location and at the same time the location that you are considering should also be evaluated thoroughly in terms of footfalls across the location in any time period. Consider their locations, business hours and how long they have been in business. These things can help you determine how hard it will be to establish a similar business in the same geographic area. You should also make note of any similar businesses in your area that have recently gone out of business. There may be a reason, such as poor location, high taxes or operating restrictions, or there may be not enough demand for the product or service in that area to sustain a business. Researching local competitor information can tell you two things: What works and what has not worked.

If you are planning to sell your products or services on a larger scale through say franchise development, or Internet sales, you need to look beyond local competition. You should look for industry databases and reports that would give you a larger view of competition across the length and breadth of the country. You can list them by industry, and by other variables to fine-tune your search. To find smaller competition, use a search engine to find businesses by key words related to your industry. For example, if you are starting on online retail outlet for speciality apparel, try searching on 'speciality apparel'. The return will show you companies selling similar products that are ranking high in search engine results and may be getting more business. Visit their websites to see what they are selling and what they are not selling. If you are not sure what keywords relate to your industry, use free, online keyword search tools to help you know what most people are searching for in your related field.

(c) How to calculate sales projections

Sales projections can be a challenge for any new business owner because there is little or no track record to support how fast you will grow or what products or services will sell best. Sales projections should factor in how much time and money will be invested into the business, and the markets you will be targeting. For example, if you get your product in the door at Big Bazaar, Spencers or some stores of this type, your sales are more likely to grow faster and your profits will be higher than if you sell your product at a few local 'mom and pop' (*kirana*) stores. For this reason, it is important that you first write market feasibility study. Your market study will help you decide where to sell your product of services, and what products and services are most likely to generate the most revenue. If you are have an Internet-based business

- estimate the total traffic (number of visitors) to your website each month;
- project anticipated site traffic volume over time;
- use traffic projections to estimate the average number of sales per every 10,000 visits to your site and
- calculate the average amount of each sale.

The more traffic you can drive to your site, the more opportunities you have for making a sale. Do you have good Search Engine Optimisation (SEO) skills? Do you have your website live and ready to go? These things are important to all Internet businesses because as your site becomes more popular, you can project an increase in sales.

(d) How to identify potential customers, clients and contract sources

This component of your small business market feasibility study should be descriptive. Your potential customers, clients and contract sources should include the following:

- A list of current customers, clients and contracts and the potential for new or renewed contracts.
- Any sales leads that may generate new customers or clients.
- A list of government contracting agencies with a brief description of what type of contracts they solicit, and how they pertain to your industry.
- A list of market types you currently, or intend to target, such as seniors citizens, working mothers, organisations, speciality retailers, etc.

Depending upon the nature of your business, it may not be possible to associate specific amounts of revenue with a particular market, but you can at least try to estimate the percentage of total revenue expected from each source.

5.3 Financial Feasibility

A financial feasibility study projects how much start-up capital is needed, sources of capital, returns on investment and other financial considerations. A financial feasibility study is an assessment of the financial aspects of something. In this case, for starting and running a business we need to consider many things including start-up capital, expenses, revenues and investor income and disbursements. Other portions of a complete feasibility study will also contribute data to your basic financial study. A financial feasibility study can focus on one particular project or area, or on a group of projects (such as advertising campaigns). However, for the purpose of establishing a business or attracting investors, one should include at least three key things in their comprehensive financial feasibility study:

- Start-Up Capital Requirements
- Start-Up Capital Sources
- Potential Returns for Investors

(a) Start-up capital requirements

Start-up capital is in simple words how much cash one will need to start a business and keep it running until it is self-sustaining. One should include enough capital funds (cash or access to cash) to run the business for at least one to two years.

(b) Calculating business start-up costs

Start-up costs will have to be calculated even if you believe you have a big idea. Whether you have already secured funding or just trying to figure out what it will take to get started, an accurate estimate of start-up costs is necessary to reasonably predict financial performance in the first few quarters. Of course, every business and every industry have different cost requirements, but these steps can help you start the number-crunching.

For example, running your own software company is going to have different start-up requirements than opening a pet store. There are six cost categories for new companies:

- Cost of sales
- Professional fees
- Technology costs
- Administrative costs/operational costs
- Sales and marketing costs
- Wages and salary

Think about how these costs categories will be weighted across your business. Going back to the earlier example, the software firm presumably would want to allocate more money to technology while the pet store presumably would need several shifts of employees, which means wages will carry a higher cost.

Look at industry leaders and other players of similar size to help predict your own business's costs. Obviously, your revenue numbers will look a little different, but break down how much a coffee chain spends on cost of sales and administrative expenses as a percentage of revenue. Keep in mind that large companies and chains will be more efficient since they have greater buying power and economies of scale than a start-up, but you can still use these percentages as goals to shoot for. Trade associations are an invaluable source of information for both new and established companies. Chances are whatever industry your start-up is in— from organic farming to independent bookstores— there will be a few entrepreneurs or a support group out there with industry information, statistics as well as several different entrepreneur forums where you can share ideas online. Also, do not be afraid to seek out other entrepreneurs who have set up shop in your industry, or perhaps a related one, and talk to them about their experience with start-up costs, especially unexpected costs.

(c) **Project start-up costs conservatively:** Business success stories, such as Pantaloons, Vishal Megamart or Shahnaz Herbal Products were not built overnight sensations. When calculating start-up costs, keep in mind that you may need a few months of funding to cover expenses even before you open for business. And once you do begin operating, it likely will take a significant amount of time until the business is self-sustaining. When approaching banks and other lenders for money, try to include a substantial cushion for beginning operations to ensure you will have enough money to set up an office, take orders, hire employees if necessary, and cover other related costs. Be reasonable with your revenue assumptions in the early stages and be conservative with cost projections. It is also possible to structure a small business loan to defer payments during the initial operating period.

(d) **Segregate one-time start-up costs from recurring costs:** Distinguish between which costs you will have to account for year-after-year, such as salaries and rent, and which upfront costs will be one-time charges, such as office furniture. This should allow you to establish a budget for after the start-up period. Look for opportunities to delay non-vital expenses, such as office decorations until after you have begun getting some business. Cash flow is the lifeblood of all businesses. Learn the Cash Flow, Ten Rules to free you from worrying about money. Use the basic rules to help you take control of your cash flow so you can create the business you have always dreamed of.

- *Never run out of cash.* Running out of cash is the definition of failure in business. Make the commitment to do what it takes so it does not happen to you.

- *Cash is king.* It is important to recognise that the basics of cash flow 101 are what keep your business alive. Manage it with the care and attention it deserves. It is very unforgiving if you do not. Remember, cash is king, because no cash means no business.

- *Know the cash balance now.* What is your cash balance right now? It is absolutely critical that you know exactly what your cash balance is. Even the most experienced person will fail if they are making business decisions using inaccurate or incomplete cash balances. This is fundamental cash flow 101. That is the reason why business failures are not limited to amateurs or people new to the business world.

- *Do today's work today.* The key to keeping an accurate cash balance in your accounting system is to do today's work today. When you do this, you will have the numbers you need— when you need them.

- *Do the work or get someone else.* Here is a simple rule to follow to make sure you have an accurate cash balance on your books. You do the work or have someone else to do it.

- *Do not manage from the bank balance.* The bank balance and the cash balance are two different forms of cash. Rarely will the two ever be the same. Do not make the mistake of confusing them. It is futile and frustrating to attempt to manage your cash flow using the bank balance. It is a prescription for failure. You reconcile your bank balance. You do not manage from it.

- *Know your six months cash balance.* What do you expect your cash balance to be six months from now? This one question will transform the way you manage your business and help you pass cash flow. This question really gets to the base of whether you are managing your business or whether your business is managing you.

- *Cash flow problems do not just happen.* You would be amazed at the number of small businesses that fail because the owner did not see a cash flow problem in time to do something about it. The key is to always be able to answer the question— what do I expect my cash balance to be six months from now?

- *Have cash flow projections.* Cash flow projections are the key to making wise and profitable business decisions. They give you the answer to the all-important question from Rule # 7. It is impossible to run your business properly without them.

- *Take care of customers.* Eliminate your cash flow worries so you are free to do what you do best-taking care of clients and making more money. Use these cash flow 101 rules to free yourself from cash flow worries. That way you can focus all your time and talents where you can make the most difference in your business.

No more wasted time worrying about what is going on with your cash flow. Instead, you can focus your unique talents and abilities each day on ways to grow your business and make more income each year. That is a recipe for success and wealth creation. The Cash Flow Projection shows how cash is expected to flow in and out of your business. For you, it is an important tool for cash flow management, letting you know when your expenditures are too high or when you might want to arrange short term investments to deal with a cash flow surplus. As part of your business plan, a Cash Flow Projection will give you a much better idea of how much capital investment your business idea needs. For a bank, the Cash Flow Projection offers evidence that your business is a good credit risk and that there will be enough cash on hand to make your business a good candidate for a line of credit or short term loan. Do not confuse a Cash Flow Projection with a Cash Flow Statement. The Cash Flow Statement shows how cash has flowed in and out of your business. In other words, it describes the cash flow that has occurred in the past. The Cash Flow Projection shows the cash that is anticipated to be generated or expended over a chosen period of time in the future.While both types of Cash Flow reports are important business decision-making tools for businesses; we are only concerned with the Cash Flow Projection in the business plan.

You will want to show Cash Flow Projections for each month over a one year period as part of the Financial Plan portion of your business plan. There are three parts to the Cash Flow Projection. The first part details your Cash Revenues. Enter your estimated sales figures for each month. Remember that these are Cash Revenues; you will only enter the sales that are collectible in cash during the specific month you are dealing with. The second part is your Cash Disbursements. Take the various expense categories from your ledger and list the cash expenditures you actually expect to pay that month for each month.The third part of the Cash Flow Projection is the Reconciliation of Cash Revenues to Cash Disbursements. As the word 'reconciliation' suggests, this section starts with an opening balance which is the carryover from the previous month's operations. The current month's revenues are added to this balance; the current month's disbursements are subtracted and the adjusted cash flow balance is carried over to the next month.

5.4 Technical Feasibility

The technical feasibility study assesses the details of how you will deliver a product or service (i.e., materials, labour, transportation, where your business will be located, technology needed, etc.). Think of the technical feasibility study as the logistical or tactical plan of *how* your business will produce, store, deliver and track its products or services.

A technical feasibility study is an excellent tool for trouble-shooting and long-term planning. In some regards, it serves as a flow chart of how your products and services evolve and move through your business to physically reach your market. Do not make the mistake of trying to entice investors with your staggering growth projections and potential returns on their investment that only includes income (revenue) to the business. With any increase in revenue there is always an increase in expenses. Expenses for technical requirements (i.e., materials and labour) should be noted in the technical feasibility study.

You also should not strictly rely on feasibility study conclusions to impress an investor. An experienced investor or lending institution will read your entire report and come to their own conclusions. Therefore, it is critical that the technical and financial data in your study reconcile. If other parts of your feasibility study shows growth, you will also have to project labour and other costs and the technical ability to support that growth. The technical component serves as the written explanation of financial data because if offers you a place to include detailed information about why an expense has been projected high or low, or why it is even necessary. It demonstrates to potential investors and lenders (and in some cases, potential clients) that you have thought about the long-term needs your business will have as it grows.

(a) Preparing an outline for writing your technical feasibility study

The order that you present technical information is not as important as making sure you have all the components to show how you can run your business. You do not have to include specific financial information in the technical portion of your feasibility study, but all information in this component must support your financial data represented elsewhere. Basic things that most businesses need to include in their technical feasibility study include as follows:

- Materials
- Labour
- Transportation or Shipping
- Physical Location
- Technology

(b) Calculating material requirements

In this section, you list the materials you need to produce a product or service, and where you will get those materials. Include information, such as if volume discounts will be available as your business grows, or if you ever plan to manufacture your own parts at some point in time.

Things to include in your list of materials are as follows:

- Parts needed to produce a product
- Supplies (glue, nails, etc.)
- Other materials that are involved in producing or manufacturing your product.

You do not need to include actual financial data in this portion of the study but financial data supporting your narrative assessment should be included in a separate spreadsheet as an attachment.

(c) Calculating labour requirements

You cannot run a business, offer services or manufacturer products for free. Even if you start your business with you as your only employee, at some point, if you plan to grow you will need to add to your labour pool. In most cases, labour will be one of your biggest small business expenses. In this section, you will list the number and types of employees needed to run your business now, and that may be employed in the future as your business grows. You can break labour into categories, if necessary, as in the following:

- Senior Level Management
- Office and Clerical Support
- Production or Distribution
- Professional Staff (i.e., lawyers, accountants, engineers, marketing)
- Fulfilment (i.e., mail room, shipping department)

If you plan to outsource (hire another company to do a job for you) order fulfilment, fundraising or other aspects of your company's business, be sure to list what functions will be outsourced and to where.

(d) Transportation and shipping requirements

If you need to ship items from one place to another, how will you transport these items? Small items can be shipped via local carriers, DHL, DTDC, but heavy or bulk items may need to be transported via a freight or trucking company. If you are shipping perishable items, you will need special overnight handling. You may also need special permits to ship certain items, and nonprofits organisations should consider applying for discounted postal rates. These are all things that affect the technical, or 'how' of moving your goods from one place to another. If you offer services, how will trainers, educators, consultants, sales personnel get to customers and clients?If you offer a product that is governed by state or federal law (such as medications or prescription medical supplies), do you need a licensed distributor or pharmacy to ship on your behalf? In the Transportation Feasibility component, list things that will affect how you get your goods or services to other businesses or individuals, including:

- the methods of transportation and shipping services that will be needed to get your product or services to a customer;
- special handling or other unique arrangements required to transport your product;
- any special permits that will be required, including postal rate discounts; and

- cars (company or privately owned) and other vehicles needed to conduct your business.

(e) Physical location of your business

Where you run your business, you will have an effect on your success. If you are starting out in a home-based office, project whether or not, and when, you might need any of the following:

- A 'Brick and Mortar' Office (office space outside your home)
- Warehouse Facilities
- Your Own Factory
- Your Own Trucking Facility
- Retail Storefront
- Any other purchased or rented facilities needed to conduct your business.

In the Physical Location Feasibility component, you should also discuss the pros and cons of where these facilities will be located. Should they be in one central location, or across state lines? Do you need to have special parking considerations for customers or trucks? Do you need to be near other facilities, such as an airport, commercial hubs, or shopping mall?

(f) Technology requirements to run your business

Every business needs at least some kind of technology to operate. The technology component includes discussions about, and a probable list of the following:

- Telephone Answering Systems
- Computer Hardware and Software
- Inventory Management
- Cash Registers, Credit Card Collection, Cheque Processing
- Special Devices to Accommodate the Disabled
- Teleconferencing Facilities and Equipment
- Cell Phones, PDAs or Other Devices Needed to Conduct Business
- Alarm or Camera Systems
- Manufacturing Equipment

The order in which you present your technical requirements is not as important as making sure that you include all the technical requirements of your business from production to customer receipt. This information will help investors know more about the operations of your business. Having a great idea for a product or business is not enough; you have to show how you can make money from the idea. The technical feasibility study addresses the physical and logistical mechanics of if, and how, you will be able to get something into product and back out the door to customers.

5.5 Why Do Ventures Fail

Even though prospective entrepreneurs put in a lot of effort to start their venture— there are times, when there is a shortfall on one or more dimensions. Some of the most common dimensions that lead to failure of new ventures are presented as follows:

(a) **Poor execution:** As many people recommend, crisp execution— rather than a clever idea— is vital to the success of new businesses. It stands to reason, therefore, that poor execution is the downfall of most startups that go bust. There are several ways you can avoid execution failure. First, you should conduct an honest evaluation of your skills and only pursue opportunities that are aligned with your strengths. Entrepreneurs who are blinded by greed or arrogance are more prone to getting in over their heads. It is also wise to surround yourself with talented people who are not afraid to speak up when you are headed off a cliff. Companies with inept leadership usually fail in the first year or two, but even established companies can stumble badly when they outgrow the capabilities of the founding team. Bill Gates led Microsoft from inception to its current position as one of the largest and most successful companies in history, but this is seldom the case. As a founder, you need the discipline to know when to hand over the reins to a professional manager who can take your business to the next level.

(b) **No viable market:** Each day, entrepreneurs from the 'build it and they will come' school of business invest their money in a cool idea with the hopes that customers will magically appear once they open the doors. All too frequently, these hopes turn out to be in vain. History is replete with ventures that crashed and burned because the founders spent all of their time and money developing a product without bothering to consider how to attract customers. Even worse, many did not really understand what customers valued and were willing to pay for. (Remember the 'dot bomb' era of the not-so-distant past?) It is imperative to research and validate the market before you launch your business. Talk to prospective customers and find out what they really need. Chances are you will end up with a much more compelling offering than what you initially dreamed up on your own. Remember, find the customers first, and then look for a solution.

(c) **Too much leverage:** Mature companies can predict revenues over the next few quarters with some degree of certainty. On one hand, these businesses can make prudent use of leverage, both financial (debt) and operating (fixed overhead costs) to improve equity returns. Revenues projections for early-stage companies, on the other hand, can be all over the map. In this environment, it can be dangerous to take on more than a modest amount of debt or other fixed obligations (rent, salaries, etc.). With little margin for error, if revenues take longer to ramp up than expected— as they nearly always do— you may find yourself handing the keys of your business over to your creditors. Itis best to keep most costs variable at first and use equity capital to finance your start-up until your company has been around a while and you develop some confidence in your ability to forecast sales. Delay making investments or taking on fixed obligations until you have a critical mass of customers. You will know when it is time to rent a larger office space or hire that second shift when you have got a backlog of orders on the books.

(d) **Undercapitalising the business:** It is all too common for entrepreneurs to grossly underestimate the amount of time and capital necessary to reach cash flow breakeven, causing many promising ventures to shut down prematurely. Be conservative with your financial projections and plan on having adequate funds when you launch to cover all sunk costs (including start-up losses) until your company becomes cash flow positive. If you do not have enough savings to cover the required investment, it may be tempting to launch your start-up under the assumption that you will be able to obtain funding at a later date. While staging investment has its advantages (preserving the option to abandon, higher valuation and, therefore, less dilution, etc.), this strategy can backfire and leave you unable to get the money when you need it most or force you to negotiate with banks and investors from a position of weakness. It is often better to change the business model to bring required investment in line with available resources.

(e) **Lack of competitive advantages:** Does your town really need another dry cleaner, pizzeria or lawn care service? Entrepreneurs frequently start these 'me-too kind' of businesses because of their simplicity and modest capital requirements. However, the lack of competitive barriers renders them extremely vulnerable to new entrants, who will gladly cut prices to the bone to steal customers. If you want your start-up to thrive, you need something that insulates it from competition. It could be a great location, a cool brand, proprietary technology or a cost structure that cannot be easily replicated. None of these advantages is likely to be permanent, but they only need to shield you long enough for your company to take root. This will give you time to make investments that create additional barriers.

(f) **Competing head-to-head with industry leaders:** A sure sign of impending failure is an entrepreneur who plans to bootstrap his/her new business while competing directly against entrenched market leaders. Large businesses have enormous resources to deter competitors from entering their markets. Big companies can undercut your prices, outspend you on advertising, and choke off access to suppliers and distributors. It is advised against making a frontal assault unless you have a world-class team and very deep pockets. Even then, your chances of success are likely to be disappointing.

(g) **Picking a niche that is too small:** Most small businesses compete successfully against larger rivals by specialising in a niche market. However, you still need to do your homework to be sure that the niche is large enough to support your business and that customers are not too expensive to find and serve. You may discover that niche markets can be just as fiercely competitive as the mass market. You need to figure out how fast your niche is growing and how much market share you will need to capture. If your financial projections require you to hold more than a few percent of market share to remain profitable, be careful. Do not press ahead unless you can convincingly demonstrate to yourself how your competitive advantages will enable you to become the market leader.

(h) Break-up of the founding team: A start-up can be a high-stress environment, especially when you are struggling to turn the corner before the lights go out. At moments like this, disagreements about the direction of the company or the division of profits among the owners can lead to a rift within the founding team. Because people wear lots of hats in start-ups, the sudden departure of a key executive can doom a fledgling organisation. This makes it imperative to structure agreements so that the founders and key hires are treated fairly and that everyone's interests are closely aligned with the success of the new venture.

(i) Poor pricing strategy: The most common method for setting prices is to start at the unit cost and then mark up the price to achieve a profit, so-called 'cost-plus' pricing. Unfortunately, cost has little to do with how a product or service is valued by customers, which can lead to systematic under pricing. For example, if a widget costs ₹20 to manufacture and you sell it to a customer for ₹25 when that customer would gladly have paid ₹35, you have left ₹10 worth of value on the table. Even worse, cost-based pricing can lead to prices that are greater than what the market will bear. Because unit cost is related to sales volume (see CVP Analysis for more info), high prices lead to fewer sales, which in turn increases unit cost, leading to a further round of price increases. In *The Strategy and Tactics of Pricing*, Thomas Nagle and John Hogan point out, , *failing to account for the effect of price on sales volume—and hence costs—has led to numerous business failures over the years once they enter a "death spiral" of price increases to allocate fixed costs across a smaller volume of sales. You should instead let anticipated prices, based on the product's perceived value to customers; determine the cost structure, not the other way around. Consequently, pricing strategy and customer value should be addressed in the earliest stages of planning a new business.*

(j) Growing too fast: Growth is generally regarded as an indication of business success, but uncontrolled growth can— and does— kill entrepreneurial companies for two primary reasons. The first is that businesses need systems and infrastructure to scale properly, but few invest the time and effort to lay the foundations for growth in those first hectic years. That is too bad, because things tend to spin out of control when you put the pedal down. This can be especially problematic for companies that receive a large infusion of outside capital. It is the equivalent of trying to break the land speed record by strapping a jet engine onto a soap box racer. Do not be surprised when the wheels come off. The second reason is that top-line growth requires additional investments in fixed assets (warehouses, machinery, trucks, etc.) and working capital (inventory, accounts receivable, etc.). At controlled rates of growth, on one hand, companies are able to finance incremental sales through internal cash flow. Hyper growth, on the other hand, can suck up large amounts of cash, forcing businesses deep into debt or bringing the whole enterprise to a screeching halt. Many times, owners are not even aware of the impending collapse, because they focus on profitability (as depicted on the income statement) rather than cash flow. Never forget that cash is the lifeblood of your business!

□□□

At a Glance

1. For feasibility analysis a significant number of activities need to be undertaken and placed in the form of a report. Following are the listed activities:
   - Economic feasibility
   - Market feasibility
   - Financial feasibility
   - Technical feasibility

   Details that emerge from these above listed activities are :

   Executive Summary, The Industry and the firm, Market research and analysis, Economics of the business, Mraketing plan, Design and development plan, Manufacturing and operational plan, Management team, Overall schedule, Critical risks, problems and assumptions, Financial plan and Appendices

2. Questions related to critical success factors are:
   - Which elements of a company's business model are most important to achieve its profit goals?
   - Out of company's business model elements which one is the most difficult to execute?
   - Will these elements change over time?

3. Things to include in a market feasibility study should include:
   - Description of the industry
   - Current market analysis
   - Competition
   - Anticipated future market potential
   - Potential buyers and sources of revenues
   - Sales projections

4. Calculate sales projection when you have an internet-based business by:
   - Estimating the total traffic (number of visitors) to the website each month
   - Project anticipated site traffic volume overtime
   - Use traffic projections to estimate the average number of sales per every

        10,000 visits to the site

- Calculate the average amount of sale

5. Three key things for comprehensive financial feasibility study are:
   - Start-up capital requirements
   - Start-up capital sources
   - Start-up capital requirements

6. There are six cost categories for new companies:
   - Cost of sales
   - Professional fees
   - Technology costs
   - Administrative costs/operational costs
   - Sales and marketing costs
   - Wages and Salary

7. Basic rules to help you to take control of your cash flow are:
   - Never run out of cash
   - Cash is king
   - Know the cash balance now
   - Do today's work today
   - Do the work or get someone else to do it
   - Do not manage from bank balance
   - Know your six months cash balance
   - Cash flow problems do not just happen
   - Have cash flow projections
   - Take care of customers

8. You can break labour into following categories:
   - Senior level management
   - Office and clerical support
   - Production or distribution
   - Professional staff (i.e. lawyers, accountants, engineers, marketing)
   - Fulfilment (i.e. mail room, shipping department)

9. Technology requirements to run a business are
   - Telephone Answering Systems
   - Computer hardware and software
   - Inventory management
   - Cash registers, credit card collection, cheque processing
   - Special devices to accommodate the disabled
   - Teleconferencing facilities and equipment
   - Cell phones, PDAs or other devices needed to conduct business
   - Alarms or camera systems

- Manufacturing equipment

10. Failure of new ventures are due to following:
   (a) Poor execution
   (b) No viable market
   (c) Too much leverage
   (d) Undercapitalising the business
   (e) Lack of competitive advantage
   (f) Competing head-to-head with industry leaders
   (g) Picking a niche that is too small
   (h) Break-up of the founding team
   (i) Poor pricing strategy
   (j) Growing too fast

Multiple Choice Questions

1. Economic analysis is used to evaluate the effectiveness of a proposed system. This method is also known as:
   (a) Financial plan
   (b) Economic feasibility
   (c) Cost/benefit analysis
   (d) Overall schedule

2. Value-cost-price comprises:
   (a) Can you justify your trade-off decisions?
   (b) Substitute one for another
   (c) Kow how your product service creates value
   (d) Are your cost-price is as low as possible ?

3. Market feasibility study should include:
   (a) Anticipated future market potential and current market analysis
   (b) Evaluate the risk involved
   (c) Avoid the pitfalls of managing probabilities
   (d) Product or services are optimally designed

4. Under critical success factors Scale v/s. Scope ask the question:
   (a) Do you know how your costs are changing as output changes?
   (b) How would you customize your product and achieve cost savings by expanding your scale?
   (c) Are all resources being used cost effectively?
   (d) Calculate the average amount of each sale

5. Comprehensive financial feasibility study comprises:
   (a) A list of current customers, clients and contracts and the potential for new or renewed contracts
   (b) Sell your product at a few local 'mom and pop' (*Kirana*) stores

    (c)   Start up capital requirements, start up capital sources and potential return for investors

    (d)   Seek out other entrepreneurs who have set up shop in your industry

6.   Cost of sales, professional fees, technology costs, administrative costs/ operational costs and sales and marketing costs are the cost categories for new companies but the sixth one is missing which is:

    (a)   Business start up costs

    (b)   Wages and salary

    (c)   Calculating material requirements

    (d)   Physical location of your business

Ans. 1. c, 2. d, 3. a, 4. b, 5. c, 6. b

Review Questions

1.   If you are starting out in a home- based office you will need to have certain facilities. Please enumerate them.

2.   Even though prospective entrepreneurs put in a lot of effort to start their venture but inspite of their best efforts at times, they as well as their new ventures fail. Write in detail the most common dimensions that lead to failure of their ventures.

3.   What is so-called 'cost plus' pricing? Give suitable examples.

4.   Growing two fast and uncontrolled growth can and does kill entrepreneurial companies for various reasons. Cite example and use your imagination liberally to list a few.

5.   What is market feasibility study in a business? Give detailed description.

6.   A technical feasibility study is an excellent tool for trouble shooting and long term planning. How?

7.   Mention those "technology requirements" that you need to run your own business.

Chapter 6
Project Planning

Introduction

The task of starting a business is preceded by the choice of what business one wants to pursue. Subsequent to the feasibility analysis for a venture it is essential that based on that feasibility a complete road map be developed that will be followed by the entrepreneur and his team while trying to establish that business. If we take the new venture as a project then what we need is a project plan to clearly state our objectives and achievable along with the time that is needed to execute the various tasks.

6.1 Projects

The project planning exercise is all about chalking out a course of action for implementing the launch of a new venture. For the purpose of understanding the whole concept of project planning, we can consider that the enterprise itself is a project. So the success or failure of an enterprise largely depends upon the project plan and its implementation. In simple words, a project is an idea or plan that is intended to be carried out. The dictionary meaning of a 'project' is that it is a scheme, design; a proposal of something intended or devised to be achieved. Some have defined project 'as the whole complex of activities involved in using resources to gain benefits'. According to *Encyclopaedia of Management*, "a project is an organised unit dedicated to the attainment of a goal—the successful completion of a development project on time, within budget, in conformance with predetermined programme specification".

A project can also be defined as a scientifically evolved work plan devised to achieve a specific objective within a specified period of time. Here, it is also important to mention that while projects can differ in their size, nature, objectives, time duration and complexity, yet they partake of the following three basic attributes:

- A Course of action
- Specific Objectives

- Definite Time Perspective

Thus, every project has a starting point and an end point with specific objectives.

(a) Project classification

Project classification is a natural consequence to the study of project idea. Different authorities have classified projects differently. Following are the major classification of projects:

(i) Quantifiable and non-quantifiable projects

Projects for which a plausible quantitative assessment of benefits can be made are called **quantifiable projects**. Projects concerned with industrial development, power generation, mineral development fall in this category. On the contrary, non-quantifiable projects are those in which a plausible quantitative assessment cannot be made. Projects involving health education and defence are the example of non-quantifiable projects.

(ii) Sectoral projects

According to this classification, a project may fall in any one of the following sectors:

- Agriculture and Allied Sector
- Irrigation and Power Sector
- Industry and Mining Sector
- Transport and Communication Sector
- Social Service Sector
- Miscellaneous Sector

The project classification based on economic sectors is found useful in resource allocation more especially at macro levels.

(iii) Techno-Economic Project

Projects classification based on techno-economic characteristics fall in this category. This type of classification includes factors intensity-oriented classification, causation-oriented classification and magnitude-oriented classification. These are discussed as follows:

- Factor intensity-oriented classification: based on factor intensity classification, projects may be classified as capital intensive or labour intensive. If large investment is made in plant and machinery, the projects will be/ termed as 'capital intensive'. On the contrary, projects involving large number of human resources will be termed as 'labour intensive'.
- Causation-oriented Classification: where causation is used as a basis of classification projects may be classified as demand based or raw material

based projects. They very existence of demand for certain goods or services makes the project demand-based and the availability of certain raw material, skills or other inputs makes the project raw material –based.

Magnitude-oriented Classification: In case of magnitude-oriented classification, based on the size of investment involved in the projects, the projects are classified into large scale, medium-scale or small-scale projects.

Project classification based on techno-economic characteristics is found useful in facilitating the process of feasibility appraisal of the project. Let us address the question: how the entrepreneurs finally select the project? The fact remains that in spite of increasing literature on entrepreneurs do finally select a project, comparatively little is known about how an entrepreneur identifies and select a project. Hence, it is somewhat difficult to state in any categorical manner as to how an intending entrepreneur should proceed to select his/her project. As a matter of fact, project selection is not a nebulous idea. It is a well outlined game plan. There is a definite procedure of selecting a project. Basically, project selection consists of two main steps: Project Identification and then Project Selection.

(b) Project identification: If we ask anyone intending entrepreneur what project he/she will select, the obvious answer would be "a project having a good market". But the question is how without knowing the product could one determine the market? Whose market will one find out without knowing the item, that is, product? Idea generation about a few projects provides a way out of above tangle.

Project selection process starts with the generation of a product idea. In order to select the most promising project, the entrepreneur needs to generate a few ideas about the possible project he/she can undertake. The project ideas can be discovered from various—internal and external sources. These may include:

- Knowledge of potential customer needs,
- Watching emerging trends in demands for certain products,
- Scope for producing substitute product,
- Going through certain professional magazines catering to specific interests, such as electronics, computers, etc.,
- Success stories of known entrepreneurs or friends or relatives,
- Making visits to trade fairs and exhibitions displaying new products and services,
- Meeting with the government agencies,
- Ideas given by the knowledgeable person,
- Knowledge about the government policy, concessions and incentives, list of items reserved for exclusive manufacture in small scale sector,
- A new product introduced by the competitor.

(c) Project selection: Project selection starts from where project identification ends. After having some project ideas, these are analysed in the light of existing economic conditions, the government regulations, SWOT analysis. The intending entrepreneur analyses his/her strengths and weaknesses as well as opportunities/competitive advantages and threats/challenges offered by each of the project idea. On the basis of this analysis, the most suitable idea is finally selected to convert it into an enterprise. The process involved in selecting a project out of some projects is also described as the "zeroing in process".

What follows from above analysis is that there is a time interval involved in between project identification and project selection. But, in some cases, there may be almost no time gap between the two. An imaginary case can illustrate it. Project identification and selection is half done in the process of establishing an enterprise. The entrepreneur needs to analyse other related aspects also, such as raw material, potential market, labour, capital, location, forms of ownership, etc. It is necessary to mention that each of these aspects has to be evaluated independently and in relation to each other. This forms a continuous and "back and forth" process.

(d) Project formulation: A project report or a business plan is a written statement of what an entrepreneur proposes to take up. It is a written description of the course of action that the entrepreneur hopes to follow and achieve his business objectives. The significance of a project report is for two purposes: first and foremost, the project report is kike a road map. It describes the direction the enterprise is going in, what its goals are, where it wants to be, and how it is going to get there. It enables the entrepreneur to know that he is proceeding in the right direction. Some hold the view that without a well-spelled statement of goals and operational methods to achieve them, the business stands little chance to see success.

The second function of the project report is to attract investors. Although, it is not mandatory for the small enterprises to prepare a project report, yet it is useful and beneficial for them to prepare the project report for various reasons. The preparation of project report is beneficial for those who desire to apply for financial assistance from financial institutions and/ or commercial banks. It is the project report that such organisations evaluate to assess whether such a venture really does need that quantum of money and would it be able to pay it back in the time it is required to do so. Similarly, other organisations that provide assistance support to new ventures, such as Business and Technology Incubators at institutes of repute.

(e) Contents of a project report

Having assessed the importance of a project report, it is now essential to look at what are the details that have to present in a systematic and planned manner. The more comprehensive, and complete the business plan is, the more likely it is to earn the respect of concerned stakeholders. A good report should contain the following contents:

- Executive Summary
- The industry and the firm
- Market Research and Analysis
- The Economics of the business
- Marketing Plan
- Design and Development Plan
- Manufacturing and Operational Plan
- Management Team
- Overall Schedule
- Critical Risks, Problems and Assumptions
- Financial Plan
- Appendices

The details that go into each of these are presented as follows:

(i) Executive summary

Should be compelling and appealing, written in one or two pages. It is usually prepared after the other sections are completed. Business concept: it should explain how product or service will change the way customers currently do certain things. In case there is any proprietary technology, trade secrets or unique capabilities they should be out rightly mentioned here. The opportunity and the strategy that you intend to follow to achieve it should be written in brief. The opportunity should be summarised here and why it is compelling should be highlighted appropriately. A brief description of the primary customer groups, how you intend to position the product(s) and service(s). How the venture would reach and service these groups of customers. The structure of the market along with its size and the anticipated share of it that you would be able to capture with this venture should be clearly stated. What price you will charge for your offering. The source of advantage that you will create and endeavour to sustain and in what form is it warrants mention here.

(ii) The industry and the firm

This is the time we commence to put the details in place. This would include a complete description of the industry that we intend to become a part of or the one that we are creating by means of a novel offering. This will include the current status and prospects that the sector holds. The prospects will relate to the expectation of any new products or developments, new markets and customers, new requirements that may emerge over the coming times. Further to these details, a description of the concept of the business, product(s) or service(s), principal customers of the product(s) and service(s). Describe in some detail each product or service and the application of the product or service and describe end use as well as any significant secondary applications. The unique features of the product or service need to be elaborated. The recent state of development of the product or service and the time and money needed to fully develop, test, and introduce it in the market. In case any patents, trade secrets or proprietary features have been obtained they need to be highlighted. What can be possible future opportunities for expansion of product line and the commensurate growth strategy need to be discussed as the investors will be keen to know any additional revenue streams that can emerge in times to come.

(iii) Market research and analysis

This part of the report is supposed to provide information about the customers whom we intend to target. The rationale and process of segmenting the customers and the basis for that should be detailed. Appropriate explanation in this regard has to be presented. Some issues related to customers that should be covered are as follows:

- Location of the customers— regional, national, international
- Whether customers are easily reachable
- Describe customers' purchasing processes
- Why they might change current purchasing decisions
- Any orders, contracts or letters of commitment that you may have from some prospective customers.

The current market size and anticipated share by market segment and/or by regions and/or country along with the potential annual growth for three years should also be presented so as to make things clear about prospects for growth. At this stage, it is also important to describe the competition and the competitive edge they may be holding. A realistic assessment of the strengths and weaknesses of competitors, comparison of the fundamental value added or created by your product or service with regard to the competition. It is a sound idea to discuss three or four key competitors and why customers buy from them and why they leave them. With respect to these information presented till now, one has to plan for ongoing market evaluation to guide product-improvement programmes.

(iv) Economics of the business

A clear picture of the economics of engaging in this business with the product and service decided and the manner in which you decide. How does this work in favour of the venture. Would include information about as in the following:

- Gross and operating margins
- Profit potential and durability
- Fixed, variable and semi-variable costs (mention relevant industry benchmarks)
- Months to breakeven
- Months to reach positive cash flow

(v) Marketing plan

A detailed presentation of how you intend to attain the sales projections shown. How you intend to approach the market with your strategy to capture a market share. Should include the following:

- Specific marketing philosophy
- Plans for identifying and contacting potential customers
- What features of the product or service will be emphasized to generate sales
- Introduction of product –regional, national, or international
- Seasonal trends that underlie the cash conversion cycle in the industry
- Plans to obtain institutional contracts
- Pricing
  - Discuss pricing strategy and compare this with that of the major competitors
  - Whether gross profit margin large enough to cover all costs and still allow a profit
  - Justify your pricing strategy in terms of economic payback to customers
  - If product priced lower than that of competitors, how will maintain profitability
  - Describe any discount allowance for prompt payment or volume purchases
- Sales tactics
  - Describe the methods
  - Discuss the value chain and the margins for intermediaries
- Special policies regarding discounts, exclusive distribution rights

- How intermediaries will be selected
- Present a selling schedule and sales budget
- Service and warranty policy
  - o Indicate importance to the customers' purchasing decisions and discuss your method of handling service problems
  - o Describe the kind and term of warranties
  - o Compare service and warranty policies to those of your competitors
- Advertising and promotion
  - o Trade show participation, direct mailing, trade magazine advertisement, use of advertising agencies
  - o Schedule and approximate costs
- Distribution
  - o Methods and channels of distribution
  - o Sensitivity of shipping cost as a percent of the selling price
  - o If international sales are involved, how these will be handled

(vi) Design and development plan

In case your product concept is a product that needs to be designed and developed, in that case the details about how you are going to complete that task and what difficulties and risk would be involved. The costs that would be incurred on doing these processes and would it lead you to owning a patent or some intellectual property protection. These matters have to place in this section.

- Development status and tasks
- Current status of each product or service and what remains to be done
- Competence and expertise of the company has or will require

Difficulties and risks

- Possible effect on the cost of design and development, on the time to market introduction

Costs

- Design and development budget
- Discuss the impact on cash flow projections of underestimating this budget

Proprietary issues

- Describe any patent, trademark, copyright you own or are seeking
- Contractual rights or agreements

(vii) Manufacturing and operational plan

Again this section is dependent on the product service concept. This section will report on how you intend to produce the product and how would different activities be performed by the organisation in order to get the product to market in the time required. Some of the important issues that will have to be included there are as follows:

Operating cycle

- Lead/lag times
- Plan for handling any seasonal production load

Geographical location

- Advantages and disadvantages of the site location

Facilities and improvements

- How and when the necessary facilities to start production will be acquired
- Equipment and space — leased or acquired
- Future equipment needs

Strategy and plans

- Describe the manufacturing process
- Potential subcontractors

Production plan

- Approach to quality control, production control, inventory control

Regulatory and legal issues

- State, national or foreign regulatory requirements
- Any pending regulatory changes that can affect the nature of opportunity and its timing

*(viii) **Management Team:*** Another very important component of the project report is presenting information about the people who have started the venture and prospectively those whom you would employ. The credibility, reputation and personality go a long way in creating success. Some of the points that need to be part of this section area follow:

Organisation

- Key management roles and individuals who will fill these

Key management personnel

- Detailed background about each key person
- Describe exact duties and responsibilities of each of the key members

- Complete resumes for each key member to be included as an exhibit

Management compensation and ownership

- Other investors
- Board of directors
- Supporting professional advisors and services

(ix) Overall schedule

The section show's the timing and interrelationship of the major events necessary to launch the venture. Milestones critical to the venture's success in terms of: Incorporation of the venture, completion of design and development, completion of prototypes, obtaining of sales representatives, ordering of materials in production quantities, starting of production or operation, receipt of first order, delivery on first sale, receiving the first payment on accounts receivable. Further, there is a need to detail out the activities that are most likely to cause a schedule slippage and impact on the venture's operation; steps to be taken correct such slippages.

(x) Critical risks

An important component of a plan is to be able to present the knowledge of major problems or risks that may arise during and after the launch and after that. Presenting tells the reader (investor) that you are well-prepared event to the extent of knowing the 'what if' and 'then what' questions. Should provide information about as in the following:

- Running out of cash before orders are secured
- Potential price cutting by competitors
- Any potentially unfavorable industry wide trend
- Sales projections not achieved
- Difficulty encountered in obtaining needed bank credit
- Running out of cash after orders pour in
- Assumptions concerning sales projections, customer orders, etc.

(xi) Financial plan

This is the most important part of the plan after the executive summary. Indicates the venture's potential and presents a timetable for financial viability. Essentially this should include information about the following:

- Pro forma income statements for at least three years
  - Fully discuss the assumptions (e.g., amount for bad debts and discounts)
  - Highlight any major risks, such as the effect of a 20 percent reduction in sales from those projected
- Pro forma balance sheets for three years

- Pro forma cash flow analysis— monthly for first year
  - Determine the need for and timing of additional financing and indicate peak requirements for working capital
  - How additional financing will be obtained
- Discuss assumptions and sensitivity of cash flow to these assumptions
- Break-even chart
  - How the break-even might be lowered
  - Cost control
  - Mechanisms for the control of various cost elements
  - Highlights
  - Maximum amount of cash required and the timing
- Amount of debt and equity needed
  - How fast can the debt be paid
- Desired financing
- Use of funds

(xii) Appendices

The last section of the document is about providing any other information that would support the case of your venture for funding. An illustrative list would include the following:

- Product specifications or photos
- List of references
- Suppliers of critical components
- Special location factors
- Facilities or technical analysis
- Reports from consultants or technical experts
- Copies of any regulatory approval, licenses, etc.

Further to these details that are presented in a business plan document and expressed in the form of a presentation to those who seek to participate with the venture in some form, it is advisable to look at the checklist for business feasibility. This checklist can be summarised as follows:

- Identify the core competency of your business
- A core competency might be:
  - Valuable (can generate large revenue)

- o   Rare (not easily found in competitors)
- o   Non Substitutable (cannot be replaced)
- o   Costly to imitate (expensive for the competitors to try to duplicate)

- Develop a Concept Test
- Conduct a Market and Industry Research
- Conduct a Technical Feasibility Analysis
- Determine whether the proposed business has sufficient management expertise, organisational competence, and available resources.
- Conduct an Economic Feasibility Analysis
- Conduct a Financial Feasibility Analysis
- Financial Feasibility Study elements:
  - o   Estimation of Sales
  - o   Estimation of Costs
  - o   Estimation of Break-even Point and Profitability

- Identify the Strength, Weaknesses, Opportunity and Threats (SWOT Analysis) of the business

(f) Project implementation

Once the project is approved by investors and other concerned stakeholder, the next stage is to begin implementing the project. The implementation has to be drawn out in such a way that various activities are completed on time as delays in one would lead to delays in others and because of this it is essential to allocate appropriate time for each activity. It is a sound idea to draw out a time line for the activities that go into the successful launch of the venture.

The schedule given in Table 6.1 can be further broken into very minute specific tasks that are involved in setting up the enterprise.

Table 6.1 Timeline for Implementation of Project Plan

Tasks / Months	1	2	3	4	5	6	7	8	9	10	11	12
Formulation of project report												
Application for funding												
Acquisition of land												
Construction of building												
Installation of Machinery												
Manpower recruitment												
Commencement of commercial activity												

6.2 Project Evaluation

Project evaluation is a systematic and objective assessment of an ongoing or completed project. The aim is to determine the relevance and level of achievement of project objectives, development effectiveness, efficiency, impact and sustainability. Evaluations also feed lessons learned into the decision-making process of the project stakeholders. Design, monitoring and evaluation are all part of results-based project management. The key idea underlying project cycle management, and specifically monitoring and evaluation, is to help those responsible for managing the resources and activities of a project to enhance performance of the venture, from short-term to long-term.

There are various methods used for evaluating projects. Some of these are as follows:

- Simple rate of return (SRR)
- Payback Period (PBP)
- Benefit Cost Ratio (BCR)
- Net present Value (NVP) and
- Internal Rate of Return (IRR)

The SRR and the PBP are the undiscounted measures while BCR, NPV and IRR are the discounted measures of project worth of Investment. A brief about these methods is given as follows:

(a) Simple Rate of Return (SRR)

The SRR is a commonly used criterion of project evaluation. It basically expresses the average net profits (Net Cash Flows) generated each year by an investment as a percentage of investment over the investments expected life. It is as

$$SRR = Y/I$$

where

Y = the average annual net profit (after allowing depreciation) from the investment

I = the initial investment

The calculated SRR should be compared with the investor's Required Rate of Return (RRR) to judge the profitability of the investment. The investment will be accepted if SRR.RRR, otherwise it will be rejected. When the SRR of all the investment opportunities is greater than the RRR of the investor, then the investment yielding the highest SRR should be selected.

(b) Pay Back Period (PBP)

The payback period is the length of time required for an investment to pay itself out. It is computed as

PBP = I/E,

When the projected net cash flows (E) are uniform or

$$PBP = I / \sum_{n} En = 1,$$ When the projected net cash flows are non-uniform.

where I = the initial investment; E = the projected net cash flows per year from the investment.

PBP = Pay Back Period expressed in number of years.

The individual investments are ranked according to their relative payback period with the shortest being the most favored. The acceptability of the investment is determined by comparison with the investor's required payback period (RPP). Accept the investment when the PBP<RPP, otherwise reject the investment. Although it is simple and easy to use, the PBP method has two major weaknesses as a measure of investment worth.

- This method fails to consider earnings after the payback period is reached.
- It fails to consider the difference in timing of cash flows.

(c) Benefit Cost Ratio (BCR)

It is the ratio of present worth of benefit stream to present worth of cost stream, i.e.,

Sum of the present worth of benefit

BCR =

Sum of the present worth of cost

Mathematically, it can be shown as

$$\sum_{t=1}^{n} Bn / (1+i)^{n}$$

$$BCR = {}_{n}\sum_{t=1}^{n} Cn / (1+i)^{n}$$

where,

Bn = Benefit in each year

Cn = Cost in each year

n = number of year

i = interest (discount) rates.

The investment is said to be profitable when the BCR is one or greater than 1. This method is widely used in economic analysis and not in private investment analysis.

(d) Net Present Value (NPV)

Net present value is computed by finding the difference between the present worth of benefit stream less the present worth of cost stream. Or it is simply the present worth of the cash flow stream since it is a discounted cash flow measure of project worth along with internal rate of return.

NPV = Present worth of Benefit Stream – Present Worth of Cost Stream.

Mathematically, it can be shown as

$$NPV = \sum_{t=1}^{n} Bn / (1 + i)^n - = \sum_{t=1}^{n} Cn / (1 + i)^n$$

Or NPV = Present worth of the cash flow stream.

Mathematically,

$$NPV = \sum_{t=1}^{n} (Bn - Cn) / (1 + i)^n$$

where,

Bn = benefits in each year of the project.

Cn = Costs in each year of the project.

n = number of years in a project

i = interest (discount) rate

Bn – Cn = Cash flow in n_{th} year of the project

The project is profitable or feasible if the calculated NVP is positive when discounted at the opportunity cost of capital.

(e) Internal Rate of Return (IRR)

Internal Rate of Return (IRR) is that discount rate which just makes the net present value (NVP) of the cash flow equal zero. It is considered to be the most useful measure of project worth and used by almost all the institutions including World Bank in economic and financial analysis of the project. It represents the average earning power of the money used in the project over the project life. It is also sometimes called yield of the investment.

Mathematically,

IRR is that discount rate 'i' such that

$$\sum_{t=1}^{n} (Bn - Cn) / (1 + i)^{n} = 0, \text{ i.e., NVP} = 0$$

where,

Bn = Costs in each year of the project.

Cn = Costs in each year of the project.

n = number of years in the project.

i = interest (discount) rate.

A project is profitable or feasible for investment when the internal rate of return is higher than the opportunity cost of capital. The computation of IRR for project involves a trial and error method. Here, alternative discount rates are used to the cash flow streams of the project under consideration till the NPV of the project reaches zero. However, it is not always possible to get a discount rate which makes the NPV exactly equal to zero through this trial and error method. We may get discount rate, which makes the NPV nearer to zero, that is, either positive or negative. Under such situation, we use interpolation to estimate the true value. Interpolation is simply finding the intermediate value between too discount rates we have chosen. The rule for interpolating the value of the internal rate of return lying between two discount rates too high on the one side and the too low on the other is IRR = Lower discount rate: Difference between the two discount rates (NPV at lower discount rate: Absolute difference between the NPVs of the two discount rates).

6.3 Project Monitoring and Control

This part of the text deals with the manner in which one has to handle the events that were not a part of the original project when it was conceived. Monitoring and control lasts for the duration of the project and covers the development process: monitors all key parameters, such as cost, schedule, risks; takes corrective actions when needed; needs information on the development process, provided by metrics. There are three main issues that have to be looked after in project monitoring and control:

- Monitoring the project: anticipating, identifying and controlling risks
- Monitoring changes to the organisation.
- Controlling changes

(a) Monitoring the project

The project manager monitors the overall project. A phase project manager monitors his phase. The phase project manager reports to the overall project manager of any risks. Jointly, phase project managers and overall project manager should

- identify risks, potential project problems, as early as possible
- identify when goals may not be met
- identify when constraints may be violated
- ensure that contingency plans occur before unrecoverable problems occur
- provide and receive project status for the phases and total project.

When there is a significant chance that the goals of the project will not be met, this risk should be reported to upper management. Also, when the constraints of the project may be violated, specifically, costs being overrun and schedules significantly slipped, these risks will be reported. When there are disagreements between the phase project manager and overall project manager, then resolution will be escalated to the change control board. Lack of resolution there could escalate to upper management.

Figure 6.3 lists types of risks, identified and not identified. Of the identified risks, these can be separated into those that the project managers consider to be important and those not considered being important; of these, the important risks can be built into the schedule. Of these identified important risks, some will be actual problems and contingency plans in the schedule would be initiated. Of the identified risks, some will be considered not important. These later may not become problems, as expected, or may indeed become problems. The other categories of problems, unidentified problems, have a higher likelihood of being overlooked. Of these, some will become problems and others will not. Thus, as shown in figure above, there are three paths that result in problems:

- Those risks that are identified as important and you do nothing about them
- Those risks that are identified as unimportant and later change into a high risk
- Those you do not identify and later become problems.

Risks in 1 should never become a problem because the project managers would build them into the schedules. Risks in 2, although probably not built into the schedule, should be recorded and remembered and periodically revisited by project managers to determine if they are now turning into problems. Unidentified risks (3.) require constant monitoring by project managers to identify and resolve.

it is very likely at points in the project that the project will be ahead of technology and ahead of standards, resulting in risks involving these areas.

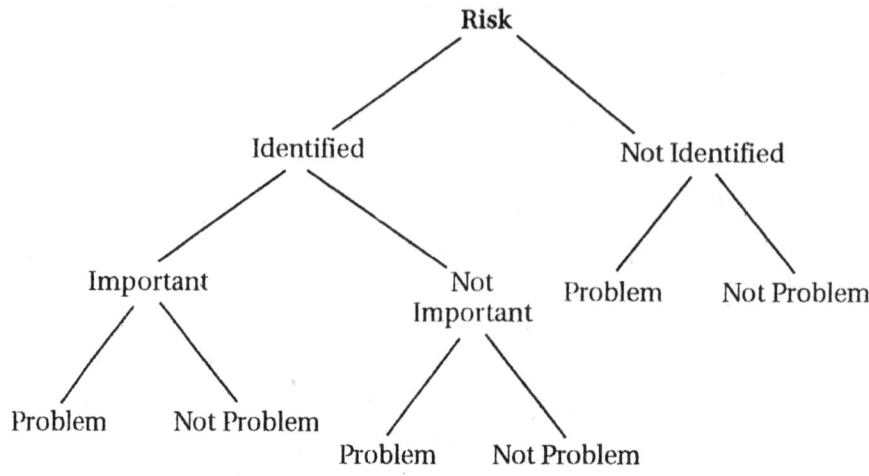

Fig.6.3 Type of Risk

There are also likely to be many generic project risks; Table 6.2 identifies the top ten project risks.

Table 6.2 Generic Project Risks

Project Risk	Importance
Lack of top management commitment to the project	9
Failure to gain user commitment	8
Misunderstanding the requirements	8
Lack of adequate user involvement	7.5
Failure to manage end user expectations	7
Changing scope/objectives	7
Lack of required knowledge/skills in the project personnel	7
Lack of frozen requirements	6.5
Introduction of new technology	6
Insufficient/inappropriate staffing	6
Conflict between user departments	5.5

(b) Monitoring changes to workflows

Reengineering workflows is not a "one shot" deal but should involve ongoing process management and improvement. Once workflows have been implemented, they should be monitored for actual improvement in business operations and for compliance with business policies.

Reengineering is imbedded both within human processes implemented in the organisation and within user interfaces. Both should be considered for further (even radical) change once the project is complete. As in the project reengineering process, the employee should be heavily involved, as reengineering is a social process in addition to a business and technical process.

(c) Monitoring system performance

A potential problem when automated systems are involved is the potential of the systems not being able to handle increased volumes of data in the future. To take care of this, performance monitoring should be a part of all automated systems that are likely to grow in size, identifying potential future bottlenecks in the system, including lack of disk space, lack or processing power, approaching transaction limits, long before they become a problem, so corrective action can be taken.

This process is very complex because automated systems will grow in size due to systems being installed incrementally (e.g., they may be installed at a pilot location first) and due to future increases in number of customers over time. It is also complex because new technology may become available that handles greater capacity but that will incur additional costs to the organisation to implement. In this book, it is proposed that information required for this planning be kept in a Performance and Adaptability Plan document that identifies future projections of increases in number of customers handled by automated systems, bottlenecks identified so far, and contingency plans for resolving anticipated future performance problems. The Performance and Adaptability Plan document would be used by business planners who would project increases in numbers of customers, performance monitors who identify bottlenecks in systems, and capacity planners who would identify requirements for changes to hardware and system software.

(d) Controlling changes

In order to provide stability to the project, project agreements must be recorded, and any changes to agreements must be evaluated for their effects upon other agreements. These agreements should, thus, be recorded in controlled documentation, and when an agreement is changed, then all other agreements that are based upon that agreement must be re-evaluated. In order to control controlled documents in the project, it is proposed that there be a *change control board* to review changes. The change control board would include the overall project manager, phase project managers, representatives of workers, users, the data processing group and business policy management, and perhaps a change control administration manager to update schedules and provide unbiased advice on business, technical and administrative decisions. Problems of interest to upper management, such as budget issues, would be escalated up to them for resolution. As the project progresses, the responsibilities of the phase managers might be consolidated and the change control board might grow smaller, eventually just handling maintenance changes rather than monitoring the project. When a phase is completed, resulting automated systems should go into maintenance mode. Changes to an automated system agreed upon by the change control board would be sent to a business group for design and to a maintenance group for implementation in the automated system. The maintenance group is often part or the entire group that did the development of the automated system. Once a phase is implemented, a help desk should take telephone calls from users of an automated system. The help desk would give advice on the use of the system and report on errors and suggested enhancements to the maintenance group who would go through the change board for review.

As the automated system matures, a user group might take over the change control board in reviewing changes. *Controlled Documents* may include the following:

- organisational objectives, priorities of objectives, strategies and goals
- project objectives, priorities of objectives, strategies, goals and constraints
- business requirements
- workflow requirements
- system requirements
- organisational business policies*
- interface plans*
- functional specifications*
- internal design documents (programming specifications)*
- vendor customisation specifications*
- programs and program code*
- databases and data dictionary*
- test plans*
- performance and scalability requirements (a "Performance, and Adaptability Plan")
- user documentation, including descriptions of user interfaces.

Once an automated system has been implemented, then the automated system must be maintained. After an automated system has been completed and goes into "maintenance mode", documents that extend beyond the project and should be maintained and kept up-to-date. Documentation that describes an automated system are functional specifications and internal design specifications. These documents should also be controlled. Doing so and enforcing that any changes to the automated system also be recorded in the functional and internal design specifications, provides control over the automated system. Technical items from which an automated system can be built—program code and databases—are also controlled. Program code and databases for previous versions of the automated system are also kept in case a severe problem occurs that requires a changed automated system to be backed out, returning to a previous version. Other documents than those listed above are less often controlled during the project, including project plans, risks and contingency plans because they are likely to change and be updated quite often, but should only be changed with careful consideration and consultations. Controlled documents can be used to control changes that may seriously harm a project and to distinguish an error in the project from a change in the project. An **error** is an inconsistency between how an agreement, workflow or automated system is implemented and how it is documented—this is either an error in the implementation or in the documentation. A **change** is a modification in the way an agreement, workflow or automated system is implemented when the implementation matches the documentation of it—for a change, both the agreement, workflow or automated system and the documentation should be changed.

❑❑❑

At a Glance

1. A project is defined as a scientifically evolved work plan devised to achieve a specific objective within a specified period of time. Projects may differ in their size, nature, objectives, time duration and complexity but they have three common attributes such as:

    *   A course of action
    *   Specific objectives
    *   Definite time perspective

2. Project classifications is a natural consequence to the study of project idea. Some of the major classifications are:

    *   Quantifiable and non-Quantifiable projects
    *   Sectoral projects
    *   Techno-economic projects

3. A good project report contains following:

    *   Executive summary
    *   The industry and the firm
    *   Market research and analysis
    *   The economics of the business
    *   Marketing plan
    *   Design and development plan

- Manufacturing and operational plan
- Management team
- Overall schedule
- Critical risks, problems and assumption
- Financial plan
- Appendices

4. In critical Risks "What if" and "then what" provides information about:
    - Running out of cash before orders are secured
    - Potential price cutting by competitors
    - Any potentially unfavourable industry-wide trend
    - Sales projection encountered in obtaining bank credit
    - Difficulty encountered in obtaining bank credit
    - Running out of cash after orders pour in
    - Assumption concerning sales projections, customer orders etc.

5. Some of the methods used for evaluating projects are simple rate of return, payback period, benefit-cost ratio, Net Present Value and Internal Rate of Return. The SRR & PBR are the undiscounted measures while BCR, NPV and IRR are the discounted measures of projects worth of investment.

6. The project manager monitors the overall project. A place project manager monitors his phase. The phase project manager reports to the overall project manager of any risks. Jointly, phase project managers and overall projects manager should identify risks and potential project problems as early as possible, identify when goals may not be met, identify when constraints may be violated and ensure that contingency plan is implemented before unrecoverable problem occur.

7. Generic project risks are lack of top management commitment to the project, failure to get user commitment, misunderstanding the requirements, lack of adequate user involvement, failure to manage user expectations, changing scope/objectives, lack of required knowledge/skills in the project personnel, lack of frozen requirements, introduction of new technology, insufficient inappropriate staffing and conflict between user departments.

Multiple Choice Questions

1. A change is a modified:
    (a) Agreement, workflow or automated system
    (b) Automated system that has been implemented
    (c) An error
    (d) None of them

2. Controlled Documents may include:
   (a) Business requirements
   (b) System requirements
   (c) Performance and scalability requirements
   (d) All of the above

3. Monitoring changes to the organisation and controlling changes are the two main issues that have to be looked after in project monitoring and control. The third one is:
   (a) Development process
   (b) Development process provided by metrices
   (c) Corrective actions when needed
   (d) Monitoring the project, anticipating, identifying and controlling risks

4. There are various methods used for evaluating projects. Net present value is one of them and is given by the formula:
   (a) Present worth of Benefit Stream – Present worth of cost stream
   (b) Past worth of benefit stream – present worth of cost stream
   (c) Present worth of cost stream – present worth of benefit stream
   (d) Past worth of cost stream – Past worth of benefit stream

5. An important component of a plan is to be able to present the knowledge of major problems or risks that may arise during and after the launch and after that means:
   (a) Flow of cash before and after orders pour in
   (b) Running out of cash after orders pour in
   (c) No difficulty encountered in obtaining needed bank credit
   (d) Sales projections achieved

6. How you intend to approach the market with your strategy to capture a market share is:
   (a) Discus spricing strategy and compare this with that of the major competitors.
   (b) Should not obtain instructional contracts
   (c) How will maintain profitability if product is priced higher than that of competitors.
   (d) Non-specific marketing philosophy

   Ans. 1. a, 2. d, 3. d, 4. a, 5. b, 6. a

Review Questions

1. What is Techno – Economic project classification? How does it facilitate the process of feasibility appraisal of the project?

2. A sectoral project has many sectors. Please enumerate them.

3. Why "executive summary" is so important that a good report should contain it in its contents?

4. Products service concept systematically defines & redefines manufacturing and operational plan. Define it.

5. Briefly describe when does a project become profitable or feasible for investment.

6. What is a controlled document? Make a list of such documents.

Chapter 7
Creative Problem Solving

Introduction

Creative ideas do not suddenly appear in people's minds for no apparent reason. Rather, they are the result of trying to solve a specific problem or to achieve a particular goal. Albert Einstein's theories of relativity were not sudden inspirations. Rather they were the result of a huge amount of mental problem solving trying to close a discrepancy between the laws of physics and the laws of electromagnetism as they were understood at the time. Albert Einstein, Leonardo da Vinci, Thomas Edison and other creative geniuses have always worked in the same way. They do not wait for creative ideas to strike them. Rather they focus on trying to solve a clearly stated, at least in their minds, problem.

This approach has been formalised as Creative Problem Solving (CPS). CPS is a simple process that involves breaking down a problem to understand it, generating ideas to solve the problem and evaluating those ideas to find the most effective solutions. Highly creative people tend to follow this process in their heads, without thinking about it. Less naturally creative people simply have to learn to use this very simple process. Although creative problem solving has been around as long as humans have been thinking creatively and solving problems, it was first formalised as a process by Alex Osborn, who invented traditional brainstorming, and Sidney Parnes. Their Creative Problem Solving Process (CPSP) has been taught at the International Centre for Studies in Creativity at Buffalo College in Buffalo, New York since the 1950s. However, there are numerous different approaches to CPS. Mine is more focused on innovation (that is the implementation of the most promising ideas). It involves seven straightforward steps.

7.1 Steps in Creative Problem Solving

The creative problem solving exercise can be structured into a number of sequential steps. These steps emerge as the following:

- Clarify and identify the problem
- Research the problem

- Formulate creative challenges
- Identify insights
- Generate ideas
- Combine and evaluate the ideas
- Draw up an action plan
- Do it! (i.e., implement the ideas)

Taking a closer look at these steps for a better understanding:

(a) **Clarify and identify the problem:** Arguably the single most important step of Creative problem solving is identifying your real problem or goal. This may seem easy, but very often, what we believe to be the problem is not the real problem or goal. For instance, you may feel you need a new job. However, if you break down your problem and analyse what you are really looking for, it may transpire that the actual issue is that your income does not cover your costs of living. In this case, the solution may be a new job, but it might also be to re-arrange your expenses or to seek a pay rise from your existing employer.

The best way to clarify the problem and understand the underlying issues is to ask yourself — or better still, ask a friend or family member to ask you— a series of questions about your problem in order to clarify the true issues behind the problem. The first question to ask is simply "why is this a problem?" or "why do I wish to achieve this goal?" Once you have answered that, ask yourself "why else?" four more times.

For instance, you might feel you want to overcome your shyness. So, you ask yourself why and you answer: "because I am lonely". Then ask yourself "why else?" four times. You answer: "because I do not know many people in this new city where I live", "because I find it hard to meet people", "because I am doing many activities alone" and "because I would like to do activities with other people who share my interests". This last "why else" is clearly more of the issue than reducing shyness. Indeed, if you had focused your creative energy on solving your shyness issue, you would not have actually solved the real problem. On the other hand, if you focused your creative energy on finding people with whom to share activities, you would be happier without ever having to address the shyness issue.

In addition, you can further clarify your problem by asking questions, such as: "what do I really wish to accomplish?", "what is preventing me from solving this problem/achieving the goal?", "how do I envision myself in six months/one year/five years [choose most relevant time span] as a result of solving this problem?" and "are my friends dealing with similar problems? If so, how are they coping?"By the time you have answered all these questions, you should have a very clear idea of what your problem or real goal is.

1.   *Criteria:* The final step is to decide what criteria you will eventually use to evaluate or judge the ideas. Are there budget limitations, timeframe or other restrictions that will affect whether or not you can go ahead with an idea? What will you want to have accomplished with the ideas? What do you wish to avoid when you implement these ideas? Think about it and make a list of three to five evaluation criteria. Then put the list aside. You will not need it for a while.

(b) **Research the problem:** The next step in CPS is to research the problem in order to get a better understanding of it. Depending on the nature of the problem, you may need to do a great deal of research or very little. The best place to start these days is with your favourite search engine. But do not neglect good old fashioned sources of information and opinion. Libraries are fantastic for in-depth information that is easier to read than computer screens. Friends, colleagues and family can also provide thoughts on many issues. For on sites, such as LinkedIn and elsewhere are ideal for asking questions. There is nothing an expert enjoys more than imparting his/her knowledge. Take advantage of that. But always try to get feedback from several people to ensure you get rounded information.

(c) **Formulate one or more creative challenges:** By now, you should be clear on the real issues behind your problems or goals. The next step is to turn these issues into creative challenges. A creative challenge is basically a simple question framed to encourage suggestions or ideas. In English, a challenge typically starts with "In what ways might I [or we]...?" or "How might I...?" or "How could I...?" Creative challenges should be simple, concise and focus on a single issue. For example: "How might I improve my Chinese language skills and find a job in Shanghai?" is two completely separate challenges. Trying to generate ideas that solve both challenges will be difficult and, as a result, will stifle idea generation. So separate these into two challenges: "How might I improve my German language skills?" and "How might I find a job in Chennai?" Then attack each challenge individually. Once you have ideas for both, you may find a logical approach to solving both problems in a coordinated way. Or you might find that there is not co-ordinate way and each problem must be tackled separately. Creative challenges should not include evaluation criteria. For example: "How might I find a more challenging job that is better paying and situated close to my home?" If you put criteria in the challenge, you will limit your creative thinking. So simply ask: "How might I find a more challenging job?" and after generating ideas, you can use the criteria to identify the ideas with the greatest potential. (Here is a more detailed article on formulating creative challenges)

(d) **Identify insights and inspiration:** You are almost ready to start generating ideas, but before you work on ideas in response to your challenge, think about what might provide insight and inspiration that will help you generate ideas. Some forms of inspiration are unrelated to the challenge. For instance, I like to go for long walks for inspiration. I also find the music of Bach provides me with deeper vision into problems. Other people like to lay down or take a bath. Whatever works for you is great. You may seek inspiration before you generate ideas, for instance by reading up on research related to the problem. Or you might seek inspiration during the idea generation session by brainstorming in a beautiful location. If the challenge is a B2B (business to business) issue, why not brainstorm in one of your customers' premises?

(e) **Generate ideas:** Finally, we come to the part most people associate with brainstorming and creative problem solving: idea generation. And you probably know how this works. Take only one creative challenge. Give yourself some quiet time and try to generate at least 50 ideas that may or may not solve the challenge. You can do this alone or you can invite some friends or family members to help you. Irrespective of your idea generation approach, write your ideas on a document. You can simply write them down in linear fashion, write them down on a mind-map, enter them onto a computer document (such as MS Word or Open Office) or use specialised software for idea generation. The method you use is not so important. What is important is that you follow these rules:

- Write down every idea that comes to mind. Even if the idea is ludicrous, stupid or fails to solve the challenge, write it down. Most people are their own worst critics and by squelching their own ideas, make themselves less creative. So write everything down. NO EXCEPTIONS!

- If other people are also involved, insure that no one criticises anyone else's ideas in any way. This is called squelching, because even the tiniest amount of criticism can discourage everyone in the group for sharing their more creative ideas. Even a sigh or the rolling of eyes can be critical. Squelching must be avoided!

- If you are working alone, don't stop until you've reached your target of 50 (or more) ideas. If you are working with other people, set a time limit, such as 15 or 20 minutes. Once you have reached this time limit, compare ideas and make a grand list that includes them all. Then ask everyone if they have some new ideas. Most likely, people will be inspired by others' ideas and add more to the list. If you find you are not generating sufficient ideas, give yourself some inspiration. A classic trick is to open a book or dictionary and pick out a random word. Then generate ideas that somehow incorporate this word. You might also ask yourself what other people whom you know; such as your grandmother, your partner, a friend or a character on your favourite TV show, might suggest. Brainstorming does not need to occur at your desk. Take a trip somewhere for new inspiration. Find a nice place in a beautiful park. Sit down in a coffee shop on a crowded street corner. You can even walk and generate ideas. In addition, if you browse the web for brainstorming and idea generation, you will find lots of creative ideas on how to generate creative ideas! If you are not in a hurry, wait until the next day and then try to generate another 25 ideas, ideally do this in the morning. Research has shown that our minds work on creative challenges while we sleep. Your initial idea generation session has been good exercise and has certainly generated some great ideas. But it will probably also inspire your unconscious mind to generate some ideas while you sleep.

(f) Combine and evaluate ideas: After you have written down all of your ideas, take a break. It might just be an hour. It might be a day or more. Then go through the ideas. Related ideas can be combined together to form big ideas (or idea clusters). Then, using the criteria you devised earlier, choose all of the ideas that broadly meet those criteria. This is important. If you focus only on the 'best' ideas or your favourite ideas, the chances are you will choose the less creative ones! Nevertheless, feel free to include your favourite ideas in the initial list of ideas. Now get out that list of criteria you mad earlier and go through each idea more carefully. Consider how well it meets each criterion and give it a rating of 0–5 points with five indicating a perfect match. If an idea falls short of a criterion, think about why this is so. Is there a way that it can be improved in order to increase its score? If so, make a note. Once you are finished, all of the ideas will have an evaluation score. Those ideas with the highest score best meet your criteria. They may not be your best ideas or your favourite ideas, but they are most likely to best solve your problem or enable you to achieve your goal. Depending on the nature of the challenge and the winning ideas, you may be ready to jump right in and implement your ideas. In other cases, ideas may need to be developed further. With complex ideas, a simple evaluation may not be enough. You may need to do a SWOT (strengths, weaknesses, opportunities and threats) or discuss the idea with others who will be affected by it. If the idea is business related, you may need to do a business case, market research, build a prototype or a combination of all of these. Also, bear in mind that you do not need to limit yourself to one winning idea. Often you can implement several ideas in order to solve your challenge.

(g) Draw an action plan: At this point, you have got some great ideas. However, a lot of people have trouble motivating them to take the next step. Creative ideas may mean big changes or taking risks. Some of us love change and risk. Others are scared by it. Draw up an action plan with the simple steps you need to take in order to implement your ideas. Ideas which involve a lot work to implement can be particularly intimidating. Breaking their implementation down into a series of readily accomplished tasks makes these ideas easier to cope with and implement.

(f) Implement: This is the simplest step of all. Take your action plan and implement your idea. And if the situation veers away from your action plan steps, do not worry. Rewrite your action plan!

7.2 Heuristics for Problem Solving

Heuristic problem solving are common sense rules drawn from experience, used to solve problems. Or simply put the heuristic method of problem solving is a rule of thumb. By contrast, algorithms are straightforward procedures that are guaranteed to work every time. Heuristic programming characterises programs that are self-learning; they are a part of artificial intelligence, they get better with experience. Heuristic programmes do not always reach the very best result but usually produce good results within a reasonable amount of search time.

General heuristics are "cognitive rules of thumb that are useful in solving a great variety of problems". Specific heuristics are used in specialised areas, often-specific subject domains or professions. There are three common methods in heuristic problem solving. First, the most powerful general heuristic is to form a sub-goal to reduce the discrepancy between your present state and your ultimate goal state. Do something to get a little closer to the end goal. Problems defy one-shot solutions; they must be broken down into smaller parts. A second heuristic method seeks to solve problems

We move from the world of optimisation to the world of 'good enough, fast enough' solution techniques. No matter how many techniques we teach you, it is inevitable that in the real world you will face many, many problems that cannot be solved by any technique you know. For a great many of these problems, no solution technique is known at all. For these problems, heuristic solution techniques may be the only alternative.

In some sense, it is very difficult to teach heuristic solution techniques. The methods are very problem specific. There are some general rules, however, that make finding good heuristics easier. One might consider these heuristics for finding heuristics. In the next few classes, we will explore these general rules, and examine a few applications were these rules have been successful.

Heuristic problem solving involves finding a set of rules, or a procedure, that finds satisfactory solutions to a specific problem. The first question that must be addressed is 'Why?' Why adopt a heuristic approach instead of an optimisation approach? Certainly, sometimes the problem addressed does not fall into any of the neat classifications and hence, is not amenable to known solution techniques. Even when the problem does fall into a known pigeon-hole, there may be resource limitations (computing time, data requirements, etc.) that make using the optimisation approach inappropriate. The following list some problem features that may indicate the appropriateness of heuristics (the categories overlap to a large extent, and I am not completely convinced that I am not just repeating myself).

- *Ill-Structure:*Problems for which there are no known algorithmic solutions are called ill-structured. A well-structured problem has the following characteristics:

  o All information relevant to the problem can be represented in an appropriate model.

  o The model should include all feasible solutions.

  o There exists an algorithm for finding the optimal solution to the model.

  o All data required should be economically practical to gather.

An ill-structured model is one that fails one or more of the above criteria. Of course, ill-structure is defined only relative to our current state of knowledge. As we develop more algorithms and devise more powerful models, problems become well-structured.

In many cases, a management scientist is tempted to force an ill-structured problem into a well-structured problem. Merely by ignoring a few cases, making a few assumptions, faking a bit of data, most ill-structured problems can look respectable. This is hardly a good method of problem solving. It is far better to recognise the problem as ill-structured and use heuristic techniques.

- Too Time Consuming: In many cases, there is an appropriate, well defined model: integer programming. The current state of the art in integer programming is not equipped to solve anything but toy problems (with a few exceptions). In general, there is a tremendous problem with the combinatorial explosion inherent in integer programming and similar combinatorial optimisation problems. By this I mean any problem that must examine a large number of possible solutions. Consider an integer program with 100 variables, each of which must be 0 or 1. Any technique that examines all possible solutions must examine solutions (roughly). If a computer can examine 100 solutions per second, it would take roughly 10,000,000,000,000,000,000 years to find the solution. Branch and bound attempts to cut down this number to a manageable size, but there are very good reasons to believe that it does no more that reduce the number by a constant factor. So even if 100 variable problems are solvable in minutes, 200 variable problems will take millennia. The theory behind this explosion is called **NP-completeness**.

In any case, due to this explosion, integer programming problems generally require heuristic solution techniques, as do many related problems due solely to the combinatorial explosion.

- Satisfying in many applications, the goal is not to find the optimal solution. Perhaps the data is uncertain enough that optimality does not mean anything. Or perhaps the decision maker has some non-quantifiable goals in mind. By optimising a model, one solution is presented. Heuristics can often generate many different solutions, each one good in some way, from which the decision maker can choose. The goal in any decision-making process is to find a satisfactory solution. Sometimes we can define satisfaction in terms of optimisation; often we cannot.

(a) Heuristic Problem Solving

Many problems have no solution technique that meets limitations on time, data, and so on. Heuristics are a natural choice in these situations. Many heuristics are extremely clever, taking great advantage of the particular structure of the problem to be solved (by the way, I make a distinction between problems and instances. A problem is a set of instances. Generally, we will look at heuristics for problems, though sometimes a particular instance is important enough to justify heuristics for itself. Furthermore, heuristics for an individual instance can often be generalised to a larger problem). But it is equally important to find general methods of creating heuristics. These provide quick and dirty solutions to many problems. Although the solution quality may not be the best, often they work well enough. In this section, we will examine some general heuristic techniques. These are random, greedy and exchanging methods

(i) Random solutions: The first heuristic is also the simplest: choose any random solution. For the TSP, this would be to visit the cities in random order.This may look like a ridiculous solution. What good is a random solution? By itself, it is not much good. But consider repeatedly finding a random solution and taking the best solution as our choice. Suddenly, the repeated solution does not look too silly. First, because it is so simple to find random solutions, we might be able to find hundreds of solutions in the time it takes another heuristic to find one. And perhaps the best of those hundred of random solutions is better than that found by a more complicated heuristic. Second, it is possible to run this repeated heuristic in whatever time is available. If only a short time is available, then at least some answer will be returned. If a long time is available, the heuristic keeps working, trying to find better solutions. Finally, we will be examining some heuristics that attempt to improve on a given solution. Random solutions provide an almost limitless source of new solutions to improve. On the negative side, the answers given by a small number of random solutions will tend to be pretty bad. This, by the way, leads to a fundamental rule of creating heuristics: Random choices are good. A heuristic with random choices can be run over and over, creating many solutions. Completely random solutions are one implementation of this idea, though it may ignore the problem too much. Note that it ignores the problem structure completely. All it requires that anything it generates be deemed valid as a solution.

(ii) Greedy Solutions: A second solution technique, and probably the most used heuristic technique, is the greedy technique. The general idea is as follows: begin with no assignments of values to variables. At each step, assign one variable a value. The choice of variable and value are that which minimises the increase in the

objective function (for minimisation). This is a general approach, not an algorithm. Let us see how to implement it for the TSP. There are a number of different possibilities.

One natural heuristic is to start at any node. From there, go to the closest (cheapest) unvisited node. Continue along until you have visited all the nodes, at which point you return to the start.

This heuristic is called **nearest neighbour,** for obvious reasons. In our example, nearest neighbour gives a solution of length 16. Is this optimal? We could try other heuristics and see if we could find a better solution. Later we will see methods, called **relaxations** that give a lower bound on the solution value.

There are many other greedy algorithms for the TSP. For instance, there is also the possibility of adding edges throughout the graph, always making certain we can complete the tour. In our example, we would first add the edge AC, then BD, then AD, then BE, then CE, for a tour with cost ₹18.

Greedy heuristics are distinguished by the property that once a decision is made, it is never changed. Once an edge is added to the solution, it is never taken out. Greedy heuristics generally do much better than random. Unfortunately, in many cases there is very little opportunity for randomisation, so we are stuck with just one (or just a few) solutions.

We will get to some more techniques for finding a good solution. Unfortunately, although these techniques are fairly robust, they do not have the generality of random and greedy. There is one more general technique to be discussed.

(iii) Exchanging heuristics: Suppose we have a solution, it is often possible to generate a better solution simply by modifying our solution in some way. For instance, if we have a TSP on a map and we see that our tour crosses itself, we can generally improve the tour by replacing two edges with two others. This method of replacing a limited number of variables with other values is called exchanging. It does not change the entire solution; it only changes parts of it.

More formally, for any integer k, we can define a k-exchange to take k variables out of the solution and add k (probably different) variables to the solution. Again, this is an idea, not an algorithm. Let us see how we can apply this to our problem. Suppose we have a tour through the cities. If we remove two edges from the tour, we generally break the tour into two pieces. We can then add two other edges to create a new tour. We can compare the cost of this tour to the old tour and keep the better of the two. To find a very good solution, we can cycle through all possible exchanges. If an exchange is found that improves the objective, then we adopt the new solution as our current solution. If an exchange is worse, then we keep our current solution. This continues until we have a solution for which no exchange is better. This solution is termed a **local optimum,** for no solution near it (in the sense that it can be reached in one exchange) is better. Depending on how good the exchange algorithm works, local optima can be very, very good, or very, very bad. For the TSP, k=3 gives wonderful answers, while k=2 gives fairly poor answers.

Of course, we could choose k equal to n for these problems and any local optimum would be a global optimum (that is, it would be an optimal solution). Clearly, though, the work per iteration is at least. Generally, in order to keep the work down, k is set to some small number, perhaps 2 or 3. This keeps most of the structure of our current solution but allows some change.

(iv) Simplification heuristics: Many academics have a passion for finding special cases that can be solved. The main reason is that they result in publications, which result in tenure, so they pay the rent. Another reason for finding special cases is that we can use them to solve general problems. The accuracy of this approach depends on how closely the special case resembles the general problem.

Again, let us take the TSP. Let us solve the 'Grand Trunk Travelling Salesman Problem.' All the major cities are on the Grand Trunk Road in North India. Suppose the salesman is restricted to this highway. How would he solve the TSP through the major Indian cities? Of course, he would simply travel up and down the highway, visiting the cities in the order he meets them. This is a particularly simple case of the TSP: the cities can be placed on a line so that the distance between any two cities is exactly the distance between them on a line. If we had a TSP to solve, we might first try to place them on a line so that the above condition holds. Normally, we will fail. We then might ask if there is a way of placing the cities on a line so that the distances on the line are almost the 'real' distances. Now there are many ways of mapping cities in 2 dimensions onto a line. We could do the sweep heuristic: rotating a line about the centre of the plane and mapping the cities in the order the line hits them. It turns out that this approach does not adequately retain distance information.

One approach that does work is that of space-filling curves, which is truly a fascinating subject. The main reason that these curves do a good job is that they tend to keep distance information. Note that this mapping is useful not just for the TSP. It can be used whenever the problem with distances on a line is easier than general distances. We can also consider the special case where the distances come from a tree (a set of edges which does not contain a cycle). Suppose the cities to be visited are nodes of a tree. One nice property of a tree is that there is a unique path between any two nodes of the tree. Suppose the edges of the tree have lengths and the distance between two nodes is defined to be the length of the unique path between them. How would you solve the TSP for such a problem?

You would simply follow the nodes around the tree, skipping any you have visited before. This turns out to be the optimal route for this type of distance. How can we use this to solve the general TSP? It strikes me that there are some more clever ways, but here is a straightforward approach. Find the minimum spanning tree for the points and solve the TSP on this tree. The closer the tree distances approximate the tree distances, the better this tour will be. In all, once there is a solvable special case, it is probably worthwhile to see if you can approximate the general case with it.

(v) Break–combine heuristics: For many problems, it is possible to solve small instances but not large instances. Furthermore, it is easy to identify parts of the problem that are largely independent from other parts. The break–combine philosophy suggests breaking the problem into small pieces and solving each one independently. The pieces are then reformed (if necessary) into one large solution.

Again, consider the TSP. If the points are on the plane, with distances Euclidean, it is clear that the upper left points will have little to do with the lower right points. This suggests some sort of break–combine algorithm. Here is one which works well (very well theoretically). Divide the points in two equal pieces, say vertically. Then divide each piece into two equal pieces horizontally. Continue alternating horizontal and vertical cuts until each piece is small enough to be solved exactly. Solve each piece exactly. This is the break phase. Now combine pairs of solutions separated by the line in the reverse order they were divided. Combine them by finding the best pair of edges to add and the best to delete to form a tour of the combined pieces. Continue until all the tours are combined. This is the combine phase. This method works best when there is a natural division of the problem (for instance, when the problem is embedded in the plane) and when the combine phase does not do too poorly.

(vi) Improving our solutions: Because of the difficulty in creating good heuristics, we would like to find methods to improve our answers whenever possible. That, of course, is the main philosophy of k-exchange: find a better solution by dropping k pieces of the solution and adding k others. This leads to an improvement method called **local optimisation**. In this section, we will discuss local optimisation.

(vii) Local optimisation: One troublesome aspect of heuristic problem solving is that sometimes the answers they give are absurdly bad. Often, a human can see immediately that a solution is not optimal. This aspect of seeing inefficiencies is very worrisome. People do not trust solutions that they can improve on easily. They are not convinced that the solution is 'good' when it can be made better so quickly. Furthermore, most heuristics can be fooled very badly in some pathological situations. Therefore, it is always good to have a second line of defence. It is normally quite straightforward to create improving heuristics that will create solutions that no human can quickly improve upon. This means that the solutions will look more reasonable and will be more likely to be implemented. Also, since every solution has gone through two stages, it is far more difficult to create examples where the answer is completely absurd.

For the TSP, 2-exchanging creates good solutions, but humans can do 3-exchanging by eye, so even 2-exchanged tours can look bad to us.

To review, given a method to do exchanges, local optimisation is as follows:

0)   Let S be our current solution.

1)   Let S' be the solution after doing some exchange of S.

2)   If S' is a better solution, set S to S', go to 1.

3)   Otherwise, determine if there is an unexamined exchange of S. If so, go to step 1. Otherwise, terminate, S is the best solution found.

The resulting solution is called a **local optimal solution**. The 'local' part of this phrase comes from the fact that it is not the overall optimal solution (probably), but it is better than any solution you can get by exchanging.

In many cases, with a good start and a good exchange rule, the local optimal solution you get is good enough. Note, however, that there might be many local optimal solutions, and you may be stuck with a bad one. This leads naturally to a search for a good local optimal solution. We look at two methods for generating good local optimal solutions: iterated local search and simulated annealing algorithms.

(viii) Iterated Local Search: The first possibility is to rerun the local search algorithm with a different starting solution. This will generally lead to different local optimal solutions. This is one of the big advantages of the random heuristic: it is very easy to generate different starts. But many other heuristics have the ability to generate different solutions. Consider nearest neighbour for the TSP: it is completely arbitrary at which city the tour is started. But different starting solutions lead to different tours.

Another area where we can generate different local optimal solutions is in the choice of exchange. Note that there may be many exchanges that improve the solution. A different choice of which exchange to accept may lead to different local optimal solutions.

The main advantage of this approach is the ease of implementation and the quickness. Unfortunately, even iterating might not provide a good enough solution.

(ix) Simulated annealing: For our next approach, we will make an analogy with the world of physics and crystal growing. To grow a crystal, one begins by heating the raw materials to a liquid state. This molten material is then slowly cooled, until the crystal structure is frozen in. If the temperature is decreased too quickly, flaws in the crystal can be locked in. Slow temperature decrease allows these flaws to 'work themselves out' forming a much better crystal. This process is called **annealing**.

One can think of the final state of a crystal as a local optimum: no small movement of the molecules can decrease the total energy content. A perfect crystal contains the minimum energy content of all the final possibilities. Because molecules only move locally, the laws of physics only require that some local optimum be found. But if annealing creates better solutions, perhaps we can simulate this annealing process. The essential aspect of annealing is that the energy contained in the heat can be used to move from one energy level to a higher level. Our goal is to move to as low a level as possible, but maybe it is useful to move uphill once in a while. Simulated annealing works just like local search in that it examines exchanged solutions and always takes a better solution. The only difference is that it sometimes (with some probability) takes a worse one. This probability decreases over time (just like the temperature decreases) until we freeze in a local optimal solution, hopefully better than one we would get to otherwise. An example of this would be to keep a counter i. We would accept a worse solution with probability $1/i$. Every 50 exchanges or so we would increment i. Once i is 1000, we would simply set the probability we would accept a worse solution to 0 and freeze our solution into a local optimum.

Most real uses of simulated annealing use a more complicated probability function, based on the amount of worsening of the solution. Solutions that are only slightly worse are much more likely to be accepted than those that are much worse.

Generally, simulated annealing gets much better answers, but it takes a very slow cooling process. Therefore, for some problems, it may be better to use iterated local search, generating many solutions. Often, however, the quality of the simulated annealing solution is unreachable by iterated local search.

7.3 Brainstorming

Brainstorming can be an effective way to generate lots of ideas on a specific issue and then determine which idea – or ideas – is the best solution. Brainstorming is most effective with groups of 8–12 people and should be performed in a relaxed environment. If participants feel free to relax and joke around, they will stretch their minds further and, therefore, produce more creative ideas. A brainstorming session requires a facilitator, a brainstorming space and something on which to write ideas, such as a white-board a flip chart or software tool. The facilitator's responsibilities include guiding the session, encouraging participation and writing ideas down. Brainstorming works best with a varied group of people. Participants should come from various departments across the organisation and have different backgrounds. Even in specialist areas, outsiders can bring fresh ideas that can inspire the experts.

There are numerous approaches to brainstorming, but the traditional approach is generally the most effective because it is the most energetic and openly collaborative, allowing participants to build on each others' ideas. Creativity exercises, relaxation exercises or other fun activities before the session can help participants relax their minds so that they will be more creative during the brainstorming session.

(a) Step by step process of brainstorming

- Define your problem or issue as a creative challenge. This is extremely important. A badly designed challenge could lead to lots of ideas which fail to solve your problem. A well-designed creative challenge generates the best ideas to solve your problem. Creative challenges typically start with: "In what ways might we...?" or "How could we...?" Your creative challenge should be concise, to the point and exclude any information other than the challenge itself. For example: "In what ways might we improve product X?" or "How could we encourage more local people to join our club?"

- Give yourselves a time limit. We recommend around 25 minutes, but experience will show how much time is required. Larger groups may need more time to get everyone's ideas out. Alternatively, give yourself an idea limit. At minimum, push for 50 ideas. But 100 ideas is even better.

- Once the brainstorming starts, participants shout out solutions to the problem while the facilitator writes them down – usually on a white board or flip-chart for all to see. There must be absolutely no criticizing of ideas. No matter how daft, how impossible or how silly an idea is, it must be written down. Laughing is to be encouraged. Criticism is not.

- Once your time is up, select the five ideas which you like best. Make sure everyone involved in the brainstorming session is in agreement.

- Write down about five criteria for judging which ideas best solve your problem. Criteria should start with the word "should", for example, "it should be cost effective", "it should be legal", "it should be possible to finish before July 15", etc.

- Give each idea a score of 0–5 points depending on how well it meets each criterion. Once all of the ideas have been scored for each criterion, add up the scores.

- The idea with the highest score will best solve your problem. But you should keep a record of all of your best ideas and their scores in case your best idea turns out not to be workable.

(b) Factors to be considered for successful brainstorming

There are a numerous approaches to brainstorming, but whichever approach you use, there are several key factors which make the difference between a successful brainstorming session and a mediocre brainstorming session.State your challenge correctly. In order to get the right ideas, you need to ensure that you are giving the brainstorm session participants the right challenge. Otherwise, you could end up with a lot of ideas which do not actually solve your problem. No squelching! Squelching is when you criticise an idea or a person contributing the idea. Squelching can be obvious, such as "That's the dumbest idea I have ever heard!" or subtle, such as "you would never get the budget to do that." No matter what the form, squelching does two terrible things to a brainstorming session. Firstly, it makes the person who contributed the idea feel bad. As a result, she is unlikely to contribute any more ideas to the session. Even if her idea was not a good one, it is likely she would have had other, better ideas to contribute. Secondly, squelching tells other participants that unusual ideas are not welcome at this brainstorming session. Since most creative ideas are also unusual ideas, a single squelching effectively prevents participants from offering creative ideas. So, if you remember nothing else about brainstorming, remember: no squelching!

(i) Mixed participants: When brainstorming works well, it is because the session taps into the combined creativity of all the participants. Clearly, then, the more varied the participants, the wider the range of creative thinking and the more creative the ideas generated. It is a common mistake for managers to think: we need marketing ideas, so let us get the marketing department together to brainstorm ideas. These people work together all the time, have similar backgrounds and know too much about marketing. As a result, their ideas will be limited in scope. Bringing together a dozen people from a dozen departments is a far better approach to generating a wide range of creative ideas.

(ii) Enthusiastic facilitator: The facilitator is the person who manages the brainstorming session. Normally, she does not contribute ideas, rather she makes note of the ideas, encourages participation, prevents squelching, watches the time and directs the session. A good facilitator will have a sense of humour and a knack for encouraging people to contribute ideas and be creative in their thinking. A good facilitator compliments ideas and gives high praise to the most outrageous ideas; that is because she knows that outrageous ideas encourage outrageous thinking which generates creative ideas. Moreover, what at first might seem a crazy idea may, on reflection, prove to be a very creative idea? Incidentally, if the facilitator is in the same company as the participants, care should be taken not to use a facilitator who is significantly higher in the corporate hierarchy. A high ranking moderator can make participants reluctant to take the risk of proposing an outrageous or highly unusual idea.

(iii) Well-stated challenge: The challenge is the problem or issue for which you will be generating ideas. It is important to indicate very clearly the challenge in such a way as to indicate the kind of ideas you want, while not making the challenge so restricting that brainstormers cannot get creative. In our experience, the most common problem is that the challenge is vaguely phrased. A manager who is looking for ideas on how to improve product X in order to make it more attractive to younger customers all too often phrases the challenge like this: 'New product ideas' or 'product improvements'. Such vague challenges encourage vague ideas, many of which do not respond to the managers' needs. Good environment with no disturbances. An uncomfortable environment, an overly small room, cell phone

calls and secretaries calling their bosses out of the room for a moment all not only interrupt a brainstorming session, but also interrupt the continuity and thinking of participants. If you want an effective brainstorming session, you must insist participants turn off their telephones and inform their staff that they are not to be disturbed short of a total catastrophe. You should find a space that is large enough for the group and comfortable. A supply of water and coffee should be provided. Sometimes a little alcohol, such as wine or beer, can loosen people up and reduce inhibitions about proposing crazy ideas. Where possible, hold the brainstorming session outside your office, in a pleasant environment where participants are less likely to be disturbed or worry about their other work obligations.

□□□

At a Glance

1. The creative problem exercise can be structured into a number of sequential steps which means clarify and identify the problem, research into the problem, formulate creative challenges, identify insights, generate ideas, combine and evaluate the ideas, draw up an action plan and implement the ideas.

2. Heuristic problem solving are common sense rules drawn from experience, used to solve problems. Heuristic programming characterises programs that are self-learing, they are a part of artificial intelligence, they get better with experience. Heuristic programmes do not always reach the very best result but usually produce good results within a reasonable amount search time. Heuristic problems solving involves finding a set of rules, a procedure that finds satisfactory solutions to a specific problem.

3. In creative problem solving generation of ideas is not that important. What is important is that one must follow the below rules i.e. write down every idea that comes to mind, even if the idea is ludicrous or fails to solve the challenge; squelching must be avoided, follow the classic trick to open a book or dictionary and pick out a random word. Then generate ideas that somehow incorporate that word.

4. Ill structure is problem for which there is no known algorithmic solution. A well structured problem must have all information relevant to the problems that can be represented in an appropriate model. It should include all feasible solutions, there should exist an algorithm for finding the optimal solution to the model and lastly data that is required should be economically practical to gather.

5. If a computer can examine 100 solutions per second, it would take roughly 10,000,000,000,000,000,000 years to find a solution. Branch and bound attempts to cut down this number to a manageable size, but there are good reasons to believe that it does no more than reduce the number by a constant factor. So even if 100 variable problems are solvable in minutes, 200 variable

problems will take millenia. The theory behind this explosion is called **NP-completeness**.

6. One natural heuristic is to start at any node. From there go to the closest (cheapest) unvisited node. Continue along until you have visited all the nodes, at which point you return to the start. This heuristic is called **nearest neighbour**. When an exhange is worse, then we keep out current solution. This continues unitl we have a solution for which no exchange is better and called local optimum.

Multiple Choice Questions

1. Brainstorming generates lots of ideas on specific issues and determine:
   (a) Which idea is the test solution
   (b) Which idea is the least solution
   (c) Which idea is the best solution
   (d) Which idea is the bad solution

2. Step by step process of brainstorming is:
   (a) give yourself a time limit
   (b) give yourself an idea limit
   (c) give yourself breathing limit
   (d) give yourself criteria limit

3. An enthusiastic facilitator is the person who manages the:
   (a) Well stated challenge
   (b) Mixed participant
   (c) Brainstorming session
   (d) Successful brainstorming

4. To grow a crystal molten material is slowly cooled so as to allow flaws to "work themselves out" forming a better crystal & this process is called:
   (a) Local search
   (b) Distance search
   (c) Optimal solution
   (d) Annealing

5. SWOT meaning:
   (a) Strength, Weakness, Opportunity and Threat
   (b) Sense, Wealth, Opportunities and Threats
   (c) Sense Weakness, Opulence and Tiredness
   (d) Strength, Weakness, Outrage and Thaw

Ans. 1. c, 2. a, 3. c, 4. d, 5. a

Review Questions

1. What do you mean by Heuristics for problems solving?
2. We move from the world of optimization to the world of "good enough, fast enough' solutions techniques. Define these techniques in detail.
3. What is local optimum solution?
4. Write in detail the factors that are to be considered for successful brainstorming.
5. Narrate
   (a) Mixed participants
   (b) Enthusiastic facilitar
   (c) Well-stated challenge

Chapter 8
Synectics, Value Analysis and Innovation

Introduction

Synectics is a creativity technique that is closely related to brainstorming. The main difference is that Synectics is more formalised and rigorous than brainstorming. It might seem inappropriate to formalise a creative process, however, many people feel the open-ended nature of free-form brainstorming overwhelming. Synectics helps by giving you a guide for generating new ideas. It is often summarised as 'making the strange familiar and making the familiar strange'.

Although normally considered as a creativity technique or process, synectics can also be considered a state of mind or even a philosophy. It is essentially about combining entities, be those entities people, existing ideas or even physical objects ("The secret is to bang the rocks together, guys!").

8.1 Synectics and Value Analysis: The Synectics Process

Synectics was formally created by William Gordon and George Prince. Gordon and Prince eventually disagreed about the details of the system; however, the basic principles are widely accepted. Synectics as we know it today is usually attributed to Gordon who published it in 1961. There are many different 'tools' in the Synectics kit.

All are based on the same principles: looking at familiar things in unfamiliar ways and combining the previously discrete. Perhaps the best known synectic technique is the use of *trigger questions*. When beginning to think about a subject, it is useful to write down a list of words that relate to it. These can be physical aspects, processes, emotional connotations, anything. The 'trigger questions' can then be used to prompt analysis and synthesis of these.

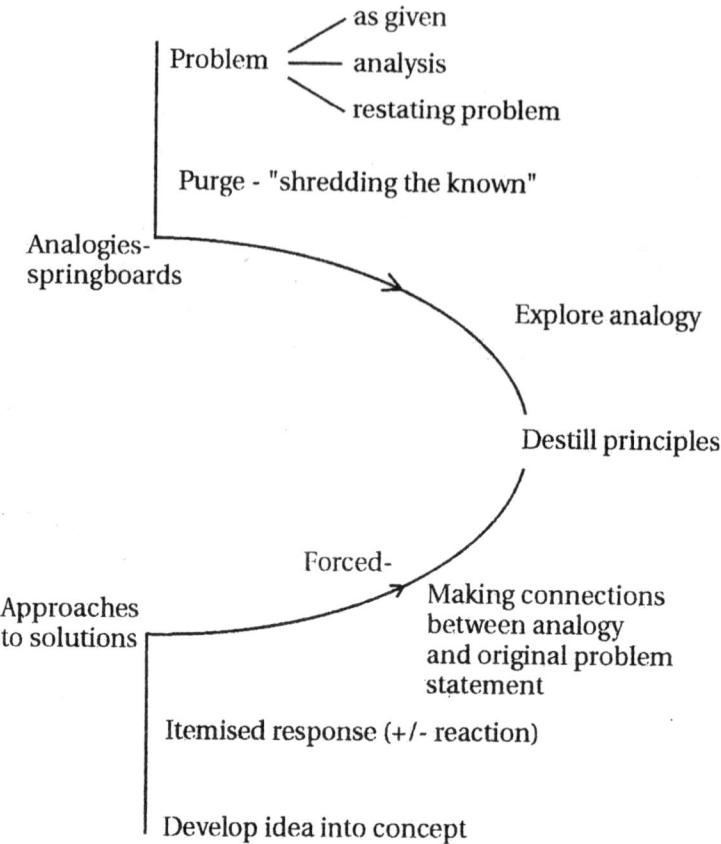

Fig.8.1 The synectics process (adopted from Tassoul, 2006)

A common list of trigger questions is based around these principles as shown in Table 8.1:

Table 8.1 A common word list of trigger questions

- Subtract	- Substitute	- Hybridise
- Add	- Fragment	- Metamorphose
- Transfer	- Isolate	- Symbolise
- Empathise	- Distort	- Mythologise
- Animate	- Disguise	- Fantasise
- Superimpose	- Contradict	- Repeat
- Change	- Parody	- Combine
- Scale	- Analogise	

The output of these transformations can be captured on paper, on a whiteboard or you can buy PC software to assist in the process. One distinguishing factor of synectics is its emphasis on metaphor and fantasy. For example, if trying to determine how to respond to a business threat then this could be likened to defeating with a fire-breathing dragon. What are the dragon's strengths (its 'fire')?, weaknesses (the 'soft underbelly')?, desires (a pile of gold? human sacrifices? worship?), what weapons would dragons layers need?, can the dragon be tamed instead of slain?, etc. All of these fantasies could give ideas on how to deal with a very real commercial 'opportunity'.

Synectics as a technique brings out the issues related to what is there in a product that is valued by customers. Synectics is best applied for more complex and intricate problems. Synectics can be used in group as well as individual. With an un-trained group, the facilitator will have to work a small step at a time; he/she must have enough experience to inspire the group through such a process. The starting point of synectics is an initial problem statement. In the design process, it continues with the design goal, problem definition and design specification generated in the problem analysis phase. The outcome of synectics is a limited amount of preliminary yet surprising ideas.

(a) Step by Step process of Synectics

- Start with the original problem statement. Invite the problem owner to present and discuss the problem briefly.
- Analyse the problem. Restate the problem. Formulate the problem as a single concrete target.
- Generate, collect and record the first ideas that come to mind (shredding the known).
- Find a relevant analogy in one of the listed categories of analogies (personal, nature, fantastic, etc.)
- Ask yourself questions in order to explore the analogy. What type of problems occur in the analogous situation? What type of solutions are there to be found?
- Force-fit various solutions to the reformulated problem statement.
- Generate, collect and record the ideas.
- Test and evaluate the ideas. Use the itemised response method to select between the ideas.
- Develop the selected ideas into concepts.
- Present your concepts to the point.

8.2 Innovation

Whenever a discussion on innovation commences, the relevance of creativity is the first to be recognised. Creativity which is the ability to develop new ideas and to discover new ways of looking at problems and opportunities is the key to innovation. At the same time, Innovation is defined as the ability to apply creative solutions to problems or opportunities to enhance or to enrich people's lives. Within this domain, ideas can come from anybody and can be found in any field of activities leads to the question that is it possible to pursue all the ideas that emerge from a creative exercise. The simple progression from a very large pool of ideas to those which become commercially viable and successful in the market can be shown as follows: For every 3,000 new product ideas, four make it to the development stage, two are actually launched, and one becomes a success in the market. On an average, new products account for 40% of companies' sales!!

There are two levels at which we can address the subject of Innovation. One is where it is considered a mindset, a pervasive attitude or a way of thinking focused on the future and beyond the present. This view is heavily driven by creativity. The other view is a more practical view that can be said is in a way an outcome of the earlier view as it is about translating thoughts into a new idea, method or device; a novelty about some existing activity. From an organisation point of view, it is also addressed as the core process concerned with renewing what the organisation offers and the ways in which it generates and delivers these. This is actually a manifestation of novelty in the case of a business organisation. The aim of innovation in a business organisational establishment is about obtaining a competitive edge— and through this surviving and growing. Schumpeter (1934), through his concept of creative destruction has very aptly suggested the role of innovation for a new firm by means of embarking upon new combinations of factors of production. Innovation could take the form of

- a new good
- a new method of production
- a new market
- a new source of supply of raw materials
- carrying out of a new organisation

Everett Rogers in his book on *Diffusion of Innovation defines innovation as* an idea, practice or object that is perceived as new by an individual or other unit of adoption. The perceived newness of the idea for the individual determines his/her reaction to it. Peter F. Drucker in his book on *Innovation & Entrepreneurship* suggests that systematic innovation consists of the purposeful and organised search for changes, and in the systematic analysis of the opportunities such changes might offer for economic or social innovation.

On the question that how do innovations emerge, there are a number of ways in which this can happen. The very first way is termed as **unexpected occurrences**. This means unplanned events that lead to a novelty. Serendipity has a role to play here. For example, DuPont surprise invention of nylon. The next way is termed as **incongruities**. This means that things that are not expected to take a certain form if we are able to come up with things in that way. For example, Minimills in steel industry. The third way is related to *Demographic changes* and an apt example is the introduction of robotics in manufacturing in a large number of countries. *Perceptual changes* are the fourth way that means changes in the way we have been seeing things. Computers long time back was considered a product for use in big established businesses only while today it has become a personal level product where each individual desires to have one for him/her. *Bright ideas* are the last of the ways that innovation emerges and good examples of these are zipper, ball point pen, spray can— some products that have become central to our lives today.

When innovations emerge the development happens in cycles of radical and incremental innovation. A radical innovation is one wherein there is a significantly high level of newness and it changes the way things are done drastically. Once this radical innovation happens, it goes through a phase of improvements over a period of time and these improvements are said to be incremental innovations.

Degree of novelty is a concern here. This is dependent on the category of people who adopt the innovation for further usage. The individual adoption curve is a normal distribution based on Table 8.2.

Table 8.2 Diffusion of innovation (adopters)

Adopter Categories	Shared Characteristics
Innovators	2.5%. Require a shorter adoption period than any other group. Venturesome, mobile, daring. Risk takers. Financial resources to absorb unprofitable innovations understand and apply complex technical knowledge to cope with a high degree of uncertainty.
Early Adopters	13.5%. Upward social mobility. Greatest degree of opinion leadership, role model within social system, respected by peers, successful.
Early Majority	34%. Interact frequently with peers, seldom holds positions of opinion leadership, deliberate before adopting a new idea.
Late Majority	34%. Responds to pressure from peers, economic necessity, skeptical, cautious.
Laggards	16%. No opinion leadership. Isolated. Point of reference is in the past. Suspicious of innovations, innovation–decision process is lengthy, resource limited.

The adoption process places adopters into categories and explores how the earlier adopters influence later adopters. This information is used to segment markets, design promotional campaigns, and can be used to develop e-business strategies. The adoption curve is used as a model to understand who is likely to be an innovator and how interpersonal influence passes to later adopters of innovations. For organisations, the role that innovation plays is mainly related to protection of the competitive advantage that the firm has created. This is done through a strategic approach for preempting, protecting against, or jumping ahead of competition. It enables a company to accelerate growth, experience incremental margin enhancement and build additional core competency to bolster competitive advantage.

ㅁㅁㅁ

At a Glance

1. Synectics is a creativity technique, which is formalised and rigorous. Brain storming synectics guides you for generating new ideas and often makes the "strange familiar and familiar strange." The best known synectic technique is the use of trigger question.

2. Everett Rogers in his book on " Diffusion of Innovation defines innovation as an idea, practice or object that is perceived as new by individual or other unit of adoption. The perceived newness of the ideas for the individual determines his/her reaction to it. Innovation is also known as unexpected occurrences and incongruities.

3. When innovations emerge, the development happens in cycles of radical and incremental innovation. A radical innovation is one where there is a significantly high level of newness and it changes the things existing activities that are done drastically.

4. Schumpeter through his concept of creative destruction has aptly suggested the role of innovation for a new firm by means of embarking upon new combination of factors of productions. Innovations can take the form of a new market, a new source of supply of raw materials and also carrying art of a new organization.

Multiple Choice Questions

1. The first way innovations emerge is called:
   (a) Expected Occurrences
   (b) Unexpected Occurrences
   (c) Explicit Occurrences
   (d) Systemic Occurrences

2. In step by step process of synectics:
   (a) Generate, collect and record the first ideas that come to mind

    (b)   Collect but do not record the 2nd idea that come to mind

    (c)   Do not collect but record the 3rd idea that come to mind

    (d)   Do not generate, do not record and also do not collect that does not come 15 min

3.   Synectics normally considered as a creativity technique, it can also be considered as a:

    (a)   State of mind

    (b)   Irrational mind

    (c)   Delirium mind

    (d)   Sound mind

Ans. 1. b, 2. a, 3. a

Review Questions

1.   Make a list of trigger questions that are required in synectics.

2.   Synectics as a technique brings out the issues related to what is there in a product that is valued by customers. Write down the "step by step process of synectics."

3.   Define these terms:

    (i)   Incongruities

    (ii)   Unexpected occurrences

    (iii) Perceptual changes

    (iv) Bright ideas

    (v)   Radical innovation

4.   What are the "Shaved characteristics" as adopted by Innovators and Laggards?

Unit III

International Entrepreneurship
Opportunities

Chapter 9

International Entrepreneurship

Introduction

With the globalisation of the world economy, interest in international markets has increased manifolds and thereby observed enhanced entrepreneurial activity in this domain also. This has been more of a recent phenomenon with more of IT firms being in this space. One of the most important features of today's global economy is the growing role of young entrepreneurial new ventures researchers have been on the lookout for the motivations for, the pattern of, and the pace of internationalisation by new ventures. We can draw on the International business and entrepreneurship theories to define and study international entrepreneurship. With its origin in the entrepreneurship literature, one stream of research suggests that some new ventures are 'born global' (such as IT firms in India) and, therefore, differ significantly from businesses that become international in scope over time as they accumulate resources or competencies to go global. This phenomenon is a function of their resources and the size of their home markets.

9.1 The Nature of International Entrepreneurship

The various proponents of International Entrepreneurship provide definitions to the concept, McDougall (1989) states that 'international entrepreneurship is the development of international new ventures or start-ups that, from their inception, engage in international business, thus, viewing their operating domain as international from the initial stages of the firm's operation.' Zahra (1993) defines international entrepreneurship as the study of the nature and consequences of a firm's risk-taking behaviour as it ventures into international markets. Oviatt and McDougall (1994) state that a business organisation that, from inception, seeks to derive significant competitive advantage from the use of resources and sale of outputs in multiple countries. Wright and Ricks (1994) suggested that international entrepreneurship is a firm-level activity that crosses national borders and focuses on the relationship between businesses and the international environments in which they operate. McDougall and Oviatt (2000) state that a combination of innovative, proactive, and risk-seeking behaviour that crosses or is compared across national borders and is intended to create value in business organisations is what international entrepreneurship is all about. As more countries become market oriented and developed, the distinction between foreign and domestic markets is becoming less pronounced. International entrepreneurship is the process of an entrepreneur conducting business activities across national boundaries. The mechanisms usually adopted can be through exporting, licensing or opening a sales office in another country. International entrepreneurship is, therefore, to do with going over the domestic boundaries of a nation in order to access markets and resources. The liberalisation and globalisation of Indian business has seen a lot of increased activity in this field. Ventures based on specialised resources are able to capitalise on markets elsewhere. Indian ventures, such as Dr. Reddy's Lab, Biocon Ltd. and many more small and medium-sized firms are in the international arena of business.

9.2 Importance of International Business to the Firm

International business is all business transactions— private and governmental— that involve two or more countries. Why should one be interested in studying international business? The simplest answer is that international business comprises a large and growing portion of the world's total business. Today, almost all companies, large or small, are affected by global events and competition because most sell output to and/or secure suppliers from foreign countries and/or compete against products and services that come from abroad.

More companies that engage in some form of international business are involved in exporting and importing than in any other type of business transaction. Many of the international business experts argue that exporting is a logical process with a natural structure, which can be viewed primarily as a method of understanding the target country's environment, using the appropriate marketing mix, developing a marketing plan based upon the use of the mix, implementing a plan through a strategy and finally, using a control method to ensure the strategy is adhered to. This exporting process is reviewed and evaluated regularly and modifications are made to the use of the mix, to take account of market changes impacting upon competitiveness. This view seems to suggest that much of the international business theory related to enterprises, which are internationally based and have global ambitions, does often change depending on the special requirements of each country.

Another core issue is the company's growth and the importance of networking and interaction. This view looks at the way in which companies and organisations interact and consequently network with each other to gain commercial advantage in world markets. The network can be using similar subcontractors or components, sharing research and development costs or operating within the same governmental framework. Clearly, when businesses formulate a trading block with no internal barriers they are actually creating their own networks. Collaborations in aerospace, vehicle manufactures and engineering have all sponsored the development of a country's or a group of countries' outlook based on their own internal market network. This network and interaction approach to internationalisation shows the substance of being able to influence decisions when knowing how the global network players work or interact.

For example, a crucial market network is that of the Middle East. Middle-Eastern countries are rich, diverse markets, with a vibrant and varied cultural heritage. This means that although there has been a harmonisation process during the past few years, differences still exist. Rather than business being simpler as a result, it should be recognised that because of regulations and the need those countries have to restructure as they enter the global market, performing any kind of business can be highly complex. It should be remembered though that the Middle-Eastern countries have a low-income average and like to have their cultural differences recognised. Those firms that will or have recognised these facts have a good chance of developing a successful marketing strategy to meet their needs. Fortunately, some firms have realised these important differences and reacted adequately when strategic decisions had to be made regarding their penetration to this kind of markets. International business as we have seen is defined as 'any commercial transaction taking place across boundary lines of a sovereign entity. Every company is trying to expand its business by entering foreign markets. International business helps in the following ways:

- Helps as growth strategy: Geographic expansion may be used as a business strategy. Even though companies may expand their business at home.

- Helps in managing product life cycle: Every product has to pass through different stages of product life cycle-when the product reaches the last stages of life cycle in present market; it may get proper response at other markets.

- Technology advantages: - Some companies have outstanding technology advantages through which they enjoy core competency. This technology helps the company in capturing other markets.

- New business opportunities: Business opportunities in overseas markets help in expansion of many companies. They might have reached a saturation point in domestic market.

- Proper use of resources: Sometimes industrial resources, such as labour, minerals, etc. are available in a country but are not productively utilised.

- Availability of quality products: - When markets are open, better quality goods will be available everywhere. Foreign companies will market latest products at reasonable prices. Good product will be available in the markets.

- Earning foreign exchange: - International business helps in earning foreign exchange which may be used for strategic imports. India needs foreign exchange to import crude oil, deface equipment, raw material and machinery.Helps in mutual growth: Countries depend upon each other for meeting their requirements. India depends on gulf countries for its crude oil supplies.Investment in infrastructure: International business necessitates proper development of infrastructure. A company entering international business must invest in roads.

(a) Complexities involved in international business

International business means presence in multiple countries. So, the complexities are also related to their working. Some of these complexities are discussed as follows:

- Controlling the market: Multinational try to control the market of the host country. Whenever they enter a new country, the first strategy is to eliminate the competitors either by taking over their business or forcing them out of market by following price reduction policies.

- Exhausting natural resources: Multinational corporations set up their production facilities in those countries where natural resources are available in sufficient quantities.

- Importance to luxuries: Multinational corporations enter those areas where margin of profits is high.

- Trade practices: Since multinational corporations have their head office in one country and the trade practices followed there are adhered to.

- Economic development: It is generally felt that the entry of businessmen from outside may help in the economic development of that country. The actual practice in many countries is different.

- Shifting of investment: International business is related to profitability of its operations. If a business is getting sufficient profits in a particular country then the investment remain there.

The various mechanisms that a firm can utilise to go international are presented with some of the major advantages and disadvantages associated with each of them.

(b) Exports

- Advantages:
  - Avoids cost of establishing manufacturing operations overseas
  - May help achieve experience curve and scale economies
- Disadvantages:
  - May compete with low-cost location manufacturers
  - Possible high transportation costs
  - Tariff barriers

o   Possible lack of control over marketing reps.

(c) Licensing: An agreement where licensor grants rights to intangible property to another entity for a specified period of time in return for royalties.

- Advantages:
  - o   Reduces development costs and risks of establishing foreign enterprise
    - ➢   Lack capital for venture
    - ➢   Unfamiliar or politically volatile market
  - o   Overcomes restrictive investment barriers
  - o   Others can develop business applications of intangible property
- Disadvantages:
  - o   Lack of control
  - o   Cross-border licensing may be difficult
  - o   Creating a competitor

(d) Franchising: when the franchiser sells intangible property and insists on rules for operating business.

- Advantages:
  - o   Reduces costs and risks of establishing enterprise
- Disadvantages:
  - o   May prohibit movement of profits from one country to support operations in another country
  - o   Quality control

(e) Joint venture

- Advantages:
  - o   Benefit from local partner's knowledge
  - o   Shared costs/risks with partner
  - o   Reduced political risk
- Disadvantages:
  - o   Risk giving control of technology to partner
  - o   May not realise experience curve or location economies
  - o   Shared ownership can lead to conflict

(f) Wholly owned subsidiary

- Advantages:

- o   No risk of losing technical competence to a competitor
- o   Tight control of operations
- o   Realise learning curve and location economies
- Disadvantage:
  - o   Bear full cost and risk

To be able to decide on which of these above mentioned mechanisms is best suited for a venture one can look at certain internal and external factors that would provide guidance in determining which way to go.

(g) Internal factors

- Financial sources/resources
- Product characteristics
- Extent of marketing presence
- Degree of market penetration
- Firm's knowledge/experience
- Speed of market entry

(h) External factors

- Level of demand
- Commercial infrastructure
- Communication with intermediaries
- Investment climate
- Licensing regulations
- Tariff levels
- Political risk
- Competition
- Protection of Intellectual Property Rights
- Availability of personnel

9.3 International versus Domestic Entrepreneurship

The dimensions on which the international and domestic entrepreneurship differ are basically to do with the reasons to go international as compared to just focus attention on domestic markets. The main reason for organisations to tread across borders has noticeably been to acquire access to larger markets. This requires making alterations to your offerings at times. Whether international or domestic, an entrepreneur is concerned about the same basic issues: sales, costs, profits. What varies is the relative importance of the factors being considered. International entrepreneurial decisions are more complex due to uncontrollable factors, such as the following:

(a) Economics: A domestic business strategy is designed under a single economic system. Creating a business strategy for multiple countries means dealing with different levels of economic development and different distribution systems.

(b) Balance of payments: A country's balance of payments affects the valuation of its currency. This economic variable will affect how companies do business in other countries.

(c) Type of system: Types of System Barter or third-party arrangements have been used to increase business activity with the Commonwealth of Independent States (CIS), the former USSR. There are still many difficulties in doing business in developing and transition economies due to:

- gaps in the knowledge of the Western system regarding business plans, marketing and profits
- widely variable rates of return.
- non-convertibility of the ruble.
- differences in the accounting system.
- nightmarish communications.

(d) Political–Legal Environment: Multiple political and legal environments create different business problems. Each element of the international business strategy can potentially be affected by multiple legal environments. Laws governing business arrangements also vary greatly in the 150 different legal systems and sets of national laws.

(e) Cultural environment: The impact of culture on entrepreneurs and strategies is significant. Understanding the local culture is necessary when developing worldwide plans.

(f) Technological environment: Technology varies significantly across countries. New products in a country are created based of the conditions and infrastructure of that country.

9.4 Social Entrepreneurship

"It's a process whereby the creation of new business enterprise leads to social wealth enhancement so that both society and the entrepreneur benefit." These benefits, include the creation of jobs, increased productivity, enhanced national competitiveness— "as in Africa desperately trying to participate in the world economy"— and better quality of life.

It is melding the enterprise and innovation often associated with the private sector with the grassroots accountability necessary to sustain solutions in the public sector. Social entrepreneurship strives to combine the heart of business with the heart of the community through the creativity of the individual.

Social entrepreneurship is clearly not defined by such measures as size or sales figures. It ranges from the work being done by large organisations, such as Hartigan's to the successes that come from projects undertaken in small communities and even by individuals.

Entrepreneurship is a central ingredient in economic growth. It serves as a critical spur for the commercial introduction of new goods and services, as well as the opening of newmarkets to innovations. Entrepreneurship plays two special roles in the process of economic experimentation. First, entrepreneurs engage in 'extreme' experiments. Start-up businesses are not constrained by the limits of old technologies, traditional ways of organising production, or the need to serve established markets. Instead, entrepreneurs can be more aggressive than established organisations in pursuing radical approaches to the creation of economic value. Second, in contrast to purely scientific experiments, economic experiments compete with one another, with entrepreneurs once again playing a crucial role. The value of start-up activity is not limited to the (substantial) value created by new businesses, but also includes the benefits from increased competitive pressure on established firms. By playing a fundamental role in the process of economic experimentation, entrepreneurship contributes decisively to the range and diversity of economically useful knowledge, which is at the base of economic prosperity. There are three types of economic experiments:

- Technological Experiments: an attempt to exploit a scientific discovery or engineering opportunity for economic gain.
- Market Experiments: an attempt to identify and exploit the market applications where the technology may be most valuable.
- Organisational Experiments: an attempt to link together individuals and organisations in the pursuit of exploiting the interaction between market and technical opportunities.

Entrepreneurship activities influence, such as national productivity, wage levels and unemployment.

In their seminal paper on the *Rise of the Entrepreneurial Society*, Bargen, Freedman and Pages (2003) suggest that if the institutional maturity is created by a nation it reflects on the quantum and quality of entrepreneurial and industrial activity. These activities have a significant impact on the productivity, wages and level of unemployment. These in turn by way of creating work and jobs for people are impacting the socio-cultural demographics of nations. Our society earlier had a view that based on the age-old caste system specific communities alone were supposed to engage in doing business. However, over the years there has been a tremendous change in this view.

Another view that was there when just after independence the government working on the socialist model and with the intent of creating a strong industrial base create jobs for people. It became a trend that if one is able to get a job it was taken as more respectful and a reflection of the capability of the individual, while somebody getting into self-employment was being looked down upon in terms of probably being not so capable. This myth has been shattered and today those who are endeavour to become entrepreneurs are being hailed as competent and courageous people who are not simply job seekers but are contributing to job creation for others as well. The social reputation of entrepreneurs has been enhanced over the last one decade as people have realised that not all can probably become entrepreneurs and not all can probably make that contribution that entrepreneurs make through their initiatives.

The role of entrepreneurship is profound in the economy and society. Entrepreneurship is closely related to small and medium sized businesses. They grow very fast and hence, are future employers. Entrepreneurship helps the society as well as the entrepreneur, himself/herself. The benefits of entrepreneurship may be divided into three distinct categories that include the benefits to the nation, benefit to the society and the benefit to the individual. An effective entrepreneurship venture fosters the production of wealth for a nation. When many of the entrepreneurship produce an output greater than the input, the economy of the nation is directly bolstered. Another advantage to the nation is the creation of jobs for its people. Such a job creation utilises the human resources of that particular country and helps the natural talent materialise. With the new inventions and development in the new technology a nation can use its resources more effectively. Since a majority of the entrepreneurship projects are private, it provides an environment of competitiveness which further increases the quality of the products in the national markets. By privatising the local economy, entrepreneurship ventures help attract eager foreign firms who are otherwise reluctant to do business with the government subsidized economy.

The income level of the average person and the standard of living of a society increase with every successful entrepreneurship project that is undertaken. There is an increase in the employment level on the regional scale. It is also noticeable that an entrepreneurship helps develop other entrepreneur businesses because of the extra incentives that it can provide to a new entrepreneur in the shape of capital, knowledge and technology. Entrepreneurship helps the societies to fulfil its basic needs in the world that calls for the 'survival of the fittest'. Entrepreneurs lead by example in assisting the society and, therefore, boost the morale of the public. An entrepreneur helps himself while creating opportunities for others. It is a fact that by doing so an entrepreneur fulfils his/her creative urge. Each successful project carried out by the entrepreneur leads to self satisfaction. The greatest satisfaction is derived from the fact that the individual is his/her own boss and, therefore, can use its creativity without any fear of repercussion. The quality of every good entrepreneur project is the profit and the fame that such a career provides. In fact, entrepreneurs always enjoy respect and high status in their communities.

According to Schumpeter, there are five basic types of entrepreneurship projects. The introduction of a new good in the market is the first of these. By new product, it means something that has been invented and has never been available in the market. In simple terms, whenever a new invention is made, it is seen as an act of entrepreneurship. The second is the introduction of the new method of production. We know that it is the production of goods that forms the pillar of the economy. By new method, it is assumed that the method that is effective and efficient and is able to improve on an existing production method. The third type of entrepreneurship is the opening of a new market. Whenever such resources are provided that enables the population to benefit, whether it is an economic, education or any other benefit, it establishes a new opportunity that is known as a new market for using that particular resource. The fourth factor is the conquest of a new source of supply. Economist believes that a new supply source allows the industry to increase its productivity. This new source can be in many forms including the discovery of a natural resource (oil, steel, etc.) or attracting a labour force that has not been exposed to that industry. The last but not the least is the carrying out the new organisation of industry that will increase human welfare.

□□□

At a Glance

1. International business is all business transactions — private and governmental — that involve two or more countries. It comprises a large and growing portion of the world's total business. Today, almost all companies, large or small, are affected by global events and competition because most sell output to and/or compete against products and services that come form abroad.

2. International business means presence in multiple countries, control the market of host countries, eliminate competitors either by taking over their business or forcing them out of the market by following price polices. International business is related to profitability of its operations. If a business is getting sufficient profits in a particular country then the investment remains there.

3. There are still many difficulties in doing business in developing and transition economies due to gaps in knowledge of the western system regarding business plans, marketing and profits, widely variable rates of return, non- convertibility of the currency, differences in accounting system and not so well established communication facilities.

4. There are three types of economic experiments such as Technological experiments which attempt to exploit a scientific discovery or engineering opportunity for economic gain. Market experiments which attempt to identify

and exploit the market applications where the technology may be most valuable and Organisational experiments that attempt to link together individuals and originations in the pursuit of exploiting the interactions between market and technical opportunities.

Multiple Choice Questions

1. Whenever a new invention is made, it is seen as an act of:
   (a) Technique
   (b) Entrepreneurship
   (c) New Business
   (d) Project work
2. Entrepreneurship contributes decisively to the range and diversity of:
   (a) Economic experimentation
   (b) Economically useful knowledge
   (c) Serve established markets
   (d) Radical approaches to the creations of economic value
3. Benefits of Social Entrepreneurship include:
   (a) Size or sales figures
   (b) Introductions of new goods and services.
   (c) Creation of jobs, increased productivity and enhanced national competitiveness
4. A country's balance of payments and _____ affects the companies doing business in other countries.
   (a) Valuation of its currency
   (b) Devaluation of its currency and business strategy
   (c) Business plans, marketing and profits
   (d) Non- Convertibility of the ruble
5. Factors that are considered for a successful venture are:
   (a) Level of demand, competition
   (b) Tight control of operations
   (c) Speed of market entry, degree of market penetration, extent of marketing presence, financial sources/resources
   (d) Bear full cost and risk
6. Exports advantages are:
   (a) May compete with low cost location manufactures
   (b) Unfamiliar or politically volatile market
   (c) Reduces costs and risks of establishing enterprises
   (d) Avoid cost of establishing manufacturing operations overseas and help achieving experience curve and scale economies

---

Ans. 1. b, 2. b, 3. c, 4. a, 5. c, 6. d

Review Questions

1. International business helps countries in many ways. Please describe in detail the preceding statement..

2. Describe the complexities that are involved with international businesses.

3. The various mechanisms that a firm can utilise to go international have some major advantages and disadvantages. Enumerate few.

4. Your neighbourhood ABC Spices Dealer is an active international firm. Enumerate the importance of international business to this firm.

5. Describe nature of international entrepreneurship.

Unit IV

Institutional Support for
New Ventures

Chapter 10

Government Policies for Small Scale Industries

Introduction

The Micro, Small and Medium Enterprises (MSME) sector has been recognised as the engine of growth all over the world. In India, with the advent of planned economy from 1951 and the subsequent industrial policy followed by Government of India, both planners and Government earmarked a special role for small scale industries and medium scale industries in the Indian economy. Due protection was accorded to both sectors, and particularly for small scale industries from 1951–91, till the nation adopted a policy of liberalisation and globalisation. Certain products were reserved for small scale units for a long time, though this list of products is decreasing due to change in industrial policies and climate.

Small and Medium Enterprises (SMEs) always represented the model of socio-economic policies of Government of India which emphasised judicious use of foreign exchange for import of capital goods and inputs; labour intensive mode of production; employment generation; non-concentration of diffusion of economic power in the hands of few (as in the case of big houses); discouraging monopolistic practices of production and marketing and effective contribution to foreign exchange earning of the nation with low import-intensive operations. It was also coupled with the policy of de-concentration of industrial activities in few geographical centres. It can be observed that by and large, SMEs in India met the expectations of the Government in this respect. SMEs developed in a manner, which made it possible for them to achieve the following objectives:

- High contribution to domestic production
- Significant export earnings
- Low investment requirements
- Operational flexibility
- Location wise mobility
- Low intensive imports

- Capacities to develop appropriate indigenous technology
- Import substitution
- Contribution towards defence production
- Technology-oriented industries
- Competitiveness in domestic and export markets

At the same time, one has to understand the limitations of SMEs, which are as follows:

- Low capital base
- Concentration of functions in one/two persons
- Inadequate exposure to international environment
- Inability to face impact of WTO regime
- Inadequate contribution towards R&D
- Lack of professionalism

In spite of these limitations, the SMEs have made significant contribution towards technological development and exports. SMEs have been established in almost all-major sectors in the Indian industry as follows:

- Food Processing
- Agricultural Inputs
- Chemicals and Pharmaceuticals
- Engineering; Electricals; Electronics
- Electro-medical equipment
- Textiles and Garments
- Leather and leather goods
- Meat products
- Bio-engineering
- Sports goods
- Plastics products
- Computer Software, etc.

As a result of globalisation and liberalisation, coupled with World Trade Organisation (WTO) regime, Indian SMEs have been passing through a transitional period. With slowing down of economy in India and abroad, particularly USA and European Union and enhanced competition from China and a few low cost centres of production from abroad, many units have been facing a tough time. Those SMEs who have strong technological base, international business outlook, competitive spirit and willingness to restructure themselves shall withstand the present challenges and come out with shining colours to make their own contribution to the Indian economy.

10.1 MSME - New Policy and Definition

The small scale industry sector output contributes almost 40percent of the gross industrial value-added 45percent of the total exports from India (direct as well as indirect exports) and is the second largest employer of human resources after agriculture. The development of small scale sector has, therefore, been assigned an important role in India's national plans.

In order to protect, support and promote small enterprises as also to help them become self-supporting, a number of protective and promotional measures have been undertaken by the Government.

The promotional measures cover

- industrial extension services
- institutional support in respect of credit facilities
- provision of developed sites for construction of sheds
- provision of training facilities
- supply of machinery on hire–purchase terms
- assistance for domestic marketing as well as exports
- special incentive for setting up enterprises in backward areas, etc.
- technical consultancy and financial assistance for technological upgradation

Today, SMEs in India are grappling with fast changes at the market place that is transiting from a controlled economy to a free market set-up. They, being the important members within the supply chain, are also exposed to the competitive pressures either directly from the market place on indirectly passed on from their higher ups in the chain. Considering the strategic role played by SMEs, it is essential to examine how they can improve their performance in international markets and how they can enhance their export competitiveness. The long, small and medium scale enterprises were clubbed together loosely, with no clear definition of what constituted medium scale units. The government has now provided clarity on this issue with the enactment of the Micro, Small and Medium Enterprises Development Act, 2006 (MSMED Act) which came into force from 2nd October, 2006.

10.2 Government Policies and Support- A Brief History

The evolution of policy framework and support of the government can be categorised into three phases:

1948–91: Office of Development Commissioner (SSI) was established in 1954 on the basis of the recommendations of the Ford Foundation. Over the years, it has seen its role evolving into an agency for advocacy, hand holding and facilitation for the small industries sector. It has over 70 offices and 21 autonomous bodies under its management. These autonomous bodies include Tool Rooms, Training Institutions and Project-cum-Process Development Centres. Office of the Development Commissioner (MSME) provides a wide spectrum of services to the micro, small and medium industrial sector. These include facilities for testing, tool menting, training for entrepreneurship development, preparation of project and product profiles, technical and managerial consultancy, assistance for exports, pollution and energy audits, etc. Office of the Development Commissioner (MSME) provides economic information services and advises Government in policy formulation for the promotion and development of SSIs. The field offices also work as effective links between the Central and the State Governments.

1991–99: Small Industries Industrial Development Bank was created, emphasis was given on the credit disbursal and industrial infrastructure development scheme was launched to set up mini industrial estates.

1999 onwards: A new ministry was formed and a new policy package was announced in August 2000 to address the problems of credit, infrastructure, marketing and technology upgradation effectively.

10.3 Present Policy Frame Work and Focus Areas

By enacting the Micro, Small and Medium Enterprises Development Act, 2006, the Government has recently fulfilled one of the needs felt and articulated by this segment for long. This Act seeks to facilitate promotion and development and enhancing competitiveness of these enterprises. It provides the first-ever legal framework for recognition of the concept of 'enterprise' (comprising both manufacturing and services) and integrating the three tiers of these enterprises, namely, micro, small and medium. Apart from clearer and more progressive classification of each category of enterprises, particularly the small, the Act provides for a statutory consultative mechanism at the national level with wide representation of all sections of stakeholders, particularly the three classes of enterprises; and with a wide range of advisory functions. Establishment of specific funds for the promotion, development and enhancing competitiveness of these enterprises, notification of schemes/programmes for this purpose, progressive credit policies and practices, preference in Government procurements to products and services of the micro and small enterprises, more effective mechanisms for mitigating the problems of delayed payments to micro and small enterprises and simplification of the process of closure of business by all three categories of enterprises are some of the other features of this legislation.

The Government has also announced a policy package for stepping up credit to small and medium enterprises assuring, inter alia, a 20 percent year-on-year growth in credit flow.

Significant improvements have also been made in the Credit Linked Capital Subsidy Scheme for technological upgradation, leading to a spurt in the number of units availing of its benefits.

Focus Areas:

- Credit/Finance
- Priority Sector Lending
- Institutional Arrangement
- Credit Guarantee Scheme
- Performance and Credit Rating Scheme

10.4 Technology Upgradation

The department of Science and Technology through its National Science and Technology Entrepreneurship Development Board facilitate the development of and upgradation of technology. They provide funding for new ventures who want to develop technology. Similarly, in the field of biotechnology the department of Biotechnology also supports new and existing ventures develop technology and build ventures with biotechnology as a basis for business.

(a) Department of Science and Technology

Department of Science and Technology (DST) was established in May 1971, with the objective of promoting new areas of Science and Technology (S&T) and to play the role of a nodal department for organising, coordinating and promoting S&T activities in the country. The department has major responsibilities for specific projects and programmes as listed in the following:

- Formulation of policies relating to S&T.
- Matters relating to the Scientific Advisory Committee of the Cabinet (SACC).
- Promotion of new areas of S&T with special emphasis on emerging areas.
- Research and Development through its research institutions or laboratories for development of indigenous technologies concerning bio-fuel production processing, standardisation and applications, in co-ordination with the concerned Ministry or Department.
- Research and Development activities to promote utilisation of by-products to development value added chemicals.
- Futurology.
- Coordination and integration of areas of Science and Technology having cross-sectoral linkages in which a number of institutions and departments have interest and capabilities.

- Undertaking or financially sponsoring scientific and technological surveys, research design and development, where necessary.
- Support and Grants-in-aid to Scientific Research Institutions, Scientific Associations and Bodies.
- All matters concern as follows:
  - Science and Engineering Research Council
  - Technology Development Board and related Acts, such as the Research and Development Cess Act,1986 (Act No. 32 of 1986) and the Technology Development Board Act,1995 (44 of 1995)
  - National Council for Science and Technology Communication
  - National Science and Technology Entrepreneurship Development Board
  - International Science and Technology Cooperation including appointment of scientific attaches abroad (These functions shall be exercised in close cooperation with the Ministry of External Affairs)
  - Autonomous Science and Technology Institutions relating to the subject under the Department of Science and Technology including Institute of Astro-physics, and Institute of Geo-magnetism
  - Professional Science Academies promoted and funded by Department of Science and Technology
  - The Survey of India, and National Atlas and Thematic Mapping Organisation
  - National Spatial Data Infrastructure and promotion of G.I.S
  - The National Innovation Foundation, Ahmedabad
- Matters commonly affecting scientific and technological departments/ organisations/ institutions; e.g., financial, personnel, purchase and import policies and practices.
- Management Information Systems for Science and Technology and coordination thereof.
- Matters regarding Inter-Agency/Inter-Departmental coordination for evolving science and technology missions.
- Matters concerning domestic technology particularly the promotion of ventures involving the commercialisation of such technology other than those under the Department of Scientific and Industrial Research.
- All other measures needed for the promotion of science and technology and their application to the development and security of the nation.

- Matters relating to institutional science and technology capacity building including setting up of new institutions and institutional infrastructure.

- Promotion of science and technology at the state, district and village levels for grassroots development through State Science and Technology Councils and other mechanisms.

- Application of science and technology for weaker sections, women and other disadvantaged sections of society.

The department of Science and Technology through its various schemes connected to the Technology development Board supports development of technology. It has funded technology development across sectors, such as Health and Medicine, Road and Air transport Engineering, Chemicals, Energy, Information Communication Technology (ICT), Food and Agriculture. They provide funding on soft collaterals and have a significantly large fund supporting this initiative. The mandate given to the department includes the following:

- Formulation of policy statements and guidelines

- Co-ordination of areas of science and technology in which a number of institutions and departments have interests and capabilities

- Support to basic and applied research in national institutions

- Support minimum infrastructural facilities for Testing and Instrumentation

- Technology Development and Commercialisation - Technology Development Board

- Autonomous Research Institutions

- Fostering International Cooperation in S&T

- Socially oriented S&T interventions for rural and weaker sections

- Support Science and Technology Entrepreneurship Development for promotion of knowledge Based Technology Driven Entrepreneurs

- Popularisation of Science and Technology

- Promotion and Development of S&T in states

- Scientific surveys and services through Survey of India and National Atlas and Thematic Mapping Organization (NATMO)

- Management of Information Systems for Science and Technology

(b) Department of Biotechnology

The setting up of a separate Department of Biotechnology (DBT), under the Ministry of Science and Technology in 1986 gave a new impetus to the development of the field of modern biology and biotechnology in India. In more than a decade of its existence, the department has promoted and accelerated the pace of development of biotechnology in the country. Through several R&D projects, demonstrations and creation of infrastructural facilities, a clear visible impact of this field has been seen. The department has made significant achievements in the growth and application of biotechnology in the broad areas of agriculture, health care, animal sciences, environment and industry.

The impact of the biotechnology related developments in agriculture, health care, environment and industry, has already been visible and the efforts are now culminating into products and processes. More than 5000 research publications, 4000 post-doctoral students, several technologies transferred to industries and patents filed including the US patents, can be considered as a modest beginning. The Department of Biotechnology has been interacting with more than 5,000 scientists per year in order to utilise the existing expertise of the universities and other national laboratories. A very strong peer reviewing and monitoring mechanism has been developed. There has been close interaction with the state governments particularly through State S&T Councils for developing biotechnology application projects, demonstration of proven technologies, and training of human resources in states and union territories. Programmes with the states of Gujarat, Rajasthan, Madhya Pradesh, Orissa, West Bengal, Haryana, Punjab, Jammu and Kashmir, Mizoram, Andhra Pradesh and Uttar Pradesh have been evolved. Biotechnology Application Centres in Madhya Pradesh and West Bengal have already been started.

A unique feature of the department has been the deep involvement of the scientific community of the country through a number of technical task forces, advisory committees and individual experts in identification, formulation, implementation and monitoring of various programmes and activities. In India, more than a decade of concerted effort in research and development in identified areas of modern biology and biotechnology has given rich dividends. The proven technologies at the laboratory level have been scaled up and demonstrated in field. Patenting of innovations, technology transfer to industries and close interaction with them have given a new direction to biotechnology research. Initiatives have been taken to promote transgenic research in plants with emphasis on pest and disease resistance, nutritional quality, silk-worm genome analysis, molecular biology of human genetic disorders, brain research, plant genome research, development, validation and commercialisation of diagnostic kits and vaccines for communicable diseases, food biotechnology, biodiversity conservation and bioprospecting, setting up of micropropagation parks and biotechnology based development for SC/ST, rural areas, women and for different states.

Necessary guidelines for transgenic plants, recombinant vaccines and drugs have also been evolved. A strong base of indigenous capabilities has been created. The field of biotechnology both for new innovations and applications would form a major research and commercial endeavor for socio-economic development in the next millennium. The department of biotechnology has a mandate for the following activities:

- Promote large scale use of biotechnology
- Support R&D and manufacturing in biology
- Responsibility for autonomous institutions
- Promote university and industry interaction
- Identify and Set up centers of Excellence for R&D
- Integrated Programme for Human Resource Development
- To serve as nodal point for specific international collaborations
- Establishment of infrastructure facilities to support R&D and production
- Evolve bio-safety guidelines, manufacture and application of cell-based vaccines
- Serve as nodal point for the collection and dissemination of information relating to biotechnology

(c) National Research and Development Corporation (NRDC)

NRDC is a government organisation involved in the task of fostering development and commercialisation of technology. Of the various functions that it is engaged in, some of the main ones are listed in the following:

(d) Commercial activities

- Commercialisation of laboratory know-how
- License indigenous technologies to industry both in India and abroad
- Provide technology development loans for setting up pilot plants to prove/scale-up laboratory processes.
- Participate in equity to facilitate formation of new ventures using indigenous technologies
- Develop technologies in priority areas
- Design and engineer laboratory processes to commercial scale
- Provide techno-commercial financial support to entrepreneurs commercialising NRDC technologies
- Execute turnkey projects abroad based on indigenous technologies
- Licensing of foreign know-how to Indian clients
- Assist export marketing of products of licensee companies

(e) Promotional activities

- Promotion and commercialisation of inventions

- Award meritorious inventions
- Arrange complimentary finance for further development through venture capital fund, PATSER, TIFAC, TDB, etc.
- Provide assistance for patenting inventive ideas of R&D organisations and universities.

(f) Development and Promotion of Rural Technology

- Identify, prove and demonstrate selected rural technologies
- Assist in commercialisation of selected rural technologies

(g) Export of Technology

- Project India as a source of technology
- Assist inventors, R&D institutes and industry to patent their new products abroad

(h) Dissemination of Information on Technology and its transfer to Industry

- Provide information on indigenous and foreign technologies
- Organise training programmes for technology development and transfer
- Hold exhibitions, publish periodicals, arrange audio-visuals to popularise indigenous technologies
  - Agro Food Processing
  - Bio-Medical Devices
  - Bio-Technology
  - Building Materials
  - Drugs and Pharmaceuticals
  - Chemical Industries
  - Environ-friendly Chemicals
  - Electronics
  - Mechanical Industries
  - Rural Industries

The recent progress (1995 onwards) made by the Indian Information Technology (IIT) sector is an outcome of planned support provided by the government on the above mentioned four support dimensions. The National Association for Software and Services Companies (NASSCOM) under the leadership of people from Dewang Mehta to Kiran Karnik has had an enormous role in guiding the government to decide the combination of support and incentives to be offered to the mushrooming IT companies. Similar growth and success is now being witnessed across other sectors, such as biotechnology and in specific geographic locations, such as Uttarakhand, etc. Further to these, the department of information and communication technology through its various activities pays attention to research and development in the field of ICT and indirectly fosters entrepreneurship as well. The following chapters will present the detailed support mechanisms laid out by the union government and some additional support put in place by some states.

□□□

At a Glance

1. Objectives achieved by SMEs:
   - (a) Low investment requirement
   - (b) Competitivenes in domestic and export markets
   - (c) High contribution to domestic production
   - (d) Operational flexibility
   - (e) Location wise mobility
   - (f) Import substitution
   - (g) Low intensive imports

2. Limitations of SMEs:
   - (a) Low capital base
   - (b) Inability to face impact of WTO regime
   - (c) Concentration of functions in one/two persons
   - (d) Inadequate export in international environment

3. Protective and promotional measures undertaken by Government for SMEs are:
   - (a) Industrial extension service
   - (b) Provision of training facilities
   - (c) Supply of machinery as hive- purchase terms
   - (d) Special incentives for setting up enterprises in backward areas etc.
   - (e) Institutional support in respect of credit facilities

4. A new ministry with a new policy package was announced in August 2000 to address problems of credit, infracture, marketing and technology upgradation effectively.

5. Focussed areas where units availed credit linked capital subsidy sheme for technological upgradation are:
   - (a) Credit/Finance
   - (b) Priority Sector lending
   - (c) Institutional Arrangement
   - (d) Credit Guarantee Scheme
   - (e) Performance and Credit Rating scheme

6. Department of biotechonology has mandate for following activities:
   (a) Promote large scale use of biotechnology
   (b) Support R & D and manufacturing in biology

Multiple Choice Questions

1. NASSCOM is:
   (a) National Association for soft & service
   (b) Only National Software Services
   (c) Services, Software of National Association
   (d) National Association for Software and Services Companies

2. National Research and Development Corporation is:
   (a) NRCD
   (b) NR and DC
   (c) DC & NR
   (d) NRDC

3. National Development and Development Corporation is involved in:
   (a) Fostering development & commercialization of technology
   (b) Fostering technology & commercialization of software
   (c) Commercialization of Industry
   (d) Commercialization support to entrepreneurs

4. The department of Science and Technology:
   (a) Provides funds on soft collaterals and its schemes are connected to the Technology Development Board
   (b) Co- ordinates areas of commerce and technology
   (c) Supports Information Management system for Science & Technology
   (d) Discourages International cooperation for Science and Technology

5. Limitations of Small and Medium Enterprises are:
   (a) Low capital base
   (b) Large capital base
   (c) Ability to face impact of WTO regime
   (d) Low intensive imports

Ans. 1. d, 2. d, 3. a, 4. a, 5. a

Review Questions

1. Mention the objectives achieved by Small and Medium Enterprises.

2. Enumerate the promotional and protective measures undertaken by GOI for MSMEs.

3. What are the mandates that are to be followed by Department of Biotechnology?

4. Write down the major responsibilities of Department of Science & Technology. Avoid any narration, to the point answer will be appreciated.

5. Write a short note on:
    (a) National Research and Development Corporation
    (b) The National Association for Software and Services Companies

Chapter **11**

Supporting Organisations, Incentives and Facilities

Introduction

The government of any nation has a critical role to play in ensuring the development of a vibrant business eco-system (see Fig.11.1). This ecosystem is built as a consequence of providing various types of support to people who are keen to starting ventures on their own. Governments across the world have found it difficult or rather impossible to create employment for one and all. Therefore, efforts to see that individuals although may start with self-employment initially but may lead to becoming job creators by way of growing their ventures to a position wherein they need to employ people to get work done. At the same time, it is important to understand that any individual desirous to start a business venture would need to have certain systems and procedures in place so that the government to be able to keep a track of the different organisations emerging.

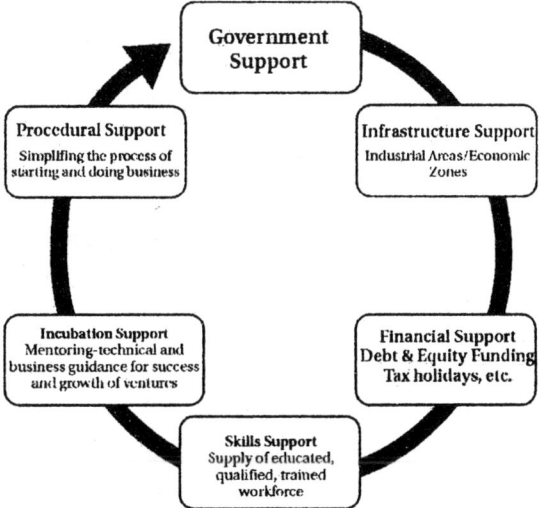

Fig.11.1 Vibrant business eco-system

Further, there are certain fundamental facilities related to starting and doing business that need to be put in place so that people can endeavour to start their own business ventures. These would be qualified and skilled workforce, infrastructure, utilities, such as electricity, water, raw material for constructing business units, financial institutions to provide funds to engage in business activities. Beside the fundamental facilities, there has to be some incentive for an individual to start a business organisation. These incentives have been found to be of great significance for those who seek support for doing business. As of now, the information technology sector with over eight thousand new ventures emerging over the past two decades and the biotechnology sector wherein about six hundred organisations have emerged over the past few years are an outcome of government support for entrepreneurship in these fields along with the efforts of qualified professionals who started ventures.

11.1 Incentive Schemes by Central Government

There are a number of schemes that the central government operates to support the small scale industries sector. Some of the main schemes are described in the following:

(a) Credit Guarantee Fund Scheme for SSI

Small scale industrial units particularly the first generation of entrepreneurs faced difficulties in accessing bank credit because of their inability to provide adequate collateral security for loans. Considering this, the Government launched the Credit Guarantee Fund Scheme for Small Industries on 30th August, 2000 with a view to alleviating the problem of collateral security and impediment to flow of credit to Small Scale Industries (SSI) sector. The Government approved Credit Guarantee Fund Scheme for small industries on 19th May, 2000 with the objective of making available credit to SSI units, particularly tiny units, for loans up to ₹ 10 lakh without collateral/third party guarantes. The scheme is being operated by the Credit Guarantee Trust Fund for Small Industries (CGTSI) set-up by Government of India and SIDBI. The Trust was incorporated on 27th July, 2000. The scheme has been operationaliseds with effect from 1st January, 2001.

Subsequently, the Government decided to increase the eligibility limit of loans to be guaranteed from ₹ 10 lakh to ₹ 25 lakh. Necessary modifications have been carried out in the indenture of the Trust to enable CGTSI to guarantee loans up to ₹ 25 lakh and to provide for counter guarantees to other institutions.

(b) Salient features of the scheme

- Eligibility and Coverage

Any collateral free credit facility (both in terms of loan as well as working capital) extended by lending institutions on or after 1st June, 2000 to new as well as existing manufacturing SSI units, including Information Technology and Software industry, particularly in the tiny sector, with a credit cap of ₹ 25 lakh per operating unit, can be extended guarantee cover. With effect from 1st September, 2003, the credit facilities up to ₹ 25 lakh sanctioned without collateral security and/or third party guarantee by the lending institutions to the new and existing Small Scale Service and Business (Industry Related) Enterprises (SSSBEs) have also been made eligible for coverage under the scheme. Any credit facility which has been sanctioned by the lending institution against collateral security and/or third party guarantee; however, is not eligible for guarantee cover under the scheme. The guarantee cover available is up to 75percent of the loans extended by the lending institutions. The guarantee cap per borrower is ₹ 18.75 lakh. The rate of interest that can be charged to the borrower by the lending institution shall not be more than 3% over the prime lending rate of the lending institution.

- Guarantee and Annual Service Fee

The lending institutions availing guarantee from the Trust have to pay one time guarantee fee of 2.5 percent of the credit facility sanctioned and the service charges of 1 percent per annum on the outstanding loan amount as on 31st March each year.

- Commencement of guarantee cover

The guarantee cover will commence from the date of payment of guarantee fee and shall run through the agreed tenure of the term credit in respect of term credit/composite credit. Where working capital alone is extended to the eligible borrower, the guarantee cover shall be for a period of 5 years or a block of 5 years, or for such period as may be specified by the Trust in this behalf.

- Invocation of guarantee

The lending institution may invoke the guarantee in respect of eligible credit facility, if the following conditions are satisfied:

o The guarantee in respect of that credit facility is in force.
o The lock-in period of 24 months from either the date of last disbursement of the loan to the borrower or the date of payment of the guarantee fee in respect of credit facility to the borrower, whichever is later, has elapsed.
o The amount due and payable to the lending institution in respect of the credit facility has not been paid and the dues have been classified by the lending institution as Non-Performing Assets. Provided that the lending institution shall not make or be entitled to make any claim on the Trust in respect of the said credit facility if the loss in respect of the said credit facility has occurred owing to action/decisions taken contrary to or in contravention of the guidelines issued by the Trust.
o The loan facility has been recalled and the recovery proceedings have been initiated under due process of law.

The Trust shall pay 75 percent of the guaranteed amount on preferring of eligible claim by the lending institution, within 30 days, subject to the claim being otherwise found in order and complete in all respects. The balance 25 percent of the guaranteed amount will be paid on conclusion of recovery proceedings by the lending institution.

(c) Eligible institutions

All scheduled commercial banks and Regional Rural Banks (categorised under 'sustainable viability') or such of those institutions as may be directed by GOI. As on 31st March 2004, 45 eligible institutions comprising 26 public sector banks, 10 private sector banks, 6 regional rural banks and 3 other institutions viz. National Small Industries Corporation Ltd. (NSIC), North Eastern Development Finance Corporation Ltd. (NEDFi) and Small Industries Development Bank of India (SIDBI) have become Member Lending Institutions (MLIs) of CGTSI for participating under the Credit Guarantee Scheme.

- Contribution to the Corpus Fund of CGTSI

The Government of India and SIDBI contribute towards the corpus fund of the CGTSI in the ratio of 4:1. The Trust was set up with an initial corpus of ₹125 crore, which was enhanced to ₹ 250 crore by the end of FY 2001–02 and to ₹427.02 crore by the end of FY 2002–03. The corpus fund was further raised to ₹ 686.19 crore during the FY 2003–04. With a view to augment the corpus so as to make the scheme self-sustaining, a budgetary provision of ₹196.29 crore has been made by the Government during the current FY 2004–05. At present, the corpus fund is of ₹767.44 crore.

- Progress of Credit Guarantee Scheme

As on 31st July, 2004, a total of 16,679 proposals have been approved by CGTSI and guarantee cover provided for credit aggregating ₹280.18 crore.

(d) Initiatives for women entrepreneurs

Women entrepreneurs have achieved remarkable success. The Small Industries Development Organization (SIDO), the various State Small Industries Development Corporations (SSIDCs), the nationalised banks and even NGOs are conducting various programmes including Entrepreneurship Development Programmes (EDPs). To cater to the needs of potential women entrepreneurs, who may not have adequate educational background and skills, SIDO has introduced process/product-oriented EDPs in areas, such as TV repairing, printed circuit boards, leather goods, screen printing, etc. A special prize to 'Outstanding Women Entrepreneur' of the year is being given to recognise achievements made by and to provide incentives to women entrepreneurs. The Office of DC (SSI) has also opened a Women Cell to provide coordination and assistance to women entrepreneurs facing specific problems. There are also several other schemes of the government, such as the Income Generating Scheme, implemented by the Department of Women and Child Development, which provides assistance for setting up training-cum-income generating activities for needy women to make them economically independent. The SIDBI has been implementing two special schemes for women namely Mahila Udyam Nidhi which is an exclusive scheme for providing equity to women entrepreneurs and the Mahila Vikas Nidhi which offers developmental assistance for pursuit of income generating activities to women. The SIDBI has also taken initiative to set up an informal channel for credit needs on soft terms giving special emphasis to women. Over and above this, SIDBI also provides training for credit utilisation as also credit delivery skills for the executives of voluntary organisations working for women. Grant for setting up a production unit is also available under socio-economic programme of Central Social Welfare Board.

(e) Incentives for North Eastern region

In view of the continuing backwardness of North East region, the need for a new and synergetic incentive package was widely felt to stimulate development of industries (the then Prime Minis er made a statement at Guwahati on 27th October, 1996 that new initiatives would be announced for the industrial development of the North Eastern region). Expert groups/committees were constituted by the Ministry of Industry and the Planning Commission to concretise the initiatives.

Subsequently, inter-departmental meetings were held under the Chairmanship of Member Secretary (Planning Commission) to consider the recommendations and finalise the proposals. Based on this proposal, Government approved the new industrial policy and other concessions in the North Eastern region which inter alia envisage the following:

- Development of Industrial Infrastructure
  - Currently the funding pattern for the growth centres envisages a central assistance of ₹ 10 crore for each Centre and balance amount to be raised by the State Government. Government has approved that entire expenditure on the growth centres would be provided as Central assistance, subject to a ceiling of ₹ 15 crore.

  - In respect of the IID centres, the funding pattern would be changed from 2:3 between GOI and SIDBI to 4:1 and the GOI funds would be a grant.

- Transport Subsidy Scheme
  - The Transport subsidy scheme will be extended further in so far as N.E. States are concerned for a period of another 7 years, i.e., up to 31st March, 2007 being coterminous with the 10th Five Year Plan on same terms and condition as are applicable now.

- Fiscal Incentives To New Industrial Units And Their Substantial Expansion o   Government has approved for converting the growth centres and IIDCs into a total tax free zone for the next 10 years. All industrial activity in these zones would be free from income-tax, excise, for a period of 10 years from the commencement of production. State Government would be requested to grant exemptions in respect of Sales Tax and Municipal Tax.

o   Industries located in the growth centres would also be given capital investment subsidy at the rate of 15percent of their investment in plant and machinery, subject to a maximum ceiling of ₹ 30 lakh. Commercial banks and the North East Development Financial Corporation (NEDFI) will have dedicated branches/counters to process applications for term loans and working capital in these centres. While sanctioning assistance NEDFI and commercial banks would take a liberal view of the debt equity ratio.

o   An interest subsidy of 3percent on the working capital loans would be provided for a period of ten years after the commencement of production. The working capital requirements would be worked out as per the Nayak Committee.

o   Similar benefits would also be extended to the new industrial units or their substantial expansion in other Growth Centres or IIDCs or industrial estates/parks/export promotion zones set up by the States in the NE region. New industrial units or their substantial expansion in the specified industries located outside these growth centres and other identified locations would also be eligible for the similar fiscal incentives.

- Relaxation of PMRY Norms

The PMRY would be expanded in scope to cover areas of horticulture, piggery, poultry, fishing, small tea gardens, etc. so as to cover all economically viable activities. PMRY would have a family income ceiling of ₹ 40,000 per annum for each beneficiary along with his/her spouse and upper age limit will be relaxed to 40 years. Project costing up to ₹ 2 lakh in other than business sectors will be eligible for assistance. No collateral will be insisted for projects costing up to Re. 1 lakh. Group financing up to ₹ 5 lakh will be eligible. Scheme will have a subsidy component @ 15percent with an upper ceiling of ₹ 15,000. The margin money may vary from 5–12.5% of the project cost to make the subsidy and margin contribution at 20percent of the project cost. PMRY would continue to have Entrepreneurship Training Component as per the existing rate.

- Other Incentives Proposed
    o   A comprehensive insurance scheme for industrial units in the North East will be designed in consultation with General Insurance Corporation of

India Ltd. and 100percent premium for a period of 10 years would be subsidised by Central Government.

o   A one-time grant of ₹ 20 crore will be provided to the North East Development Financial Corporation (NEDFI) by the Central Government through NEC to fund techno-economic studies for industries and infrastructure best suited to this region.

o   State Government may consider setting up of a "Debt Purchase Windows" by the NEDFI which buys the debt of the manufacturing units particularly in respect of the supplies made to the Government Department so as to reduce the problem of blocking of funds for these units.

o   For development of markets in north east possibilities of exports of products of north east to the neighbouring countries particularly Bangladesh, Myanmar and Bhutan would be explored.

o   It may be considered to provide assistance for restructuring State PSUs from National Renewal Fund.

o   The community pattern of land holding in large parts of NE region does not lend itself to providing collateral security as required under conventional bank lending. RBI has constituted a committee to look into this issue. An appropriate system of guarantees will be evolved for NE region.

- Procedure for Release of Assistance Under the New Initiatives

o   It is approved that the transport subsidy budget may be released by a designated agency on the basis of the recommendations of the S.L.C. It is proposed that NEDFI may be designated as the nodal agency for release of transport subsidy in N.E. States. NEDFI may be paid administrative expenses for this service which may be decided in consultation with IDBI.

- Development of Village and Small Industries (VSI) Sector

o   Weavers' Service Centres (WSCs) in NE region and Indian Institute of Handloom Technology at Guwahati would be suitably strengthened to provide technology and training support to the weavers. National Handloom Development Corporation will give priority in supply of hank yarn to the NE region. All the four varieties of silk would be covered under the Mill Gate Price Scheme. Priority would be given to the N.E. region in scheme of setting up of market complexes and permanent exhibition facilities. A new design centre for development of handicraft would be set up in NE region. To upgrade the skill of artisan, advance training programme through master craftsmen would be organised. New emporia will be set up and financial assistance for renovation of existing emporia would be provided. The Central Silk Board will give priority to NE region in implementation of its schemes.

11.2 Incentive Scheme of Reimbursement of Acquiring Quality Management System (QMS) (ISO 9000/ Environment Management System (EMS) ISO-14001 Certification)

The Govt. of India has been operating an Incentive Scheme of reimbursement of expenses of acquiring Quality Management System (QMS) ISO-9000 certification in the Small Scale Sector to the extent of 75percent of the amount limited to ₹ 75,000 to each unit. The scope of this Scheme now has been extended to provide reimbursement of expenses of acquiring EMS –ISO 14001 Certificate. The Salient features of the Scheme are as under: The Scheme envisages reimbursement of charges of acquiring ISO-9000/ISO-14001 certifications to the extent of 75percent of the expenditure subject to a maximum of ₹ 75,000 in each case. The scheme is valid up to 31st March, 2007. The Permanent Registered Small Scale/ancillary/Tiny/Small Scale Service Business Enterprises (SSSBE) units are eligible to avail the Incentive Scheme. The Scheme is applicable to those SSI/ancillary/Tiny/SSSBE units who have already acquired ISO-9000/ISO-14001 certification. It is an all India Scheme administered by Development Commissioner (SSI), Ministry of SSI, Govt. of India. A Screening Committee under the Chairmanship of AS and DC (SSI) has been set up to consider the applications for approval of reimbursement. The Scheme shall provide one time reimbursement only against a Permanent SSI registration Certificate. The amount of incentive/subsidy/grant already availed for acquiring ISO 9000 or ISO 14001 Certification under any Central Govt. (including DCSSI Incentive Scheme)/State Govt. /Financial Institution shall be adjusted against the entitlement of reimbursement. It means the total entitlement of reimbursement of acquiring one or more than on certifications shall be up to the maximum limit of ₹ 75,000 only. In case a unit has received reimbursement/subsidy/grant from Central Govt./State Govt./Financial Institution against any one of the certifications for an amount less than maximum limit of ₹ 75,000, the unit shall be eligible to receive the balance amount only.

- Only one time reimbursement is allowed against a Permanent SSI registration for acquiring ISO-9000/ISO-14001 certification; irrespective of the fact whether the concerned SSI has one or more than one unit(s) within the same premises/location or outside.

- In case an ISO-9000/ISO-14001 certificate is obtained jointly by SSI units (even having a separate Permanent SSI registration certificates) under the corporate/group of industries category, the total reimbursement shall be limited to 75percent of the total expenditure incurred by the concerned units or ₹ 75,000 whichever is less; and each SSI unit shall get the amount on pro-rata basis.

The scheme contemplates norms of reimbursement as under:

- Payments made to Certification Agency = Full Amount (excluding travel and hotel expenses and surveillance charges)
- Payments made towards
  - Consultancy; = Up to ₹ 30,000
  - Training; and Calibration (Rupees Thirty Thousand only)
  - The entitlement for reimbursement = 75% ((a) full Amount + (b) up to ₹ 30,000) up to ₹ 75,000

❏❏❏

At a Glance

1. Incentive schemes by Central Government for Small Scale Industries are:
   - Credit Guarantee Fund Scheme for SSI
   - Categorised Eligible Institutions
   - Initiatives for Women Entrepreneurs
   - Incentives for North Eastern Region
2. NSIC, NEDFi and SIDBI are the other eligible institutions categorised by GOI, which have become Member Lending Institutions of CGTSI for participating under the credit guarantee scheme.
3. Only one time reimbursement is allowed against a permanent SSI registration for acquiring ISO-9000/ISO-14001 certification.

Multiple Choice Questions

1. Credit Guarnantee Fund Scheme for Small Industries was launched by GOI on:
   - (a) 30th Sept 2009
   - (b) 30th Aug 2000
   - (c) 30th Aug 2003
   - (d) 30th November 2006
2. Under Incentive schemes by Central Government collateral free credit facility was extended to:
   - (a) Information Techonology and Software Industry
   - (b) Only Software industry
   - (c) By SIDBI only
   - (d) CGTSI
3. Under credit Guarantee scheme GOI selected _____ Public sector Banks as eligible instititution:
   - (a) 26 Banks

    (b)   20 Banks

    (c)   50 Banks

    (d)   Only 5 Banks

4.   SIDBI provides training for credit utilisation as also credit delivery skills for the executives of voluntary organization working for:

    (a)   Listed PSUs

    (b)   Listed instititutions

    (c)   For women only

    (d)   For both women & men

Ans. 1. b, 2. a, 3. a, 4. c

Review Questions

1.   Describe the various schemes operated by Central Government to support small scale industries.

2.   Write short notes on:

    (a)   SIDO

    (b)   SSIDC

    (c)   SIDBI

3.   Describe in detail regarding "Incentives for North Eastern Region."

4.   Please define "Development of village and Small Industries Sector" in detail.

5.   List the "Other Incentives Proposed" for North East Regions of India.

Chapter 12
Financial Institutions and Small Scale Industries

Introduction

The chapter presents a brief description of some of the most important financial institutions and their role in fostering entrepreneurship in India.

12.1 Industrial Development Bank of India (IDBI)

IDBI Bank Ltd. is a Universal Bank with its operations driven by a cutting edge core banking IT platform. The bank offers personalised banking and financial solutions to its clients in the retail and corporate banking arena through its large network of branches and ATMs, spread across length and breadth of India. We have also set up an overseas branch at Dubai and have plans to open representative offices in various other parts of the globe, for encashing emerging global opportunities. As on 31st March, 2010, the bank had a network of 720 branches and 1210 ATMs and plans to roll out another 300 branches during FY 2010–11. The bank's total business, during FY 2009–10, reached ₹ 3.06 lakh crore (up by 41.7%), Balance sheet reached ₹ 2.34 lakh crore (up by 35.5%) while it earned a net profit of ₹ 1031 crore (up by 20%). The vision for the bank is for it to be the trusted partner in progress, by leveraging quality human capital and setting global standards of excellence, to build the most valued financial conglomerate. They are experienced in financial markets helps us to effectively cope with challenges and capitalise on the emerging opportunities by participating effectively in our country's growth process.

MSME finance

MSME Finance takes care of the funding needs of micro, small and medium enterprises. Keeping in view the specific requirements of these units, IDBI Bank has introduced a range of attractive products. The products are designed to cater to various segments among MSME borrowers. The bank has the products that cater to all the stakeholders in a value-chain viz., the vendors, the manufacturers as well as the dealers. In addition there are tailor-made products for special category of borrowers, such as medical practitioners, transport operators, professionals and self-employed, IT service providers, etc. The bank also has a product for start-up ventures where finance is provided in the form of seed capital. With a view to make business easy for the MSMEs, the bank has introduced collateral free loans. The bank not only offers finance to its MSME customers but also takes care of their all banking needs under one roof with specific current accounts and full range of other banking products and services. The bank is in constant endeavour to introduce new products with a view to offer wide array of solutions to the MSME units.

IDBI Bank SME products:

- Sulabh Vyapar/Business Solutions
- Dealer Finance/Dealer Solutions
- Vendor Financing/Vendor Solutions
- Funding under CGFMSE
- Loans to Small Road and Water Transport Operators
- Finance to Medical Practitioners
- Loans to Professionals and Self-employed
- Working Capital Financing to IT and ITES entities
- Lending Against the Security of Future Credit Card Receivables
- Entrepreneurial Development Fund
- Laghu Udhyami Credit Cards (LUCC)
- SME Hosiery Current A/c

12.2 Small Industries Development Bank of India (SIDBI)

SIDBI has a vision to emerge as a single window for meeting the financial and developmental needs of the MSME sector to make it strong, vibrant and globally competitive, to position SIDBI brand as the preferred and customer-friendly institution and for enhancement of shareholder wealth and highest corporate values through modern technology platform.

There are four basic objectives set out in the SIDBI Charter. These are as follows:

- Financing
- Promotion
- Development
- Co-ordination for orderly growth of industry in the small scale sector.

The Charter has provided SIDBI considerable flexibility in adopting appropriate operational strategies to meet these objectives. The activities of SIDBI, as they have evolved over the period of time, now meet almost all the requirements of small scale industries which fall into a wide spectrum constituting modern and technologically superior units at one end and traditional units at the other.

(a) Development outlook

The major issues confronting SSIs are identified to be as follows:

- Technology obsolescence
- Managerial inadequacies
- Delayed payments
- Poor quality
- Incidence of sickness
- Lack of appropriate infrastructure
- Lack of marketing network

There can be many more similar issues hindering the orderly growth of SSIs. Over the years, SIDBI has put in place financing schemes either through its direct financing mechanism or through indirect assistance mechanism and special focus programmes under its P&D initiatives. In its approach, SIDBI has struck a good balance between financing and providing other support services.

(b) Co-ordination and understanding

As an apex institution, SIDBI makes use of the network of the banks and state level financial institutions, which have retail outlets. SIDBI supplements the efforts of existing institutions through its direct assistance schemes to reach financial assistance to the ultimate borrowers in the small scale sector. Refinancing, bills rediscounting, lines of credit and resource support mechanisms have evolved over the period of time to route SIDBI's assistance through the network of other retail institutions in the financial system. Improved levels of co-ordination for development of the small scale sector is also achieved through a system of dialogue and obtaining feedback from the representatives of institutions of small scale industries who are on the SIDBI's National Advisory Committee and Regional Advisory Committees.

SIDBI has entered into Memoranda of Understanding with many banks, governmental agencies, international agencies, research and development institutions and industry associations to facilitate a coordinated approach in dealing with the issues for development of small scale industries. SIDBI has signed memorandum of understanding with 18 banks and the following agencies:

- Swiss Agency for Development and Co-operation
- Small Industries Development Organisation
- Auto Components Manufactures Association
- Asia and Pacific Centre for Transfer of Technology
- Council for Scientific and Industrial Research

- United Nations Industrial Development Organisation
- Confederation of Indian Industry
- National Research Development Organisation
- Government of India for channelising TREAD assistance
- Small Enterprise Assistance Funds (SEAF)
- For setting up of SEAF India SME Equity Fund and for other capacity building initiatives for SMEs

12.3 State Bank of India

The State Bank of India, the country's oldest bank and a premier in terms of balance sheet size, number of branches, market capitalisation and profits is today going through a momentous phase of change and transformation— the 200-year old public sector behemoth is today stirring out of its Public Sector legacy and moving with an agility to give the Private and Foreign Banks a run for their money. The bank is entering into many new businesses with strategic tie-ups— Pension Funds, General Insurance, Custodial Services, Private Equity, Mobile Banking, Point of Sale Merchant Acquisition, Advisory Services, structured products, etc.— each one of these initiatives having a huge potential for growth. The bank is forging ahead with cutting edge technology and innovative new banking models, to expand its Rural Banking base, looking at the vast untapped potential in the hinterland and proposes to cover 100,000 villages in the next two years.

It is also focusing at the top end of the market, on whole sale banking capabilities to provide India's growing mid/large corporate with a complete array of products and services. It is consolidating its global treasury operations and entering into structured products and derivative instruments. Today, the bank is the largest provider of infrastructure debt and the largest arranger of external commercial borrowings in the country. It is the only Indian bank to feature in the Fortune 500 list. The bank is changing outdated front and back end processes to modern customer-friendly processes to help improve the total customer experience. With about 8500 of its own 10000 branches and another 5100 branches of its associate banks already networked, today it offers the largest banking network to the Indian customer. The bank is also in the process of providing complete payment solution to its clientele with its over 8500 ATMs, and other electronic channels, such as Internet banking, debit cards, mobile banking, etc. With four national level Apex Training Colleges and 54 learning centres spread all over the country, the bank is continuously engaged in skill enhancement of its employees. Some of the training programmes are attended by bankers from banks in other countries. The bank is also looking at opportunities to grow in size in India as well as internationally. It presently has 82 foreign offices in 32 countries across the globe. It has also 7 subsidiaries in India— SBI Capital Markets, SBICAP Securities, SBI DFHI, SBI

Factors, SBI Life and SBI Cards— forming a formidable group in the Indian banking scenario. It is in the process of raising capital for its growth and also consolidating its various holdings. Throughout all this change, the bank is also attempting to change old mindsets, attitudes and take all employees together on this exciting road to transformation. In a recently concluded mass internal communication programme termed 'Parivartan', the bank rolled out over 3300 two-day workshops across the country and covered over 130,000 employees in a period of 100 days using about 400 trainers, to drive home the message of change and inclusiveness. The workshops fired the imagination of the employees with some other banks in India as well as other public sector organisations seeking to emulate the programme. The CNN IBN Network 18 recognised this momentous transformation journey, of the State Bank of India and has awarded bank's Chairman, Mr. O. P. Bhatt the prestigious Indian of the Year – Business in January 2008.

State Bank of India has been playing a vital role in the development of small scale industries since 1956. The bank has financed over ₹ 8 lakh SSI units in the country. It has 55 specialised SSI branches, 99 branches in industrial estates and more than 400 branches with SIB divisions. The bank finances for small business activities which are of special significance to a large number of people as many of these activities can be started with relatively lower investment and with no special skills on the part of the entrepreneurs.

The various schemes for SMEs are in the following:
- Commodity Backed Warehouse Receipt Financing
- Surabhi Deposit Scheme
- Code Of Banks Commitment To Micro And Small Enterprise
- Debt Restructuring Mechanism
- Traders Easy Loan Scheme
- SSI Loans
- Business Current Accounts
- Open Term Loan
- Retail Trade
- Doctor Plus
- Dental Doctor Plus
- SBI Shoppe
- Cyber Plus
- SME Credit Plus
- Small Business Credit Card

- SME Petro Credit
- Dal Mill Plus
- Paryatan Plus
- Transport Operators
- Auto Loan
- Charter For SSI
- Artisan Credit Card
- Rice Mills Plus
- School Plus
- Swarojgar Credit Card

12.4 Punjab National Bank

With over 56 million satisfied customers and 5002 offices including 5 overseas branches, Punjab National Bank (PNB) has continued to retain its leadership position amongst the nationalised banks. The bank enjoys strong fundamentals, large franchise value and good brand image. Besides being ranked as one of India's top service brands, PNB has remained fully committed to its guiding principles of sound and prudent banking. Apart from offering banking products, the bank has also entered the credit card, debit card; bullion business; life and non-life insurance; Gold coins and asset management business, etc. Since its humble beginning in 1895 with the distinction of being the first *Swadeshi* Bank to have been started with Indian capital, PNB has achieved significant growth in business which at the end of March 2010 amounted to ₹ 43,5931 crore. PNB is ranked as the second largest bank in the country after SBI in terms of branch network, business and many other parameters. During the FY 2009–10, with 40.85 percent share of CASA deposits, the bank achieved a net profit of ₹ 3905 crore. Bank has a strong capital base with capital adequacy ratio of 14.16 percent as on Mar'10 as per Basel II with Tier I and Tier II capital ratio at 9.15 percent and 5.01 percent respectively. As on March'10, the bank has the Gross and Net NPA ratio of 1.71 percent and 0.53 percent respectively. During the FY 2009–10, its ratio of Priority Sector Credit to Adjusted Net Bank Credit at 40.5 percent and Agriculture Credit to Adjusted Net Bank Credit at 19.7 percent was also higher than the stipulated requirement of 40 percent and 18 percent respectively.

The bank has been able to maintain its stakeholders' interest by posting an improved NIM of 3.57 percent in Mar'10 (3.52% Mar'09) and a Return on Assets of 1.44 percent (1.39% Mar'09). The Earning per Share improved to ₹ 123.98 (₹ 98.03 Mar'09) while the Book value per share improved to ₹ 514.77 (₹ 416.74 Mar.'09). Punjab National Bank continues to maintain its frontline position in the Indian banking industry. In particular, the bank has retained its Number One position among the nationalised banks in terms of number of branches, deposit, advances, total business, assets, operating and net profit in the year 2009–10. The impressive operational and financial performance has been brought about by Bank's focus on customer based business with thrust on CASA deposits, Retail, SME and Agri Advances and with more inclusive approach to banking; better asset liability management; improved margin management, thrust on recovery and increased efficiency in core operations of the Bank. PNB has always looked at technology as a key facilitator to provide better customer service and ensured that its 'IT strategy' follows the 'Business strategy' so as to arrive at 'Best Fit'. The Bank has made rapid strides in this direction. All branches of the bank are under Core Banking Solution (CBS) since Dec'08, thus covering 100 percent of its business and providing 'Anytime Anywhere' banking facility to all customers including customers of more than 3000 rural and semi urban branches. The bank has also been offering Internet banking services to its customers which also enables on line booking of rail tickets, payment of utilities bills, purchase of airline tickets, etc. Towards developing a cost effective alternative channels of delivery, the bank with more than 3700 ATMs has the largest ATM network amongst nationalised banks.

With the help of advanced technology, the bank has been a frontrunner in the industry so far as the initiatives for Financial Inclusion is concerned. With its policy of inclusive growth, the bank's mission is "Banking for Unbanked". The bank has launched a drive for biometric smart card based technology enabled Financial Inclusion with the help of Business Correspondents/Business Facilitators (BC/BF) so as to reach out to the last mile customer. The Bank has started several innovative initiatives for marginal groups, such as rickshaw pullers, vegetable vendors, dairy farmers, construction workers, etc. Under Branchless Banking model, the bank is implementing 40 projects in 16 states. Backed by strong domestic performance, the bank is planning to realise its global aspirations. The bank continues its selective foray in international markets with presence in 9 countries, with 2 branches at Hong Kong, 1 each at Kabul and Dubai; representative offices at Almaty, Dubai, Shanghai and Oslo; a wholly owned subsidiary in the UK; a joint venture with Everest Bank Ltd. Nepal and a JV banking subsidiary DRUK PNB Bank Ltd. in Bhutan. The bank is pursuing upgradation of its representative offices in China and Norway and is in the process of setting up a representative office in Sydney, Australia and taking controlling stake in JSC Dana Bank in Kazakhastan. Their policy for Micro, Small and Medium Enterprises (SME) 2008–09 states as follows:

- The bank shall continue to lay emphasis on financing Micro, Small and Medium Enterprises and our existing SME credit portfolio shall be enlarged. Policy Package of Govt. of India 2006 shall be supported and popularised amongst our branches.
- Endeavour will be to achieve high growth in SME advances and to increase the share of the Micro Enterprises advances (i.e., manufacturing/service

enterprises having investment in plant and machinery/equipment up to ₹ 25 lakh/₹ 10 lakh) in the advances to Small Enterprises to 60 percent.

- The Reserve Bank of India guidelines on financing to SMEs shall continue to be followed and incorporated in various schemes for financing SMEs. These guidelines on timely sanctioning of SME applications, margin, rate of interest, collateral security, etc. shall continue to be adhered to.

- The bank is financing artisans, craftsmen, village and cottage industries and industries falling under KVIC schemes. The small non-farm sector units in rural areas and women, minorities, SC/ST and other special groups are being financed in terms of Government of India/RBI policy and shall continue to be given attention.

- Industrial units in the clusters shall be financed. The finance shall also be given for developing industrial estates, industrial parks, etc.

- The bank has specialised SME branches to support finance to SME units. The bank has plans/approvals to open more such branches during 2008–09. These branches shall be developed as centres of excellence in SME financing.

- The various service sector enterprises shall be financed taking advantage of the new investment limits in equipment under MSMED Act, 2006.

- The bank is financing loans up to ₹ 50 lakh for small enterprises under the Credit Guarantee Scheme of CGTMSE. The Bank proposes to continue the coverage under the Scheme. The bank is also charging concessional guarantee fee/annual service charges in special category of advances/ geographical areas as per the scheme.

- The bank has approved independent rating agencies, such as SMERA, CRISIL, etc. for rating of the SME units.

- With the revised policy guidelines on definition of medium enterprises under Micro, Small and Medium Enterprises Development Act, 2006, the bank shall focus on these units for financing and increasing our share.

- The bank shall continue to work with SIDBI, Ministry of Micro Small and Medium Enterprises (MSME) to better serve the SME sector.

12.5 ICICI Bank

ICICI Bank is India's second largest bank with total assets of ₹ 3,634.00 billion (US$ 81 billion) at 31st March, 2010 and profit after tax ₹ 40.25 billion (US$ 896 million) for the year ended 31st March, 2010. The bank has a network of 2,044 branches and about 5,546 ATMs in India and presence in 18 countries. ICICI Bank offers a wide range of banking products and financial services to corporate and retail customers through a variety of delivery channels and through its specialised subsidiaries in the areas of investment banking, life and non-life insurance, venture capital and asset management. The bank currently has subsidiaries in the United Kingdom, Russia and Canada, branches in United States, Singapore, Bahrain, Hong Kong, Sri Lanka, Qatar and Dubai International Finance Centre and representative offices in United Arab Emirates, China, South Africa, Bangladesh, Thailand, Malaysia and Indonesia. Its UK subsidiary has established branches in Belgium and Germany. ICICI Bank's equity shares are listed in India on Bombay Stock Exchange and the National Stock Exchange of India Limited and its American Depositary Receipts (ADRs) are listed on the New York Stock Exchange (NYSE).

ICICI Ventures: ICICI Venture is one of the largest and most successful private equity firms in India with funds under management to the tune of USD 2 billion. ICICI Venture, over the years has built an enviable portfolio of companies across sectors including pharmaceuticals, information technology, media, manufacturing, logistics, textiles, real estate, etc. thereby building sustainable value. It has several 'firsts' to its credit in the Indian private equity industry. Amongst them are India's first leveraged buyout (Infomedia), the first real estate investment (Cyber Gateway), the first mezzanine financing for a acquisition (Arch Pharmalabs) and the first 'royalty-based' structured deal in Pharma Research and Development (Dr Reddy's). ICICI Venture is a subsidiary of ICICI Bank, the largest private sector financial services group in India.

12.6 National Small Industries Corporation Ltd. (NSIC)

National Small Industries Corporation Ltd. (NSIC), an ISO 9001 certified company, since its establishment in 1955, has been working to fulfil its mission of promoting, aiding and fostering the growth of small scale industries and industry related small scale services/business enterprises in the country. Over a period of five decades of transition, growth and development, NSIC has proved its strength within the country and abroad by promoting modernisation, upgradation of technology, quality consciousness, strengthening linkages with large medium enterprises and enhancing exports, projects and products from small industries. NSIC operates through more than 120 offices, supported by a team of over 500 professionals spread across the country. To manage operations in African countries, NSIC operates from its office in Johannesburg. NSIC carries forward its mission to assist small enterprises with a set of specially tailored schemes designed to put them in a competitive and advantageous position. The schemes comprise facilitating marketing support, credit support, technology support and other support services.

(a) Marketing: Marketing, a strategic tool for business development, is critical to the growth and survival of small enterprises in today's intensely competitive market. NSIC acts as a facilitator to promote small industries products and has devised a number of schemes to support small enterprises in their marketing efforts, both in an outside the country. These schemes are briefly described as in the following:

- Consortia and Tender Marketing: Small enterprises in their individual capacity face problems to procure and execute large orders, which inhibit and restrict their growth. Accordingly NSIC adopts consortia approach and forms consortia of units manufacturing the same products, thereby easing out marketing problems of SSIs. The corporation explores the market and secures orders for bulk quantities. These orders are then distributed to small units in tune with their production capacity. Testing facilities are also provided to enable units to improve and maintain the quality of their products conforming to the standard specifications.

- Single point Registration for Government Purchase: NSIC operates a single point Registration Scheme under the Government Purchase Programme, wherein the registered SSI units get purchase preference in Government purchase programme, exemption from payment of Earnest Money Deposit, etc.

- Issue of tender sets free of cost.

- Advance intimation of tenders issued by DGS&D.

- Exemption from payment of earnest money.

- Waiver of security deposit up to the monetary limit for which the unit is registered.

- Issue of competency certificate in case the value of an order exceeds the monetary limit, after due verification.

- Exhibitions and Technology Fairs: To showcase the competencies of Indian SSIs and to capture market opportunities, NSIC participates in selected International and National Exhibitions and Trade Fairs every year. NSIC facilitates the participation of the small enterprises by providing concessions in rental, etc. Participation in these events exposes SSI units to international practices and enhances their business prowess.

- Buyer-Seller meets: Bulk and departmental buyers, such as the railways, defence, communication departments and large companies are invited to participate in buyer–seller meets to enrich SSI unit's knowledge regarding terms and conditions, quality standards, etc. required by the buyer. These programmes are aimed at vendor development from SSI units for the bulk manufacturers.

- Export of Products and Projects: NSIC is a recognised export house and exporting products and projects of small industries of India to other countries. The major areas of operation are as follows:

  o Export of products, such as handicrafts, leather items, hand tools, pipes/fittings, builders' hardware, etc.

  o Supply of small isndustry projects on turnkey basis.

- Credit Support: NSIC facilitates credit requirements of small enterprises in the following areas:

    o Financing for procurement of Raw Material (Short term)

NSIC's Raw Material Assistance Scheme aims at helping small scale industries/enterprises by way of financing the purchase of raw material (both indigenous and imported). The salient features are as follows:

➢ Financial assistance for procurement of raw materials up to 90 days.

➢ Bulk purchase of basic raw materials at competitive rates.

➢ NSIC facilitates import of scares raw materials.

➢ NSIC takes care of all the procedures, documentation and issue of letter of credit in case of imports.

    o Financing for Marketing Activities (Short term)

NSIC facilitates financing for marketing actives, such as Internal Marketing, Exports and Bill Discounting.

➢ Finance through syndication with Banks .

In order to ensure smooth credit flow to small enterprises, NSIC is entering into strategic alliances with commercial banks to facilitate long term/working capital financing of the small enterprises across the country. The arrangement envisages forwarding of loan applications of the interested small enterprises by NSIC to the banks and sharing the processing fee.

➢ Performance and Credit Rating Scheme for small industries

To enable small enterprises to ascertain the strengths and weaknesses of their existing operations and take corrective measures to enhance their organisational strength, NSIC is operating a Performance and Credit Rating Scheme through empanelled agencies, such as ICRA, ONICRA, Duns and Bradstreet (D&B), CRISIL, FITCH, CARE and SMERA. Small enterprise has the liberty to choose among any of the rating agencies empanelled with NSIC. Rating agencies will charge the credit rating fee according to their policies. The benefits to small enterprises are as follows:

- An independent, trusted third party opinion on capabilities and credit worthiness of SSI units.

- Good rating to enhance the acceptability of the SSI units with banks. FIs, SSI's customers and buyers.

- Facilitate prompter credit decisions from banks on proposals of SSI units.

- 75 percent of the credit rating fee subject to a maximum of ₹ 25,000 will be reimbursed to the small enterprise having a turnover up to ₹ 50 lakh by way of grants.

- 75 percent of the credit rating fee subject to a maximum of ₹ 30,000 will be reimbursed to the small enterprise having a turnover above ₹ 50 lakh to ₹ 200 lakh by way of grants.

- 75 percent of the credit rating fee subject to a maximum of ₹ 40,000 will be reimbursed to the small enterprise having a turnover above ₹ 200 lakh by way of grants.

- Technology Support: Technology is the key to enhancing a company's competitive advantage in today's dynamic information age. Small enterprises need to develop and implement a technology strategy in addition to financial, marketing and operational strategies and adopt the one that helps integrate their operations with their environment, customers and suppliers. NSIC offers small units the following support services through its Technical Services Centres and Extension Centres:

  o Advising on application of new techniques

  o Material testing facilities through accredited laboratories

  o Product design including CAD

  o Common facility support in machining, EDM, CNC, etc.

  o Energy and environment services at selected centres

  o Classroom and practical training for skill upgradation

NSIC Technical Services Centres are located at the following places (see Table 12.1):

Table 12.1 NSIC Technical Services Centres

Name of the Centre	Focus area
Chennai	Leather and Footwear
Howrah	General Engineering
Hyderabad	Electronics and Computer Application
New Delhi	Machine Tools and related activities
Rajkot	Energy Audit and Energy Conservation activities
Rajpura (Pb)	Domestic Electrical Appliances
Aligarh (UP)	Lock Cluster and Die and Tool making

(b) Infomediary services: Information today is becoming almost as vital as the air we breathe. We need it every minute of our working lives. With increase in competition and melting away of international boundaries, the demand for information is reaching new heights. NSIC, realising the needs of MSMEs, is offering

Infomediary Services which is a one-stop, one-window bouquet of aids that will provide information on business, technology and finance and also exhibit the core competence of Indian SMEs.

Membership Benefits

- Tender and Trade Information
- Banner display on NSIC Website
- Access to a wide range of technologies from India and abroad
- Access to national and international business leads, JV opportunities and trade information
- Comprehensive information on Government policies, rules and regulations, schemes and incentives
- Access to industrial databases and member's directory
- Various value-added, specialised services for members of Infomediary Service

(c) Software Technology Parks

NSIC Software Technology Parks (STPs) facilitate small industries in setting up 100 percent export-oriented units for software exports. They also act as nodal points to activate software exports directly through NSIC. These STPs extend support in terms of the requisite infrastructure to the SSI units to start business operations with a minimum lead time. The scheme is governed by STPI regulations of the Ministry of Information Technology, Government of India. NSIC established the first STP at Okhla, New Delhi in 1995 and second in Chennai in 2001. Several small scale units have taken advantage of these parks and contributed export earnings to the exchequer.

- Technology Business Incubators: Enterprise development is one of the thrust areas for nurturing the development and growth of micro and small enterprises in the country that is being facilitated by providing handholding support to the micro and small enterprises in every field of business. Incubation is one of the appropriate tools to achieve this goal, as it provides necessary facilities for the prospective entrepreneurs and start-up companies to learn product manufacturing processes coupled with technology development, business development under one roof. In these incubators, working projects depicting appropriate technology for small enterprises are displayed in working conditions.

- Small Enterprise Establishment Programme (SEEP): This programme facilitates setting up of new enterprises all over the country by creating self-employment opportunities for the unemployed persons. The objective of this scheme is to facilitate establishment of new small enterprises by way of providing integrated services in the areas of training for entrepreneurial skill development, selection of small projects, preparation of project profiles/reports, identification and sourcing of plant, machinery and equipments, facilitating sanction of credit facility and providing other support services in order to boost the development of small enterprises in manufacturing and services sectors.

- International Cooperation: NSIC facilitates sustainable international partnerships. The emphasis is on sustainable business relations rather than on one-way transactions. Since its inception, NSIC has contributed to strengthening enterprise-to-enterprise cooperation, south south cooperation and sharing best practices and experiences with other developing countries, especially those in the African, Asian and Pacific regions. The features of the scheme are in the following:

  o Exchange of business/technology missions with various countries.

  o Facilitating enterprise to enterprise cooperation, JVs, technology transfer and other form of sustainable collaboration.

  o Explore new markets and areas of cooperation

  o Identification of new export markets by participating in sector-specific exhibitions all over the world.

  o Sharing of Indian experience with other developing countries

- International Consultancy Services: For the last five decades, NSIC has acquired various skill sets in the development process of small enterprises. The inherent skills are being networked to offer consultancy services for other developing countries. This activity has been started during 2004–05 and is expected to occupy a place in the future service profile of the corporation. The areas of consultancy are listed as follows:

  o Capacity Building

  o Policy and Institutional Framework

  o Entrepreneurship Development

  o Business Development Services

- Insurance of Export Credit for Micro and Small Enterprises: NSIC is facilitating micro and small enterprises to insure their export credits by entering into strategic alliance with Export Credit Guarantee Corporation of India Limited (ECGC). MSEs would be helped in insuring their export credits through any office of the Corporation, located all over the country. This arrangement is made to strengthen promotion of exports from small enterprises.

12.7 Micro, Small and Medium Enterprises-Development Institute (MSME-DI)

Micro, Small and Medium Enterprises-Development Institute (MSME-DI), are field Institution office of the Development Commissioner (MSME) under the Ministry of Micro, Small and Medium Enterprises, Government of India, has been playing a key role for development of Micro, Small and Medium Enterprises through counselling, consultancy and training. These were established in 1960 as Small Industries Service Institute Extension Centre, thereafter upgraded as Small Industries Service Institute in 1975 and renamed as MSME-Development Institute since June, 2007 as a follow-up of the merger of the two Ministries of Small Scale Industries and Agro and Rural Industries into a newly formed Ministry of Micro, Small and Medium Enterprises. The Institute has made significant contributions for promotion and development of MSME in various states. The Institute strives to achieve its avowed objective through a gamut of operations ranging from training, consultancy, buyer–seller meet, vendor development programme as well as various awareness and modernisation programmes.

ⵔⵔⵔ

At a Glance

1. As on 31st March, 2010 IDBI bank had a network of 720 branches and 1210 ATMs and planned to roll out another 300 branches during FY 2010- 2011.

2. IDBI Bank SME Products:
   - Sulabh Vyapar/Business solutions
   - Dealer Finance/Dealer Solutions
   - Vendor Financing/ Vendor solutions
   - Funding under CGFMSE
   - Loans to Small Road and water transport operators
   - Finance to Medical Practitioners
   - Loans to Professionals and Self-employed
   - Working Capital Financing to IT and ITEs entities
   - Lending against security of Future Credit Card Receivables
   - Entrepreneurial Development Fund
   - LUCC
   - SME Hosiery Current A/c

3. Four basic objectives set out in SIDBI Charter are:
   - Financing
   - Promotion
   - Development

- Co-ordination for orderly growth of industry in the small scale sector
4. Major issues confronting SSIs are identified to be as follows:
    - Techonology obsolescence
    - Managerial inadequacies
    - Delayed payments
    - Poor quality
    - Incidence of sickness
    - Lack of appropriate infracture
    - Lack of marketing network
5. SIDBI has signed memorandum of understanding with 18 banks and eleven agencies.
6. SBI's various schemes for SMEs are as follows:
    - Commodity backed warehouse Receipt Financing
    - Surabhi Deposit Scheme
    - Code of bank commitment to Micro and Small Enterprises
    - Debt Restructuring Mechanism
    - Traders Easy Loan Scheme
    - SSI loans
    - Business Current Accounts
    - Open term loan
    - Retail trade
    - SME Credit Plus
    - SBI Shoppe
    - Cyber Plus
    - Small Business Credit Card
    - SME Petro Credit
    - Dal Mill Plus
    - Paryatan Plus
    - Auto Loan
    - Swarojgar Credit Card
7. Punjab National Bank's policy for Micro, Small and Medium Enterprises 2008-2009 states as follows:
    - Policy package of Govt. of India 2006 shall be supported and popularised amongst its branches
    - The Bank in financing artisans, craftsmen, village and cottage industries and industries falling under KUIC Schemes
    - Industrial units in the clusters shall be financed

- The bank shall continue to work with SIDBI Ministry of Micro Small and Medium Enterprises (MSME) is better serve the SME sector
- The bank has approved independent rating agencies such as SMERA, CRISIL etc. for rating of SME units
- NSIC is facilitating Micro, Small and Medium Enterprises to insure their export credit by entering into strategic alliance with Export Credit Guarantee Corporation of India Limited (ECGC)

Multiple Choice Questions

1. Full form of SEEP:
    (a) Small Establishment Enterprise Programme
    (b) Small Establishment Entrepreneur Programme
    (c) Small Enterprise Establishment Programme
    (d) Small programme enterprise Establishment

2. NSIC Chennai Technical Services Center's focused area is:
    (a) General Engineering
    (b) Domestic Electrical Appliances
    (c) Leather and footwear
    (d) Machine Tools

3. ICICI Bank's equity shares are listed in India on:
    (a) New York Stock Exchange
    (b) Bombay Stock Exchange
    (c) Bombay Stock Exchange and the National Exchange of India Limited
    (d) ADRs

4. NSIC operates a single point registration for Government purchase wherein:
    (a) The registered SSI units get preference in Government purchase prgramme exemption for payment of EMD etc.
    (b) The non-registered SSI units get preference in Government purchase prgramme but are not exempted form payment of EMDs
    (c) Only exemption form payment of EMDs etc.
    (d) Issue of tender set at cost

5. Punjab National Bank has _____ overseas branches:
    (a) Ten
    (b) Twelve
    (c) Nine
    (d) Five

Ans. 1. c, 2. c, 3. c, 4. a, 5. d

Review Questions

1. What is SIDBI? Write a detailed note on SIDBI.
2. Identify the major issues that are confronted by SSI units in India.
3. Can you name the four basic objectives set out in the SIDBI charter?
4. Name all those Agencies with whom SIDBI has signed memorandum of understanding.
5. Enumerate main function of SBI & PNB.

Chapter 13

Procedures to be Followed While Starting a Business

Introduction

When one endeavours to start his/her new business unit, the procedures to be followed to register the entity with respective stakeholder departments and organisations involves two activities: registration and clearances/approvals to be able to start a business unit. The clearances/approvals to be obtained are as follows:

As per an estimate and depending upon the place where one is starting a business it would require anything between 30–60 days to complete all the file work and office work. For foreign firms, it is mandatory to obtain government approval for incorporating in India or forming a joint venture in India. Certain restrictions apply in some sectors. One is advised to seek proper legal advice before setting up a formal business in India. Table 13.1 illustrates the various procedures and the government departments involved in those activities. The government has reduced the legal formalities for starting a business in recent years; a good number of legal requirements are still up there.

Table 13.1 Activities and corresponding government departments

Approvals/Clearances Required	Department to be Approached and Consulted
Incorporation of Company	Registrar of Companies
Registration/IEM/Industrial license	District Industries Centre for SSI/SIA for large and medium industries
Allotment of land	State department of Industries/SIDC/Infrastructure Corporation/SSIDC
Permission for land use (in case industry is located outside an industrial area)	a. State Department of industries b. Dept. of Town and Country Planning c. Local authority/District Collector
NOC and consent under Water and Air Pollution Control Acts	State Pollution Control Board

Approval of construction activity and building plan	a. Town and country planning b. Municipal and local authorities c. Chief Inspector of Factories d. Pollution Control Board e. Electricity Board/Power Utilities
Sanction of Power	State Electricity Board/Power Utilities
Use and storage of explosives	Chief Controller of Explosives
Use and storage of explosives	Chief Controller of Explosives
Boiler Inspection Certificate	Chief Inspector of Boilers
Finance	a. State Finance Corporation/ State Industrial Development Corporation for term loans b. For loans higher than ₹ 15 million, all India financial institutions, such as IDBI, ICICI, IFCI, etc.
Registration under States Commercial Tax Act, and Central and State Excise Act	a. Commercial Tax Department b. Central and State Excise Depts.
Other Registrations and Clearances	
Extraction of Minerals	State Director of Mines and Geology
ISI Certificate	Regional Office of the Bureau of Indian Standards (BIS)
Quality Marking Certificate	Quality Marking Centre of the State Government
Weights and Measures	Inspector of Weights and Measures
Code Number for Export and Import	Regional Office of Director General of Foreign Trade

13.1 Example on Procedures for Starting a Business

The following will be the steps to be taken if one desires to start a business in New Delhi, India. The legal form of the example venture is Private Limited Company. The following are the procedures in chronological order:

Procedure 1: Present application to the Registrar of Companies (ROC) for availability of company name (Takes 7 days and an expense of INR 500).

Procedure Details:

To check whether the name is acceptable or available, the entrepreneur can use the website of the Ministry of Company Affairs (MCA) – www.mca.gov.in.

After the name has been finalised, six names in order of preference can be inserted in the prescribed Form 1A for making the application to the agency notified by the MCA for seeking availability of desired name. The said Form 1A is thereafter forwarded to the office of RoC for further processing. While filing Form 1A, it should be ensured that

- the details are filled in correctly as no change is entertained in the Form once the Form is filed;
- Guidelines/instructions issued by the Department of Company Affairs for deciding the availability of name for the formation of a company are compiled with.
- As per the provisions of the Emblems and Names (Prevention of Improper Use) Act, 1950, use of improper names is prohibited.

The status of application filed can be ascertained from the MCA's website.

The MCA has laid down guidelines as regards the use of key words in a company's name. In order to have a key word as part of the company's name, the following minimum authorised share capital requirements have to be fulfilled (see Table 13.2):

Table 13.2 Minimum authorised share capital requirements

Sl. No.	Key Words	Required Authorised Capital
1.	Corporation	₹ 50,000,000
2.	International. Globe, Universal, Continental, Inter-Continental, Asiatic, Asia, being the first word of the name	₹ 10,000,000
3.	If any of the words at (2) above is used within the name (with or without brackets)	₹ 5,000,000
4.	*Hindustan*, India, *Bharat*, being the first word of the name	₹ 5,000,000
5.	If any of the words at (4) above is used within the name (with or without brackets)	₹ 500,000
6.	Industries/*Udyog*	₹ 10,000,000
7.	Enterprise, Product, Business, Manufacturing	₹ 1,000,000

Procedure 2: Engross Memorandum and Articles of Association according to the Delhi Stamp Act (takes one day and an expense of INR 200 (for MOA) + 0.15% of Authorised Capital (for AOA) + INR 10 (stamp paper for declaration in Form 1).

Procedural details: The Memorandum and Articles of Association is drafted on plain paper and then presented to the Officer of Stamps for stamping. Special adhesive stamps are affixed on the MOA and AOA.

The application should be accompanied necessarily by the following:

- Two blank copies of the Memorandum of Association and Articles of Association

- Payment receipt

Ensure that the copies submitted to the Superintendent of Stamps for stamping are unsigned and no promoter or subscriber has written anything on it by hand. The Superintendent returns the copies one of which is duly stamped, signed and engrossed evidencing the payment of the requisite stamp duty. The rate of stamp duty varies among states.

Procedure 3: Present the required documents along with the registration fee to the Registrar of Companies to get the certificate of incorporation (Takes about 8 days).

Procedural Details: The print out of the Memorandum and Articles of Association of the Company on the non-judicial stamp paper are to be signed by at least two subscribers, each of whom shall also write in his own hand, his father's name, occupation, address and the number of shares subscribed for. There will at least be one witness to these signatures, who shall also sign and write in his own hand, his father's name, occupation and address. Get the following documents prepared:

- Form 1 (Declaration of Compliance) - This is to be given by an advocate of the Supreme Court or of a High Court or a Secretary or a Chartered Accountant, in whole time practice in India who is engaged in the formation of a Company or by a person named in the Articles of the company as a director, manager, or secretary of the company that all the requirements of the Companies Act, 1956. This declaration should be on the non-judicial stamp paper ₹ 10 of the appropriate value with reference to the state in which the office of the Registrar of Companies situate.

- Form- 18 (Notice of situation of the registered office)- This form is to be signed by the First Director of the Company named in the Articles and must be lodged with the Registrar together with the Memorandum and Articles of Association at the time of lodgement for the incorporation of the proposed company.

- Form 32 (in duplicate) (Particulars of Directors)

- Power of Attorney (on non-judicial stamp paper ₹ 100) to be given in favour of one of the promoter/subscriber or chartered accountant or company secretary or an advocate for fulfilling various formalities at Registrars' office for incorporation of a company.

The fees paid to the Registrar for registration are scaled according to the amount of the share capital of a company as stated in its memorandum. The schedule is as following:

For registration of a company whose nominal share capital does not exceed

₹100, 000: ₹ 4,000?

For registration of a company whose nominal share capital exceeds ₹100,000, the above fee of ₹4,000 with the following additional fees regulated according to the amount of nominal capital:

- o ₹ 300 for every ₹10,000 of nominal share capital or part of ₹10,000 after the first ₹1,00,000 up to ₹5,00,000;
- o ₹ 200 for every ₹10,000 of nominal share capital or part of ₹10,000 after the first ₹5,00,000 up to ₹50,00,000;
- o ₹ 100 for every ₹10,000 of nominal share capital or part of ₹10,000 after the first ₹50,00,000 up to ₹1 crore;
- o ₹ 50 for every ₹10,000 of nominal share capital or part of ₹10,000 after the first ₹1 crore.

The above stated fees are required to be paid in the office of the ROC by way of a Demand Draft/Treasury Challan.

The DD has to be drawn in favour of either the office of the concerned ROC or in favor of the Pay and Accounts Officer, Department of Company Affairs.

Schedule of 'RoC' filing fees for the Articles and for the other forms 1, 18 and 32:

- ₹ 200 In respect of a company having a nominal share capital of ₹ 100,000 or more but less than ₹ 500,000;
- ₹ 300 In respect of a company having a nominal share capital of ₹ 500,000 or more but less than ₹ 2,500,000;
- ₹ 500 In respect of a company having a nominal share capital of ₹ 2,500,000 or more.

The ROC will then scrutinise the documents filed by the company and if necessary the authorised person will on intimation make the necessary corrections under his initials. Obtain the Certificate of Incorporation of the company from the office of the ROC. The company can commence its business on getting incorporation certificate from RoC. The other procedures given below can be done after the business is started.

Although the process of electronic filing has begun to take place, as of April 2006, the person incorporating has two choices. He/she can either file the company documents in the traditional manner, or can prepare a soft copy of all forms (which are now available online), save them in a floppy or CD, and take it to the registry where it is uploaded to the new system and filed. Once the electronic system is fully implemented, the goal is that an entrepreneur will be able to incorporate the company from any computer. All documents for company incorporation will be available for electronic filing subject to the condition that the person has obtained a Digital Signature Certificate. To obtain a Digital Signature Certificate, an application is required to be submitted with the agencies, which are notified by the MCA.

Another new requirement is the Directors Identification Number (DIN); which will be mandatory for every person who is a director on the board of the company. Directors can receive a provisional DIN through the web. The provisional number is used in the same way as the final number, which will be issued in about 30 days. A person can only have one DIN and it is used for all companies for which he/she is a director.

Procedure 4: Obtain a company seal (Takes about 2 days and an expense of INR. 300).

Procedure 5: Visit the UTI Investor's Services Limited to obtain a Permanent Account Number (Takes about 15 days, can be done simultaneously with procedure 4 and costs about INR 72 (INR 60 + service tax at 12.24% for fee and INR 5 for application form).

The company is required to apply for allotment of the PAN from the Income Tax Department under Section 139 A of the Income Tax Act, 1961 by making an application in form 49A or before 31st May of the relevant assessment year.

Income Tax department has outsourced the allotment of PAN to Unit Trust of India (UTI) and National Security Depository Limited (NSDL). Accordingly, application can be submitted to the centres of UTI/NSDL. Documents required will be Certificate of Incorporation issued by the Registrar of Companies and Situation of Registered Office (Form 18) which is filed with the RoC. Related website is www.incometaxindia.gov.in.

Procedure 6: Obtain a Tax Account Number for income taxes deducted at source from the Assessing Office in the Income Tax Department (takes about 15 days, can be done simultaneously with procedure 5, and costs about INR 56 (INR 50 + service tax at 12.24% for fee).

Procedural details: The Company is required to apply for allotment of the Tax Deduction Account Number from the Income Tax Department under section 203A of the Income Tax Act, 1961 by making an application in form No. 49B. Income Tax department has outsourced the allotment of PAN to Unit Trust of India (UTI) and National Security Depository Limited (NSDL). Accordingly, application can be submitted to the centres of UTI/NSDL. Related website is www.incometaxindia.gov.in.

Procedure 7: Register for Value Added Tax (takes about 15 days and cost about INR 525).

Procedural details: In Delhi, Value Added Tax is applicable with effect from 1st April, 2005 as per the provisions of the Delhi Value Added Tax Act, 2004. Delhi State Government has formulated the VAT Act and the VAT is levied and collected as per the provisions in force from time to time.

In addition, inter-state sales are subject to levy of central sales tax as per the provisions of the Central Sales Tax Act, 1956. It is mandatory to get registered under the Delhi Value Added Tax Act, 2004. In the case of Central Sales Tax Act, registration is mandatory to engage in the business of sales of goods from one state to another. For obtaining the registration under the Delhi Value Added Tax Act, 2004, and the Central Sales Tax Act, 1956, application in the prescribed form is required to be made to the Sales Tax Officer of the ward in which the principal place of business is located along with the following documents:

- Latest rent receipt (if premises are taken on lease) or ownership documents, as the case may be.
- Proof of legal and physical possession of the business premises.
- Four photographs of the authorised signatory and his identification proof.
- List of directors of the company.
- Bank statement of the company from the date of incorporation till the date of making the application.
- Copy of first sale and purchase document.
- List of products for which registration is required.
- A copy each of the Certificate of Incorporation, Memorandum of Association and the Articles of Association.
- A certified true copy of the Board Resolution.
- A self attested copy of the Permanent Account Number of the company.
- Bank guarantee for a sum of ₹ 100,000; however, subject to compliance of certain additional requirements; for example, if the premises is owned by the company, bank guarantee of ₹ 50,000 may also accepted by the Department. Alternatively, in lieu of furnishing a bank guarantee surety may also be given by an already registered dealer if the said dealer is registered for a period of at least 12 months.

After examining the aforesaid documents, registration certificate under Delhi Value Added Tax Act, 2004 and Central Sales Tax Act, 1956 are issued by the Department within 8 to 12 working days. Generally a visit is made by the Sales Tax/VAT Inspector within 2 to 3 days from the date of issue of certificate of registration and a report about the functioning of the Company is submitted by the said inspector to the Department. VAT registration will be effective from the date of application.

Procedure 8: Registration for Professional Tax, takes about one day and can be initiated alongwith procedure 7.

Procedure 9: Registration under the Employees Provident Fund (Miscellaneous Provisions) Act, 1952. (Takes 30 days and there is no specific costs involved. Can be done simultaneouslywith procedure 7).

Procedural details: The Employees' Provident Fund and Miscellaneous Provisions Act, 1952 provides for the institution of compulsory Provident Fund, Pension Fund and Deposit Linked Insurance Fund, for the benefit of the employees in factories and other establishments. The Act applies to every factory and establishment in which 20 or more persons are employed and which is engaged in any industry as specified. The company would be required to cover its employees under the provisions, once it crosses the limit of 20 employees.

An application in the Employer's Registration Form is required to be submitted with the office of the Regional Provident Fund Commissioner, Office of Provident office situated at Mayur Bhawan, 9th Floor, Connaught Circus, New Delhi-110001.

Procedure 10: Registration under Employees' State Insurance Act, 1948 (Takes about 30 days, can be undertaken along with procedure 7.

Procedural Details: The Employees' State Insurance Act, 1948 provides for grant of cash benefits to the employees in the recognised contingencies of sickness, maternity and employment injury. It also provides for medical benefit, in kind, to the employees and their families. The Act is applicable to all non-seasonal factories and certain establishment. For registration under the Act, an application in the prescribed form is required to be made to Regional Office of Employee State Insurance Corporation

(ESI Corporation, DDA Shopping Cum-Office Complex, Rajendra Place, New Delhi-110008).

ESIC Registration is optional if employee strength is less than 20. This procedure can be commenced simultaneously with procedure 7.

Procedure 11: Register under Shops and Establishment Act (Takes 11 days and costs about INR 600).

Procedural Details: Registration is required to be made under the Delhi Shops and Establishment Act, 1954. For this purpose, an application is required to be submitted with the inspector of the area concerned, along with the applicable fee (depending on number of workers working in the establishment) for registration of the establishment.

The statement shall consist of the following information:

- The name of the employer and the manager, if any;
- The postal address of the establishment;
- The name, if any, of the establishment;
- The category of the establishment; and
- Such other particulars as may be prescribed.

13.2 List of Approvals/Clearances for Provisional Registration as a Small Scale Enterprise

Following are the formalities that need to be fulfilled for provisional registration of small scale industries:

- Application form for Provisional Registration as SSI
- Project Profile

NOC from Pollution Control Board

- Application for NOC from Pollution Control
- Annexure to Pollution Control NOC Application
- Form-1: Application for Authorisation/Renewal of Authorisation for Collection/Reception/Treatment/Transport/Storage/Disposal of Hazardous Wastes
- Annexure to Form-1

Approval of Building Map under Factories Act

- Application for Approval of Building Map under Factories Act
- Factories Act: Questionnaire annexed to Form No.-1
- Factories Act: Form 1
- Factories Act: Form 2 (Rule 3 (3))
- Schedule 5 Material Safety Data Sheet
- Schedule 7 Notification of Activities/Sites
- Schedule 8 Safety Report

NOC from Fire Department

- Application for No Objection from Fire Department

Building Map Approval from Dev. Authority

Provisional Registration Trade Tax

- Form 14: Registration/Renewal of Registration under Trade Tax Act, 1948
- Form A (Annexure to Form - 14)
- Form B (Annexure to Form - 14)

Central Sales Tax Registration

- Application for Registration under Section 7(1)/7(2) of the Central Sales Tax

Trade Tax Validity Certificate

- Form 18: Application for Recognition Certificate under Sub Section (2) of Section 4-B of the U.P. Trade Tax Act, 1948
- Trade Tax - Treasury Challan

Electric Connection for Construction

- Application for Electric Connection for Agricultural/Industrial Use (for Load approved by District Udyog Bandhu) Power Sanction
- Application for Electric Connection for Agricultural/Industrial Use (for Load approved by District Udyog Bandhu)
- Application for Approval of Industrial Connection (For Load of 100 HP - 1000 KVA, approved by Zonal Udyog Bandhu)
- Application for Electric Connection for Industrial Use (power more than 1000 KVA)

License under Drug/Cosmetic Act

- Form 24: Application for the grant of or renewal of a license to manufacture for sale [or for distribution of] drugs other than those specified in [Schedule C, C(1) and X]
- Form 24A: Application for the grant of or renewal of a loan license to manufacture for sale [or for distribution of] drugs other than those specified in [Schedule C, C(1) and X]
- Form 24B: Application for the grant or renewal of a loan license to repack for sale or distribution of drugs, being drugs other than those specified in Schedule C, C(1) [excluding those specified in Sch. X]
- Form 24C: Application for the grant or renewal of a license to manufacture for sale [or for distribution] of Homoeopathic medicines or a licence to manufacture potentised preparations for back potencies by licenses holding licence in Form 20-C
- Form 24D: Application for the grant/renewal of a license to manufacture for sale of Ayurvedic/Siddha or Unani drugs
- Form 24E: Application for the grant or renewal of a license to manufacture for sale of Ayurvedic (including Siddha) or Unani drugs

- Form 24F: Application for the grant or renewal of a license to manufacture for sale [or for distribution of] drugs specified in Schedule X and note specified in Schedule C or C (1)

- Form 27: Application for grant or renewal of a licence to manufacture for sale [or for distribution of] drugs specified in Schedules C and C(1) [excluding those specified in [Part XB and Sch. X]

- Form 27A: Application for grant or renewal of a loan licence to manufacture for sale [or for distribution of] drugs specified in Schedules C and C(1) [excluding those specified in [Part XB and Sch. X]

- Form 27B: Application for grant or renewal of a license to manufacture for sale [or for distribution of] drugs specified in Schedules C and C(1) and X

- Form 27C: Application for grant or renewal of licence for the operation of Blood Bank, processing of Whole human blood for components and/or manufacture of blood products

- Form 27D: Application for grant or renewal of a license to manufacture for sale or for distribution of large Volume Parenterals/Sera and vaccines excluding those specified in Schedule X

- Information Data submitted with the application for grant of drug manufacturing licence regarding items to be approved

- Form 30: Application for licence to manufacture drugs for purpose of examination, test or analysis

- Form 31: Application for the grant or renewal of a licence to manufacture cosmetic for sale [or for distribution]

- Form 31A: Application for grant or renewal of a loan licence to manufacture cosmetic for sale [or for distribution]

- Form 36: Application for grant or renewal of approval for carrying out tests on drugs/cosmetics or raw materials used in the manufacture thereof on behalf of licensees for manufacture for sale of drugs/cosmetics

NOC from Forest Department

- NOC from Forest Department to Setup Saw Mill

Licence / Allotment from Excise Department

- Form P.D. 32: Application to Establish a Distillery
- Form P.D. 34: Application for grant of licence in form P.D.1 or P.D. 2 under rule 2(1) of the UP establishment of Distillery Rules, 1910
- Form B 19: Application to establish a brewery
- Form B 21: Application for grant of a licence to work a brewery in Form B-1 under rule 4(1) of the UP Brewery Rules, 1961

- Form 1A 2: Application for Industrial Alcohol
- M&T.P. Series No. 1: Application for licence to manufacture goods liable to duty or excise under the Medicinal and Toilet Preparations (Excise Duties)
- M&T.P. Series No. 2: Application for licence to Manufacture Ayurvedic preparation by an Ayurvedic Practitioner

HSD Storage NOC

- Form 4: Application for grant or amendment of licence to possess and sell explosives

13.3 Application Forms Needed for Permanent Registration of SSI

For permanent registration of SSI, the following forms have to be filled and submitted to the respective offices.

- Annexure - 1 (To be filled by Ancillary Units Only)
- Appendix A (Details of Machinery)

Consent from Pollution Control Board

- Application for Consent for Discharge/Continuation of Discharge under Section 25/26 of the Act
- Annexure to Form
- Application for Consent of Emission/Continuation of Emission u/s 21 of Air (Prevention and Pollution)

Annexure to Form

- Form 1: Application for Authorisation/Renewal of Authorisation For Collection/Reception/Treatment/Transport/Storage/Disposal of Hazardous Wastes
- Annexure to Form-1

Registration under Factories Act

- Form No - 4: Notice of Occupation for registration and grant or renewal of licence.
- Treasury Challan for Payment of fees

Shop and Commercial Establishment Registration

- Form - L: Application for Registration Statement of Facts

NOC from Electrical Safety Directorate

- Application form for Initial Inspection of High/Extra High Voltage Installation
- Statement Showing the requirement for H.V. Installation
- Application form of Initial Inspection of Medium Pressure Installation

- Application form for Initial Inspection of Electrical Installation of Generation Set

Trade Tax Exemption/Deferment

- Application for exemption from or reduction in rate of tax to new units (u/s 4-A of the U.P. Trade Tax Act)

Licence from Food Department

- Form A: U.P. Scheduled Commodities Dealers (Licenseing and Restriction on Hoarding)

Permanent Registration of Trade tax

- Form XIV: Application for registration/renewal of registration u/s 8-A of U.P.T.T. Act 1948
- Form A: Annexure to Form XIV
- Form B: Annexure to Form XIV
- Form A: Application for registration u/s 7(1)/7(2) of the Central Sales Tax, 1956 :Trade Tax Treasury Challan

Licence under Drugs and Cosmetics Act

- Form 24: Application for the grant of or renewal of a license to manufacture for sale [or for distribution of] drugs other than those specified in [Schedule C, C(1) and X].
- Form 24A: Application for the grant of or renewal of a loan license to manufacture for sale [or for distribution of] drugs other than those specified in [Schedule C, C(1) and X].
- Form 24B: Application for the grant or renewal of a loan license to repack for sale or distribution of drugs, being drugs other than those specified in Schedule C, C(1) [excluding those specified in Sch. X].
- Form 24C: Application for the grant or renewal of a license to manufacture for sale [or for distribution] of Homoeopathic medicines or a licence to manufacture potentised preparations for back potencies by licenses holding licence in Form 20-C.
- Form 24D: Application for the grant/renewal of a license to manufacture for sale of Ayurvedic/*Siddha* or *Unani* drugs.
- Form 24E: Application for the grant or renewal of a license to manufacture for sale of Ayurvedic (including *Siddha*) or *Unani* drugs
- Form 24F: Application for the grant or renewal of a license to manufacture for sale [or for distribution of] drugs specified in Schedule X and note specified in Schedule C or C(1).

- Form 27: Application for grant or renewal of a licence to manufacture for sale [or for distribution of] drugs specified in Schedules C and C(1) [excluding those specified in [Part XB and Sch. X]

- Form 27A: Application for grant or renewal of a loan licence to manufacture for sale [or for distribution of] drugs specified in Schedules C and C(1) [excluding those specified in [Part XB and Sch. X]

- Form 27B: Application for grant or renewal of a license to manufacture for sale [or for distribution of] drugs specified in Schedules C and C(1) and X

- Form 27C: Application for grant or renewal of licence for the operation of Blood Bank, processing of whole human blood for components and/or manufacture of blood products.

- Form 27D: Application for grant or renewal of a license to manufacture for sale or for distribution of Large Volume Parenterals/Sera and Vaccines excluding those specified in Schedule X.

- Information Data Submitted with the Application for grant of Drug Manufacturing licence regarding items to be approved.

- Form 30: Application for licence to manufacture drugs for purpose of examination, test or analysis

- Form 31: Application for the grant or renewal of a licence to manufacture cosmetic for sale [or for distribution]

- Form 31-A: Application for grant or renewal of a loan licence to manufacture cosmetic for sale [or for distribution]

- Form 36: Application for grant or renewal of approval for carrying out tests on drugs/cosmetics or raw materials used in the manufacture thereof on behalf of licensees for manufacture for sale of drugs/cosmetics.

Excise Licence (U.P.)

- Form P.D. 32: Application to establish a distillery
- Form P.D. 34: Application for grant of licence in form P.D.1 or P.D. 2 under rule 2(1) of the UP establishment of Distillery Rules, 1910
- Form B 19: Application to establish a brewery
- Form B 21: Application for grant of a licence to work a brewery in Form B-1 under rule 4(1) of the UP Brewery Rules 1961
- Form 1A 2: Application for Industrial Alcohol
- M & T. P. Series No. 1: Application for licence to Manufacture goods liable to duty or excise under the Medicinal and Toilet Preparations (Excise Duties)
- M & T. P. Series No. 2: Application for licence to Manufacture Ayurvedic preparation by an Ayurvedic Practitioners.

❑❑❑

At a Glance

1. Following procedures are to be followed for starting a business as a company:
   - (a) Present application to the Registrar of Companies for acceptability or availability of Company name
   - (b) Prepare Memorandum and Articles of Association
   - (c) Present the required documents along with the registration fee to the Registrar of companies to get the certificate of incorporation
   - (d) Obtain a Company seal
   - (e) List with the UTI Investor's Services Limited to obtain a permanent Account Number
   - (f) Obtain a Tax Account Number for income taxe deducted at source
   - (g) Register for Value Added Tax
   - (h) Registration for Professional Tax
   - (i) Registration under the Employees Provident Fund Act, 1952
   - (j) Registration under Employee's State Insurance Act, 1948
   - (k) Registration under Shops and Commercial Establishment Act

2. To get a license under Drug/Cosmetic Act following forms are required to be filled — Form 24, Form24A, Form 24B, Form 24C, Form 24D, Form 24E, Form 24 Form 27, Form 27A, Form 27B, Form 27C, Form 27D, Form 30, Form 31, Form 31A, and Form 36.

3. To establish a distillery follwing forms are needed to be filled — Form PD 32, Form PD 34, Form B 19, Form B 21, Form 1 A2, M and T.P. series no. 1 and M and T.P. series no. 2.

Multiple Choice Questions

1. Website of the Ministry of Corporate Affairs (MCA) is:
   - (A) www. mCA.gov/in
   - (B) www.mca.gov.in
   - (C) www.mca.in.gov
   - (D) www.gov.in

2. Registration fee of a company whose nominal share capital does not exceed ₹ 1,00,000 is:
   - (a) ₹ 15,000
   - (b) ₹ 2,000
   - (c) ₹ 11,000
   - (d) ₹ 4,000

3. Registration under Employees Provident Fund (miscellaneous Provisions) Act 1952 takes 30 days and can be done simultaneously with:
   - (a) Procedure 5
   - (b) Procedure 7

(c) Procedure 1

(d) Procedure 2

4. Approval of Building Map under Factories Act required filling up of:
   (a) Schedule 8 safety report
   (b) Factories Act: Form 1
   (c) Factories Act: Form 2(Rule 3(3))
   (d) All three above

5. Application form(s) needed for permanent Registration in Trade Tax of SSI:
   (a) Form XIV
   (b) Form A, Form B
   (c) Trade Tax Treasure Challan
   (d) All of the above

6. As per estimate and depending upon the place where one is starting a business it would require anything between _____ to complete all the file work and office work:
   (a) 30-45 days
   (b) 10-15 days
   (c) 30-55 days
   (d) 30-60 days

Ans. 1. b, 2. d, 3. b, 4. d, 5. d, 6. d

Review Questions

1. Define in detail MOA & AOA requirement as needed in starting of a business.

2. List only those documents which are required for obtaining registration under Delhi Value Added Tax Act, 2004 and CST Act, 1956.

3. What are the formalities needed to be fulfilled for provisional registration of Small Scale Industries?

4. What are the Application forms needed to be filled for permanent registration of SSI?

Unit V

Family and Non-Family Entrepreneurs

Chapter 14
Family Businesses

Introduction

The Indian family business dates back to the latter half of the 19th century, which also marks the beginning of business in India. It is not surprising then that family-run businesses currently account for a whopping 95 percent of all Indian companies. Considering that one-third of the companies listed in Fortune 500 fall under this category, including the currently second Wal-Mart, family businesses have undoubtedly paved their place in the world economy. The Indian economy, currently in a state of rapid development, is burgeoning with innumerable small and medium-sized family-run enterprises. Family businesses in India initially started in the 1890s as a means to promote import substitution and attain economic freedom from the British. These enterprises were an integral part of India's freedom struggle, and as part of the *Swadeshi* movement, got special treatment and subsidies from the government.

The businesses consolidated their positions as near monopolies under the protective environment of the *licence raj* and their inefficiencies did not get exposed to the indefatigable market realities. Some of the prominent business families during the 1960s were the Modis, Thapars, Shrirams, Singhanias, Birlas, Wadias and Godrej. Indian society's dynastic tendency ensures that promoters will continue to control their companies for some time, unlike in the West where professionals take over once the firm achieves scale. India has an almost unique system of promoters who own and manage much of the corporate sector. There are the eponymous promoter groups that have been around for decades, such as the Tatas, Birlas, Mahindras, Bajajs, Goenkas and Godrejs. Then there are the relative newcomers, such as the Ambanis of Reliance, the Mittals of Bharti, the Agarwals of Vedanta, the Biyanis of the Future Group, the Singhs of erstwhile Ranbaxy, etc. There are also the single-company promoters, such as Hamied of Cipla, Saldhana of Glenmark, the Puris of Moser Baer, Premji of Wipro, etc. In some cases, there are multiple promoters as in the case of Infosys, or professional promoters as in HDFC. In short, there are promoters of all types.

What makes India such a fertile ground for the concept of promoters? And how come other countries don't have such a wealth of promoters? Is it beneficial for India to have such a corporate landscape? If we look at the US market, almost all entrepreneur-promoted companies move on to being run by non-promoter, professional management. Take the case of the Rockefellers and the Waltons. Even in relatively new companies, such as Microsoft, eBay, Yahoo and Google, the founders have given way to others with a background in scale and complexity to manage the business. Typically, this happens once the company gets listed and other stakeholders enter the picture. In the US, the institutional investor base is organised and powerful, and pushes its interests that much harder. There are many reasons that make the concept of promoters so sustainable in India. First, the fact that most Indian promoters own pretty sizeable chunks in their companies means that they are able to exercise significant shareholder rights that, in turn, helps them stay in control. Most promoters would today typically own more than 35–40% of their companies. Older conglomerate groups, such as the Tata's and Birlas have been busy shoring up their ownership levels. The days when the Tata's-controlled Tata Steel with a lower shareholding than the Birlas' 8 percent are long gone. The second reason is the lack of a countervailing strong institutional investor base. Indian insurance companies and asset management companies do not have the maturity and ability where they can forcefully push a different point of view.

It also does not help that most institutional investors, such as insurance companies and asset management companies are controlled by the same promoter groups. In such a scenario, their incentive to rock the boat is minimal and this is revealed by a cursory look at the leading insurance companies: Tata AIG, Birla Sun Life, Bajaj Allianz, Bharti Axa, Reliance, etc. The case of asset management companies is similar. The only large financial investors that could be considered non-promoter-driven are LIC, ICICI Prudential and HDFC. But they are also unlikely to take a more activist role given their deep ties with industry. Of course, there are genuinely independent institutional investors too and we should hope that they become more significant. One class of independent investors that has not yet shown activist tendencies are foreign institutional investors and, to some extent, private equity funds investing in the public markets. While public markets accept the existence of promoter groups, the banking system requires promoter backing of companies. Banks typically require minimum shareholding by promoters and sometimes promoter guarantees. Obviously, the banking system finds comfort in dealing with promoters. Remarkably, the list of non-promoter companies is quite short. Among the larger companies, one might argue that ITC, L&T, ICICI and perhaps the HDFC group, including IDFC, would qualify. The fact is that most Indian companies have an entrepreneur/ promoter actively driving them, being the face of the company.

Is this likely to change? Should it change? Do promoters perhaps take the longer term view about growing businesses and provide a more investing mindset with less regard to short-term quarterly performance? Is this better for India given the current stage of development? Do promoter-led groups perform better from a shareholder return standpoint? And is it better from the point of view of the broader stakeholder community including employees, consumers, the government and society at large?

It is certainly true that promoters in India take the longer view and, in this respect, provide a more solid foundation for the development of industry. It is also true that some promoters take a more 'nation-building' and societal approaches, while others focus on value creation. One cannot say with certainty whether promoter-led companies or groups provide better shareholder returns than others — no specific studies exist in this respect. How will this phenomenon evolve over time? It is likely that India will follow a path different from the west. Unlike in those countries, second and third generation Indian families also typically enter the family business. This has something to do with the Indian society that encourages dynastic tendencies: from politics to business to Bollywood to agriculture and so on. The model of following one's individual urges and doing something different is not common. As a result, separation of family ownership from active management is not normal in India. The other interesting impact is in philanthropy. Since everything stays in the family and the companies along with their ownership are passed on, the concept of monetising ownership and doing great philanthropic activities, such as Bill Gates or Warren Buffet— who between them are donating more than $60 billion—is in its infancy in India.

It would be great if some more promoters decided to monetise their assets and directly invested in building the country's social and physical infrastructure. This way, India would be able to take advantage of their energies and their wealth creation for the good of all people. That is not to say that all promoters should immediately divorce ownership from management and rush to doing philanthropic or other activities. Clearly, at this point in India's economic evolution, promoters provide that much-needed entrepreneurial spark and management bandwidth that is still essential for the growth of the corporate sector. However, it will be interesting to see whether second and third generation promoters want to stay in the business, whether they make the best managers, and whether the external stakeholder community is able to separate good from the bad, and has the ability to encourage only the better promoter managers to stay. This may take a few decades but, once again, India will have evolved its own model for development— one where promoters and professionals work together to create value for all stakeholders.

14.1 Role of Professionals

The real professional is able to see trends and value them in the emerging patterns of relationship and is able to value it. The professional has an understanding of the way things work in the sphere of activity that he/she is and has adequate knowledge. He/she brings more professionals into the organisation from other field to understand and get things done. A professional is continuously on work towards his/her development and growth professional should be able to guide social establishment by way of training and competence development on his/her part.

In the words of Guy Le Boterf, a French expert on the development of competencies, *A Professional is a person who possesses a personal body of knowledge and of know-how which is recognised and valued by the market. Because of this market recognition, the Professional benefits from an advantage not available to other workers: he or she can personally manage internal or external professional mobility, in a specific firm or in the international market. A person who is recognized as a Professional possesses a social standing which is larger than the specific job he or she holds down.*

In addition to ability, confidence, responsibility, belief and respect other key personal qualities that define a professional are honour, reputation and trustworthiness. Trustworthiness comes from an assurance of reliability. Reputation is not only a signal to your customers but also a commitment mechanism that keeps you up to the mark. Paul Seabright, a British economist states that *those who can convince others of their intrinsic honesty, may thereby prosper, and it may be easier for the genuinely honest to be thus convincing—the more so if honesty, or at least the true and honorable performance of a certain trade or skill, requires a degree of style, confidence and even grace, built up over a long period of commitment to the task, that are hard for an opportunist to feign.*

Professionalism is actually the process by which given occupation becomes profession in the sense of attaining professional status. Professionalism is an aspirational standard, rather than a set of minimum requirements, the essential elements of which are competence personal integrity, responsibility and accountability service. The aspiration should be to meet the highest standards that the public has a right to expect of its professionals.

Elements of professionalism

- Altruistic: showing unselfish concern for the welfare of others
- Accountability responsibility and reliability
- Excellence
  - Knowledgeable, skilful
  - Competency to retrieve and handle information
  - Appropriate decision making skills
  - Competency in communication
- Integrity the quality of being honest moral soundness undivided or unbroken
- Dutiful appreciation of the role aptitude for personal development
- Respect to others

Professionalism is the essence of professionalism is a commitment to develop one's skills to the fullest and to apply (them) responsibly to the problems at hand. Professionalism requires adherence to the highest ethical standards of conduct and willingness to subordinate narrow self-interest in pursuit of the more fundamental goal of public service.

14.2 Professionalism v/s Family Entrepreneurs

Family entrepreneurship is defined as ownership control by members of a family strategic influence of a family in the management of the firm concern for family relationship the dream of continuity across generation.

Professionalism v/s Family entrepreneurs

- Degree of open mindedness: Professional are open-minded, receptive to new ideas, ready to experiment, while family entrepreneurs generally lack this.
- New practices: They include quality certification, participative management, change in working style, financing pattern. Professionals are always leaders in adopting them, experimenting with them. While there is lack of this attitude in family entrepreneurs, probably because of the control that they desire to wield on the venture.
- Impartial HRM: Professionals do not show partiality towards any particular gender. But family business houses employ their relative or friends or people belonging to same social caste in responsible position.
- Organisation oriented financial management: Professionals tend to make financial decision in the way which is best for the organisation. But family entrepreneurial firms give first priority to their familiar concern and interests.
- Decision making style: The decision making process in professional run organisation tends to be qualitative better and vision to be broader. It is mostly participative. While in family run businesses is more autocratic in nature. Here, it is mostly owner entrepreneur himself/herself who makes the decision sometimes with the help of his family members or friends.

❑❑❑

At a Glance

1. Elements of professionalism are:
    (a) Altruism
    (b) Accountability, responsibility and reliability
    (c) Excellence
    (d) Integrity
    (e) Respect to others
    (f) Dutiful appreciation of the role aptitude

2. Professionals v/s Family entrepreneurs:
   (a) Professionals are open-minded while family entrepreneurs generally lack this
   (b) Professionals are always leaders in adopting new practices while family entrepreneurs always desire to wield on to the practices
   (c) Professionals do not show partiality towards any particular gender. But family business houses employ their relative or friends or people belonging to same social caste in responsible position
   (d) Professionals tend to make financial decision in the way which is best for the orgnisation. But family entrepreneurial firms give first priority to their familiy concerns and interest

3. Decision making process is qualitatively better and taken with a broader vision. It is mostly participative. While in family run business it is more autocratic in nature.

Multiple Choice Questions

1. On the development of competencies French expert Guy Le Boterf says:
   (a) A professional possesses a social standing which is larger than the specific job he or she holds
   (b) The professional form a disadvantage
   (c) Professionals do not possess a social standing
   (d) All the above are true

2. Altruistic means:
   (a) Showing selfish concerns for others
   (b) Showing unselfish concern for the welfare of others
   (c) Showing neither selfishness nor unselfishness
   (d) All the above are wrong

3. Indian family business dates back to the latter half of _____ which also marks the _____ of _____ in India.
   (a) 18th Century, beginning, business
   (b) 19th Century, beginning, business
   (c) 20th Century, end of, commercial business
   (d) None of these

Ans. 1 a, 2. b, 3. b

Review Questions

1. Write in detail about Indian family business.
2. Enumerate role of professionalism in Indian businesses.
3. Compare professionals versus family entrepreneurs in Indian business.

Chapter 15

Women Entrepreneurs

Introduction

In the traditional Indian society, a distinction was made between men's work and women's work. Women have been traditionally been around family responsibilities. It had curtailed the employment opportunities for women in conventional and unconventional fields of economic activity. As times have changed, there has been a significant change in the way women are looked at specifically with respect to jobs and doing something of their own. There have been examples of women in India who have done well by initiating action in choosing their own line of interest. A lot of people question that are women entrepreneurs different from the men entrepreneurs? The entrepreneur represents distinct qualities, skills, and competences, beliefs and values. Irrespective of whether one is a man or a woman, if they possess these qualities they can easily become an entrepreneur. In today's times where the number of women in employment has increased manifolds, a similar shift in the number of women entrepreneurs is also happening. Whether it is a business of printing T-shirts or it is about gifts, chocolates, candles, you would find a lot of women actively pursuing an interest in business.

There are a number of reasons why women have started looking towards entrepreneurial careers in today's time:

- Limited job opportunities
- Pressing need to earn income to supplement the family income due to the high cost of living
- Social pressure of increasing standard of living
- Utilisation of spare time
- Self-esteemed need
- Increasing socio-economic awareness
- Impact of role models in industry and business

- Constant motivation by government institutions
- Impact of media
- Attractive incentives, subsidies and schemes

The existing women entrepreneurs in India can be classified into three main categories quite similar to as it in the case of men:

- Forced entrepreneurs who are compelled by circumstances or family business responsibilities to take up the career in business and industry.
- Chance entrepreneurs who went into business by luck or accident without any preparation.
- Created entrepreneurs, who are specifically identified, motivated, trained, equipped and developed as entrepreneurs. In recent years, there is an overwhelming response from women for the entrepreneurship developed training programmes, which is increasing the band of women entrepreneurs in India.

Generally speaking, there are certain areas of activity wherein it is considered that there are opportunities that can be pursued by women entrepreneurs. At the same time, it would not be appropriate to limit them to this list of opportunities.

15.1 Opportunities for Women Entrepreneurs

Considering the flow of women entrepreneurs in the traditional and conventional industries and product lines, it is often said that the women entrepreneurship in India is caught up in '3 Ps' (papads and pickles, food industry, petticoats, readymade garment industry, paintings and handicrafts). The entry of women entrepreneurs in the conventional product is justified on the grounds that they have acquired the skills required for these products traditionally. If they could excel in these product lines, let them excel. But many all-India levels surveys have proved that in recent years, women entrepreneurs have entered all fields of business and industry. In the last decade, there has been a remarkable shift in emphasis from the manufacturing industry to the service industry. Considering this, some important opportunities are identified for the women in urban areas:

- Beauty parlours
- Communication centres
- Community kitchens
- Computer maintenance
- Computer services and information dissemination
- Computer training at various levels
- Crèches

- Culture centres
- Distribution and trading of household provisions as well as saris, dress materials, etc.
- Health clubs
- Job contracts for packaging of goods
- Mini laundry, community eating centre
- Nutrition clubs in schools and offices
- Photocopying, typing centres
- Poster and indoor plant library
- Quality testing, quality control laboratories
- Recreation centres for old people
- Screen printing, photography and video shooting
- Stuffed soft toys, wooden toys
- Sub-assemblies of electronic products
- Trading in computer stationery
- Travel and tourism

15.2 Opportunities for Women in Semi-Urban Sectors

- Production of liquid soap, soap powder, detergents, deodorants, etc.
- Office stationary, such as cushion pads, gums, inks, ink pads
- Convenience, readymade, instant food packaging including pickles, spices, papads, etc.
- Community kitchens
- Communication services
- Different type of training and coaching classes
- Child care centres and culture centres
- Nursery classes
- Garment

15.3 Opportunities for Women in Rural Sectors

In recent times, the government has been giving tremendous importance to agro-based and allied products. Only two to four percent of the total production of fruits and vegetables is processed every year in India. This reveals a huge scope for the fruit, vegetable processing industry. Women have a natural flair and instinct for food processing and preparation. At the same time, the variety of handicraft that is developed in the various rural parts of India is so huge that if that can be channelised in an organised way it would lead to a large number of ventures. In total in any area urban, semi-urban or rural the number of opportunities that can be availed is enormous and, therefore, if women take up such initiatives they can be a good contributor to the income of their respective families.

In the non-profit domain of activity, women's non-profit organisations have long played an important role in the lives of women in many parts of the world. In India, well-educated and affluent women found socially sanctioned work outside the home in the voluntary sector. They worked as volunteers under the aegis of religious organisations and for social service dedicated to the alleviation of poverty. Participation in non-profit sector in India gave women an opportunity to enter the social and political spheres in ways often denied to them by the for-profit and public sectors. *Entrepreneurship*, has been defined in the for-profit literature as "the catalytic agent in society which sets into motion new enterprises, new combinations of production and exchange". Although the concept of entrepreneurship is closely linked with the for-profit sector and may seem strange in the NGO world, it is not. The same entrepreneurial spirit is the key to initiating projects and mobilising resources, whether it is for promoting a social cause in the non-profit sector or promoting a profit-making enterprise. Both kinds of enterprises are the result of the entrepreneur's innovation, leadership, imagination, efforts and ability. Thus, sing the definition from the for-profit literature, a *non-profit entrepreneur* is a self-directed, innovative leader who starts a non-profit enterprise.

The critical questions the answers to which can shed more light on the role of women on the non-profit sector are as follows:

- What are the characteristics of women entrepreneurs in the non-profit and social sectors?

- What motivates them?

- Are there any structural and cultural factors relevant to women's entrepreneurship of non-profit organisations?

The women working in non-profit sectors are involved in providing basic services for mainly rural women and children, including counseling, primary health services, family planning, literacy training and a variety of legal and administrative services. Many are also involved in advocacy of women's rights with local politicians and the judicial system. These women typically start their NGOs at ages ranging from 24–65 years. Although they come to entrepreneurship through a variety of paths, they share the feminist conviction that attention to women's issues is paramount for social justice. Their commitment to further the cause of women is evident from their personal histories, self-evaluation and professional experiences.

- *Desire to Serve Others*

Most of the women are motivated by the need to serve others and believe they could best do so under the aegis of an NGO. They want to provide female leadership in the work for the downtrodden, to make women's groups powerful tools of empowerment for women and children. Some women had frustrations in the social work jobs they had held previously. Some of the women believe that their work did not address problems relevant to them, such as make women conscious of the human and constitutional rights; hence, they wish to start their own enterprise.

- *Needs in Community*

Many women perceive a need in the community that was not being fulfilled. Many of the women are motivated by the rural women's needs, which have been ignored or call for specific political or judicial action. These women are driven by the motivation to bring about self-awareness among women and stimulate a wider and deeper knowledge of the problems faced by women and children.

- *Self-Actualisation*

It is not surprising that most of the women that start an NGO dealing with women's issues have a reason for self-actualisation for them. Many believe that "Only women can create a platform and empathise with other women at a grassroot level" and that "women require women to create space for themselves."

- *Desire to Achieve Change*

Many women in an NGO come from families involved in issues of social justice or were motivated to found the NGO in order "to achieve change". For example, many are motivated to change people's outlook towards unwanted children"; some believe that it is necessary to make changes in the structural and legal facilities to fight injustices towards women.

- *Other*

Some women join NGO because the NGO allows them to enhance their social connections and "try something new," and that they were "expected to do social service" by their peers.

- *The Problems*

An ILO report on Women Entrepreneurs - *Women have a proportionately greater presence in the informal economy and in microenterprises; and they are less represented in formal, registered SMEs.*

For women there are several handicaps. These have resulted in restricting and inhibiting the growth of women entrepreneurship in India. Some of the limiting factors are in the following:

- *Lack of Confidence*

In India, the women usually take a subordinate position, where they get into the habit of order taking. Even at home the family members do not trust the women of the family with decision making. All of this results in lack of confidence in the Indian women entrepreneurs.

The male–female competition is another factor, which develop hurdles to women entrepreneurs in the business management process. Despite the fact that women entrepreneurs are good in keeping their service prompt and delivery in time, due to lack of organisational skills compared to male entrepreneurs, women have to face constraints from competition. The confidence to travel across day and night and even different regions and states are less found in women compared to male entrepreneurs. This shows the low level freedom of expression and freedom of mobility of the women entrepreneurs.

- *Lack of Working Capital*

Indian women have lack of access to the funds from the market as they usually do not possess tangible security and credit in the market. They usually do not have enough property rights and have limited access to external sources of fund. Even getting loans from banks or financial institutions is difficult. The financial institutions are skeptical about the entrepreneurial abilities of women. The bankers consider women loonies as higher risk than men loonies. The bankers put unrealistic and unreasonable securities to get loan to women entrepreneurs. According to a report by the United Nations Industrial Development Organization (UNIDO), "despite evidence that woman's loan repayment rates are higher than men's, women still face more difficulties in obtaining credit," often due to discriminatory attitudes of banks and informal lending groups (UNIDO, 1995b).

Women in developing nations have little access to funds, due to the fact that they are concentrated in poor rural communities with few opportunities to borrow money. The women entrepreneurs are suffering from inadequate financial resources and working capital. The women entrepreneurs lack access to external funds due to their inability to provide tangible security. Very few women have the tangible property in hand.

- *Socio-Cultural Barriers*

In the Indian society, particularly the lower and middle strata preference is given to the male child with respect to the girl child. Therefore, this sometimes results in inadequate educational support given to the females. As a result this impediments the progress of women and handicap them in the world of work.

A kind of patriarchal– male dominant social order is the building block to them in their way towards business success. Male members think it a big risk financing the ventures run by women.

Women's family obligations also bar them from becoming successful entrepreneurs in both developed and developing nations. The financial institutions discourage women entrepreneurs on the belief that they can at any time leave their business and become housewives again. The result is that they are forced to rely on their own savings, and loan from relatives and family friends. Indian women give more emphasis to family ties and relationships. Married women have to make a fine balance between business and home. More over the business success depends on the support the family members extend to women in the business process and management. The interest of the family members is a determinant factor in the realisation of women's business aspirations.

- *Lack of the right public/private institutions*

Although, government policies do exist to make it easier for women small business owners to find funding and markets, these are most often misused by men who use it with their wives fronting through the entire process. Most of the people running these schemes are also well-aware of this potential for misuse and often take the extremely patriarchal view that loans will not be disbursed to a woman unless she is accompanied by her husband or father. Also, government policies cannot be designed at a national level, or inspired by those in existing in other countries. Policies need to be customised to be gender-, location- and culture-sensitive.

The International Labour Organisation (ILO) report has published as main findings on women entrepreneurship in India as follows:

o Women's entrepreneurship as an untapped source of economic growth
o Women have a lower participation rate in entrepreneurship than men
o Women choose different industries than men do
o Such industries are perceived as being less important to economic growth and development
o Mainstream government policies and programmes do not take into account specific needs of women entrepreneurs

But in spite of all of these problems, women have carried over there organisational skills developed in managing one of the most complex organisations— the household, to their workplace. Women have learnt over the centuries the art of negotiation, reconciliation and qualities of patience and understanding, along with an inherent quality of emotional intelligence. All these transferable skills are brought to bear upon the workplace, making it richer from these valuable experiences.

It is estimated that women entrepreneurs presently comprise about 10 percent of the total number of entrepreneurs in India, with the percentage growing every year. If the prevailing trends continue, it is likely that in another five years, women will comprise 20 percent of the entrepreneurial force. With corporates eager to associate and work with women-owned businesses, and a host of banks and non-governmental organisations keen to help them get going, there has rarely been a better time for women with zeal and creativity to start their own business.

Endowed with the famous female intuition that helps them make the right choices even in situations where experience and logic fail, women have innate flair for entrepreneurship. Although men and women may be motivated by different goals and expectations women entrepreneurs are just as competent, if not better, than their male counterparts.

Women are more likely than men to admit when they do not know something and ask for help. They are natural networkers and relationship builders, forging powerful bonds and nurturing relationships with clients and employees alike. They are also more inclined to seek out mentors and develop supportive teams. In business, this translates into establishing rapport with clients and providing great customer service. This perhaps is the reason why many women tend to launch businesses that are client based or service-oriented.

Several women organisations have taken birth to overcome the difficulties the women face in getting into business. Few of the organisations are SEWA (Self-Employed Women's Association), Mahila Griha Udhyog (famous for its product *Lijjat Papad*) and FIWE (Federation of Indian Women Entrepreneurs).

The most important service that these types of organisations are providing is that of counseling because most of the time women do not know where to start or what kind of enterprise they should take up.

These types of organisations try to see that most of the women get help with the formalities required by the government and with acquiring financing. Government purchases are important to many businesses and learning how to tender offers to the government is important to their success. For example, someone may have a tailoring shop but does not know how to sell its services to the military. These types of organisations try to help them out in filling out the tenders, getting their organisation registered, etc. It is a form of marketing support.

Other than the counseling and marketing support, training programmes are another service that they provide. There are women running very small enterprises who don't even have the most basic level of business know-how. In India, the Ministry of Industry has established the small industries' institute that has facilities in all the major cities where women can get training on manufacturing agricultural products, jewellery and other products. These organisations assist women entrepreneurs to obtain training at these government-owned facilities, as well as at others established by some private companies.

Women often are not able to get the information they need to run their businesses. These organisations provide it to them because often their involvement in family affairs is so great that they do not have time or they are not able to gain access to information they need for their businesses. These organisations also encourage them to come at least two or three times to one of our local chapters and interact with other members. Newsletters are also an important means of providing essential information to their membership.

The principal goal of these types of organisations is to foster the economic empowerment of women by helping them to become successful entrepreneurs. Another objective is to bring women business persons together to voice their needs and demands in such a way that government enacts policies beneficial to their interests and to interact with national government policy makers so that they understand the needs of women entrepreneurs. Government sees the non-profit organisations and NGOs as alternative providers of public services and sometimes encourages such activity through tax subsidies and other means. Thus, it is not unreasonable to assume, from a public policy perspective, the need to encourage the founding of such organisations and to ensure that those founded are sustainable and successful. Furthermore, donors— local and international, who are keen to promote women's issues— are interested in encouraging start-ups and ensuring that the organisations they fund are successful. Government and donors can make an effort to ensure that more women, especially of lower castes, receive higher education and training in interpersonal skills and are recruited to volunteer. Furthermore, there is a need for public support to enable wider diffusion of some of the key themes that are part of the feminist perspectives, namely, concern for equity and social justice. If more people, both men and women, are exposed to such ideology, more may take action in the form of starting NGOs or support the entrepreneurs that do.

It may be of value to ensure that those involved in social work and in volunteering be targeted to receive publicly available resources to support the formation of organisations. These include training programmes and mentoring services to facilitate the formation of NGOs. If such programmes can be made available to those who are contemplating starting non-profit organisations, or who are in the process of doing so, they may be able to increase the new entrepreneurs' chances of success. Because the initial volunteer experience seems to be a factor that helps women see the need to start non-profit organisations, policies that expose more young women to volunteer work in social service increase the number who may eventually start such organisations. For example, international donors can help existing non-profit organisations to recruit more volunteers and offer interested volunteers training in the different skills they will need— interpersonal skills, negotiating bureaucracies, legal and administrative aspects of starting, managing and running a non-profit organisation. Governments can make volunteering part of educational training so as to expose youth to social problems and thereby increase the pool of likely entrepreneurs. Volunteering may also give women a chance to expand their social connections, which is necessary in recruiting volunteers and donations. The salient feature that is evident here is that most of the women entrepreneurs in the non-profit sector share a feminist ideology and a desire to help others. By having a non-profit organisation whose mission is closely related to their ideology, they are able to actualise their beliefs and this affords them a high level of satisfaction and accomplishment.

Earnings and independence seem to be secondary to pursuing the mission of their non-profit organisation. Lack of access to financial capital does not pose a major challenge to women entrepreneurs in this sector; what is essential is access to volunteers and donations, initially through personal networks. Parental role models and early professional and volunteer experience serve to raise the awareness and motivate many of these women to pioneer non-profit organisations to pursue social justice. Because they are self-professed feminists, it is not surprising that they choose to start NGOs addressing women's issues to remedy social injustices and work for change. These women entrepreneurs are persistent, hardworking and willing to take risks. They are self-confident, extroverted and energetic.

❑❑❑

At a Glance

1. Women have started looking towards entrepreneurial careers in today's time because of :
    - Limited job opportunities
    - Pressing need to earn income to supplement the family income due to high cost of living
    - Social pressure of increasing standard of living
    - Utilisation of spare time
    - Self-esteem need
    - Increasing socio-economic awareness
    - Impact of role models in industry and business
    - Constant motivation by government institutions
    - Impact of media
    - Attractive incentives, subsidies and schemes

2. Opportunities for women in semi-urban sectors are as:
    - Production of liquid soap, soap powder, detergents etc.
    - Community kitchens
    - Communication Services
    - Different types of training and coaching classes
    - Nursery classes

3. ILO report on women Entrepreneurs in India says:
    - Its an untapped source of economic growth
    - Women have lower participation rate in entrepreneurship than men

- Women choose different industries than men do
- Mainstream government policies and programmes do not take into account specific needs of women entrepreneurs

4. Some women join NGO because it allows them to enhance their social connections and "try something new", and they are "expected to do social service" by their peers.

5. ILO report says: Women have a proportionately greater presence in the informal economy and in microenterprises, and they are less represented in formal, registered SMEs.

Multiple Choice Questions

1. Self Actualism is a trait found in:
   (a) Women Entrepreneurs
   (b) Both men & women Entrepreneurs
   (c) Both a & b are correct
   (d) Both a & b are wrong

2. SEWA, FIWE and Mahila Griha Udyog are:
   (a) All women organization
   (b) All business organisation
   (c) Federation of India Women Entrepreneurs
   (d) All the above above are wrong

3. Women Entrepreneurship in India is caught up in '3 Ps' which is:
   (a) Passion, Papads, Professionalism
   (b) Papads, Petticoats, Paintings
   (c) A and B both are correct
   (d) Placement, Passion, Pain reliever

Ans. 1. a, 2. a, 3. b

Review Questions

1. What are the characteristics of women entrepreneurs in the non-profit and social sector?

2. The existing women entrepreneurs in India can be classified into three main categories, what are these, write in detail.

3. List the opportunities that are available to women entrepreneurs in India.

Unit VI

Venture Capital

Chapter 16

Venture Capital: Nature and Overview

Introduction

Venture Capital (VC) is one of the many ways in which a growth-oriented venture can obtain funds in exchange for certain equity in the venture. VC is a fund which is managed by a class of people/organisations that support stimulate and sustain entrepreneurship by way of providing for equity capital at different stages of a venture depending upon their fund requirements and growth aspirations. To the very fundamental question as to why would a venture need to raise funds, we may have the following answer that a typical business will need to define its proposed product/service offering and protect it, develop the product/service to a marketable stage, establish manufacturing to make the new product or a service group to provide the service and set up a sales and marketing group to promote it and expand the product/service range and geographic reach of the company to increase revenues to a point where the company 'breaks even'. For all these tasks, an entrepreneur may seek funds. Further, in order to initiate, build and grow a venture there is always a requirement of funds. Usually, VC funding is for supporting innovative ideas and concepts that are new to the context in which they are being presented. Further a VC fund is available to those sectors where there is high growth potential.

If innovation is the fuel for igniting the entrepreneurial engine, venture capital provides the much needed momentum so that it attains sustainable speed to change the gears from idea to IPO stage. Entrepreneurship is a key factor in promoting growth in output and employment. Consequently, to encourage new start-ups, most governments in developed countries have created public venture capital programmes and encourage promotion of private venture capital firms. Venture capital is a means of financing growing private companies. Finance may be required as seed capital, for the start-up, development/expansion or purchase of a company via a mechanism, such as in a management buyout. Both establishing a new business as well as growing business always requires capital. There are a number of different ways to fund new business and its growth. These include the owner's own capital, arranging debt finance or seeking an equity partner, as is the case with venture capital. With venture capital, the venture capitalist acquires an agreed proportion of the equity of the company in return for the requisite funding. Equity finance offers the significant advantage of having no interest charges. It is patient capital that seeks a return through long-term capital gain rather than immediate and regular interest payments. Venture capital investors are, therefore, exposed to the risk of the company failing. When venture capitalists invest in a business they become part-owners and typically require a seat on the company's board of directors. They tend to take a minority share in the company and usually do not take day-to-day control. Rather, professional venture capitalists act as mentors and aim to provide support and advice on a range of management and technical issues to assist the company to develop its full potential. Surveys, worldwide, consistently rate the management support as the most important contribution of a venture capital firm. There are many sources of capital, but only a venture capitalist can provide experienced management input gained by helping many other companies successfully conquer the inevitable problems and growing pains. Venture capitalists provide funds and at the same time support to the extent of

- *Being like a business partner* -sharing the risks and rewards.
- Being like a *mentor* by providing strategic, operational and financial advice to the company based on past experience with other companies in similar situations. The venture capitalist also has a *network* of contacts in many areas that can add value to the company, such as in recruiting key personnel, providing contacts in international markets, introductions to strategic partners and, if needed. Can tell you when is the right time to prepare a company for an initial public offering (IPO).

Risk finance and venture capital environment can bring about innovation, promote technology, and harness knowledge-based ventures. In this sense, venture capital is different from other types of financing as in the following:

- Development finance
- Seed capital, (at times, venture capitalists provide)
- Term loan/conventional financing
- Passive equity investment support
- R&D funding sources.

The concept of venture capital is relatively new to the Indian economy, and is gaining prominence in the recent years. In developed countries, such as U.S.A. and the U.K., venture capital financing is mainly through private initiative, with hardly any involvement of the government institutions. It has done great service in stimulating entrepreneurial growth in unproven and risky ventures which offered high potential for growth. In developing countries, such as Taiwan, Singapore, South Korea and Israel, venture capital has played an important role in economic growth. Indian venture capital approach is modelled on the U.S.A./U.K. pattern. Government not only plays a pro-active role in creating a regulatory environment to secure benefits to the small and medium enterprises (SMEs) but also provides venture support through different arms.

16.1 Historical Background

USA is the birth place of Venture Capital industry. During most its historical evolution, the market for arranging such financing was informal. Entrepreneurs primarily relied on the resources of wealthy families. It was in 1946 that American Research and Development Corporation (ARD), a publicly traded, closed-end investment company was formed. The best known investment of ARD was the start-up financing it provided in 1958 for computer maker Digital Equipment Corp. ARD provided its original investors with a 15.8 percent annual rate of return over its twenty-five years as an independent firm though it had difficult times in the beginning. The number of such specialised investment firms, which later were called **venture capital firms**, began to boom in the late 1950s.The creation of federal Small Business Investment Company (SBIC) programme in 1958 aided the growth of venture capital firms. Hundreds of SBICs were formed in the 1960s, and many remain in operation today.

During the 1960s and 1970s, venture capital firms focused their investment activity primarily on starting and expanding companies. These companies were exploiting breakthroughs in electronic, medical or data-processing technology. As a result, venture capital came to be almost synonymous with technology finance. The initial success generated further success in 1990s which were the best years for the Venture Capital Industry. The favourable economic climate in the US coupled with the advent of the Internet boom was the engine for growth. The decade saw low interest rates and high P/E ratio compared to historical averages. This triggered mergers and acquisition activities creating more opportunities for small, venture-backed companies to exit (cash out) at high prices. The Internet became a new medium for both personal and business communications. It created tremendous opportunities for entrepreneurs and venture capitalists in the mid and late 1990s. The industry, in turn, experienced extraordinary growth both in the number of firms, and in the amount of capital they have raised. It is estimated that over 1000 venture capital firms sprang up in the United States. The 21st century, however, is seeing declining trend in venture capital activities. Global venture capital (GVC) is an important phenomenon that has a significant impact on global entrepreneurship. Despite this, the understanding and analysis of GVC is very limited in academic and practitioner research. It is estimated that US$ 800 billion was raised globally between 1998 and 2002 out of which US$ 94 billion is currently under management in Asia. Though the sums under management is huge, very little has been studied that will enable these

GVC firms to successfully deploy these funds in emerging Asian markets. Asia is an especially difficult market for foreign investors, with its diverse sets of political systems, laws and cultural challenges. This diversity makes successful investing in Asia a uniquely difficult proposition. Venture capital firms today are more globalised than ever before. It has an estimated 5,162 professionals in 1,560 firms operating in Asia, the majority being foreign firms (Asian Private Equity, 2003).

16.2 Venture Capital in India

Research and Development Cess Act, 1986 introduced in the fiscal budget for the year 1986–87, is the precursor of the concept of venture capital as a new financial service in India. This Act imposed 5 percent cess on all know-how import payments to create a pool of funds for, inter alia, venture capital activities. Technology Development Fund (TDF) was set up in the year 1987–88, through the levy of this cess on all technology import payments. TDF was meant to provide financial assistance– to innovative and high-risk technological programs through the Industrial Development Bank of India. This measure was followed up in November 1988, by the issue of guidelines by the (then) Controller of Capital Issues (CCI). These stipulated the framework for the establishment and operation of funds/companies that could avail of the fiscal benefits extended to them. However, another form of venture capital which was unique to Indian conditions also existed. That was funding of green-field projects by the small investor by subscribing to the IPO of the companies. In March 1987, Industrial Development Bank of India (IDBI) had become the first to introduce Venture Capital Fund (VCF) scheme for financing ventures seeking development of indigenous technologies/adaptation of foreign technology to wider domestic applications. Thereafter, Industrial Credit and Investment Corporation of India (ICICI) started financing technology-oriented innovative companies. ICICI in association with Unit Trust of India (UTI) formed a venture capital subsidiary called TDICI— Technology Development and Information Company of India— with headquarters at Bangalore, for taking up venture capital activity. Industrial Finance Corporation of India (IFCI) formed Risk Capital and Technology Finance Corporation (RCTC), with headquarters at New Delhi. TDICI is now known as ICICI Venture Funds Management Company Ltd. or ICICI Venture; and RCTC is now known as IFCI Venture Capital Funds Ltd. (IVCF). Their main focus is on development and commercialisation of viable indigenous, often, untried technologies. Almost at the same time, Credit Capital Venture Finance Limited was started in the private sector. This has mobilised funding from global funding agencies, with the joint sponsorship of Commonwealth Development Corporation, London (U.K.), Credit Capital Finance Corporation, Asian Development Bank (ADB) and Bank of India, a public sector bank in India.

Government of India, in November 1988, announced the first venture capital guidelines in the Parliament. These guidelines provided venture financing of technology start-ups, promoted primarily by first generation entrepreneurs. Soon thereafter in 1989, four institutions were selected by the World Bank under its Industrial Technology Development Project to start venture capital activities in different parts of the country. ICICI at Mumbai, Gujarat Industrial Investment Corporation (GIIC) in Ahmedabad, Andhra Pradesh Industrial Development Corporation (APIDC) in Hyderabad, and Canara Bank in Bangalore were selected under this scheme. IFCI at New Delhi, and Infrastructure Leasing and Financial Services Ltd. (IL & FS) at Mumbai were added later under the scheme. These institutions formed separate companies for handling venture capital activity and have been following Government of India guidelines.

The venture capital industry has grown manifold over the last decade and a half. The number of venture capital funds increased from 12 in 1990 to 31 in 1997, and 45 in 2000. The total corpus increased from ₹ 200 crore in 1990 to ₹ 4, 000 crore in 1997 and ₹ 5, 000 crore in 2000. However, there has been almost stagnant growth in the domestic funds, whereas 19 offshore private equity funds have started making investment in Indian companies. From 2001, inflow of venture capital from offshore funds has been quite substantial, after the implementation of the recommendations of the Report of the Working Group on Structure of Venture Capital Funds (VCF), chaired by K.B. Chandrasekhar, an NRI (Non-Resident Indian) from Silicon Valley, U.S.A.

State Bank of India (SBI) and Canara Bank took the lead in promoting venture financing among the public sector banks. SBI Capital Markets, promoted by SBI is operating VCF. Later several PSU Banks started venture financing. From 1996, there has been an increased level of activity in the venture capital industry. More funds have been set up both by existing companies and by new ones in the public and private sectors. There has also been an increased availability of foreign funds for Indian venture capital investments.

World Bank has been instrumental in the development of Venture Capital industry in the country. It provided initial support through providing funds as well as giving international exposure. Further, it contributed in developing manpower resources and networking among venture capital companies in India to foster cohesiveness. This resulted in professionalisation of venture capital companies. The venture capital industry started maturing and in 1992, twelve domestic VCFs formed the Indian Venture Capital Association (IVCA). The association took vigorous steps and influenced Government of India to streamline the guidelines for venture capital industry in the country. The IVCA became the nodal centre for all venture activity in the country. It has built up an impressive database. According to the IVCA, the pool of funds available for investment to its 20 members in 1997 was ₹ 25.6 billion. Out of this, ₹ 10 billion had been invested in 691 projects.

With the liberalisation in economy and financial reforms, several foreign equity funds started investing in India from 1996, more so from 2001. Though venture financing in India is growing, it is still in its infancy.

16.3 Characteristics of Venture Capital

Ideas and innovations, which have potential for high growth but with inherent uncertainties, are financed by Venture capitalists. Further, venture capitalists provide networking, management and marketing support as well. Therefore, venture capital refers to risk finance as well as managerial support. This blend of risk financing and handholding of entrepreneurs by venture capitalists creates an environment particularly suitable for knowledge and technology-based enterprises. Start-ups are seldom funded by venture capitalist. However, a rare combination of product opportunity, market opportunity and proven management may attract venture fund.

Though the fundamental principle underlying the operations of a venture capital fund is "No return without risk; and greater the risk, greater will be the returns", the ultimate aim of the venture capitalist is the same as that of the promoters, that is, the long-term profitability and viability of the invested company. Venture capitalists play dual role; that of strategic advisor and financial partner. In the process, they continuously monitor and evaluate the projects till their exit. As partners, they get involved in the management of the invested unit where they bring expertise and drive which ensures the survival and growth of the enterprise. They, generally, have wider horizon and innovative solutions which maximise the chances of the project success. In India, venture capitalists have followed a broad approach in funding the enterprise. They have supplied funds to new, high risk, not necessarily high tech ventures, and have also extended management, marketing and financial skills to assisted ventures. In the beginning, they supported high tech unproven technologies but with the experience of the first few years, it has been broad based now. They

- expect a very high growth rate in the assisted enterprise;
- bring management and business skills;
- expect medium term gains (5–10 years) and
- do not insist for any collateral to cover the capital provided.

The majority of venture capital funds create their funds under the Indian Trust Act, 1882. The industry has either a two or three-tier structure. In the two-tier structure, an Asset Management Company (AMC) is formed which also acts as a trustee to the funds. The funds are settled as close-ended funds. In the three-tier structure, an asset management company and a separate Trustee Company are formed. The policy guidelines to the AMC for making investments and disinvestments are provided by the Board of Trustees. This facilitates launching of more funds, each with a different objective or focus by the VC companies which normally act as the AMC. Both the structures are very similar to the Limited Partnership Act which is the structure through which VC funds are operated in U.S.A. and the U.K as well. IDBI operated its venture capital activities through a separate division. SIDBI, which also operated VC earlier through a separate division, has formed an asset management company and a Trustee Company in 1999–2000 to operate venture capital activities.

The venture capitalist may invest in an enterprise through different mechanisms, such as equity, quasi-equity, conditional loans and income notes. The equity form of investment is the most desirable form of venture financing, as it reflects an approach of sharing risks and rewards; and does not put any pressure on the cash flow of the company in the initial teething period. Equity contribution from the venture capitalist should be slightly lower than that of the promoters' equity so that promoter feels secure and carries on with innovation and business development. The quasi-equity instruments are converted into equity at a later date. Convertible debentures and convertible preference shares are the convertible instruments. The conditional loan is a misnomer. It is really not a loan because there is no repayment of principal; and there is no interest on such loans. In this instrument, the company pays royalty to the venture capital undertaking that is linked to the turnover, after the unit goes into regular production. This is based on the true concept of sharing risk and reward. Income Notes is a hybrid of simple loan and conditional loan. The outstanding debt carries concessional rate of interest and royalty attached to the turnover.

The most crucial stage in any venture capital investment is its exit from the enterprise. Generally, the goal of the venture capitalist is to sell the investment in a period ranging from three to seven years at a considerable gain. The different possible routes for exit from venture investment or disinvestments or divestment are in the following:

- Initial Public Offer (IPO): The most preferred exit route for a venture capitalist is the IPO. The company can go to the public through stock exchanges.
- Trade Sale: In a trade sale, the venture capitalist sells his/her stake to a strategic buyer, which already owns a business similar/complementary or plans to enter into the target industry. This helps the strategic buyer to produce a synergistic increase in its value. The promoter may or may not sell this stake to the strategic buyer.
- Promoter Buy Back: In this pattern, the promoter buys back the venture capitalist's stake at a pre-determined price. This is not very popular since the promoter as a first generation entrepreneur is hard pressed for money.
- Company Buy Back: In this, the company buys back the venture capitalists stake at a pre-determined price. The company buy back has been recently announced.
- Management Buy Out: In this, the operating management group acquires the business by buying the equity held by the promoters. It usually involves revitalising an operation with entrepreneurial management acquiring a significant equity interest.

16.4 Venture Capital Process

The venture capital model typically works by way of an investment made by investors in a fund (Trust). This fund has a fixed time period of 5 +2 years. The Asset Management Company manages the investments for the trust and charges the fund an annual operating cost of approx. 2.5 percent per annum. To obtain returns from this fund, the AMC invests in several companies. The upside of this whole equation is shared between the AMC and investors approx 25:75 subject to a minimum invested return. Typically, a venture fund may invest in up to 20 companies out of which 10 would fail, four will succeed and 6 may do okay. The venture capital funds do not shy away from risk but manage them by way of a balanced portfolio of investments, focusing on the people and the ideas and mentoring, coaching, adding value to the companies they fund. All new ventures are high risked— there is a significant chance of loss. That is why the expectations of a VC fund are of gaining the typical 300–400 percent returns on investment in each venture. When four out of 20 succeed in the expected manner, the fund is able to obtain more than the type of returns that they had in mind while investing. Table 16.1 shows the expectations that VCs have at different stages of the firm's growth and the investments made.

Table 16.1 Return on investment typically sought by VCs

Stage of Business	Expected Annual Return on Investment	Expected Increase in initial investment
Start up (idea) stage	60%	10–15 x investment
First Stage financing (new business)	40–60%	6–12 x investment
Second Stage financing (development stage)	30–50%	4–8 x investment
Third stage financing (expansion stage)	25–40%	3–6 x investment
Turnaround situation	50%	8 15 x investment

16.5 Angel Investors

Informal investors who invest because of interest in a sector or an offering are angels. There are different types of angels. Angel investors are individuals who are interested in investing in early-stage or startup companies in exchange for an equity ownership interest. Such investors are likely to invest only upon seeing a business plan that indicates clear potential for profit and growth. These investors are often willing to invest in ventures that are too risky for banks or that are not potentially profitable enough for venture capitalists. Nevertheless, angel investors are primarily motivated by a return on their investments. Additionally, angel investors may be willing to invest smaller amounts of money than venture capitalists or other financing resources.

Angel investors can be a good source of advice, guidance, networking opportunities and other financing resources, in addition to their own angel financing. Angel investors tend to invest in businesses they believe in, are interested in, or in which they have experience.

Angel investors are also typically more interested in a business's founders and management team than other investors. And although like other investors angel investors will want to cash out of their investment after a set period of time, that timeframe tends to be longer, typically five to seven years, compared to two to four years for venture capitalists. To asses why do Angels invest the way they do, there are several reasons.

First, angel investors must believe in the business opportunity and know enough about it to become personally committed. Most experienced angel investors will not invest in a venture that is outside their personal realm of experience— unless it is an idea that intrigues them so much that they cannot pass it up. Even then, they will often rely on the expertise of co-investors with whom they have a prior relationship.

Second, angel investors are usually keenly interested in the management team or the founders of the company— who are they and what kind of backgrounds and experience do they bring to the project? Can they implement the company's ideas? Will the angel investor enjoy and feel comfortable working with this group of people? Typically, angel investors do not just want to invest their money— they also want hands-on involvement in the company. Last, is this a business to which they can add value? Do they know enough about the industry to be supportive? And, is this a venture that captures their interest— do they want to invest their personal time in it? Angel investing is as much as lifestyle as it is a business.

There are various types of Angel investors.

Some of these are as follows:

- Corporate Angels
- Entrepreneurial Angels
- Enthusiast Angles
- Micromanagement Angels
- Professional Angels

In India, there are Angel networks in different geographies. One of the prominent networks of Angels is the Indian Angel Network (IAN). The network looks at investing from USD 100,000 to about USD 1 million, exiting over a 3–5 year period through an IPO, M&A or strategic sale. IAN may consider investments over a million dollars but is likely to do so through syndication. Indian Angel Network is India's first and largest Angel network with successful entrepreneurs and high profile CEOs interested in investing in early stage businesses across India, which have potential to create disproportionate value. The Network has invested in multiple sectors as follows:

- Information Technology
- Intellectual Property
- Hospitality
- Mobile
- Education
- Internet, etc.

The network, in addition to money, provides constant access to high quality mentoring, vast networks and inputs on strategy as well as execution. The network members, because of their background are better able to assess the potential and risks at the early stage.

The other is the Mumbai Angels Funding which started in November 2006.It is a unique forum where its members may interact and exchange ideas and knowledge. The Mumbai Angels provides a unique platform to start up and very early stage companies by bringing them face to face with successful entrepreneurs, professionals and executives who are interested in and have the funds available to invest in startup companies.

Many members of Mumbai Angels have prior Silicon Valley experience. In addition to the capital of its members, the Mumbai Angels provides access to high quality mentoring, vast networks in India and abroad and inputs on strategy as well as execution. The Mumbai Angels are interested in a diverse range of sectors including

- IT products and services
- Business Process Outsourcing (BPO)/Knowledge Process Outsourcing (KPO)
- Retail
- Biotechnology and Pharmaceuticals
- Internet
- Media and Entertainment
- Telecommunication, in addition to any other area that interests the members.

The members of the Mumbai Angels typically consider investments of US$ 200,000 to US$ 500,000 and remaining as an investor in the company for a three to five year period prior to an exit pursuant to an initial public offering, trade sale or merger or acquisition. Larger investments may also be considered, although these may be in syndication with other groups of investors.

16.6 How VCs Evaluate Businesses

The precise dynamics of the manner in which VCs evaluate businesses for investment is quite tricky. However, some of the general rules that they follow are as follows:

- Large Market Opportunity, and the venture has demonstrated potential to get to 25 percent of the markets share in 5 years
- Product value proposition
- Competitive edge should be durable
- Team of entrepreneurs— willingness, preparedness, vision

Overall they like to take a more complete assessment of the situation in terms of nature of the proposed business, the economic environment conditions of the proposed industry, proposed business strategy of the entrepreneur to be able to make money, financial information on the proposed business in terms of the economics of the business and how cash flow would happen to achieve a break even and then go on to earn profits, scalability of the venture and the entrepreneur/team characteristics. The entrepreneur/team has to be sound on all fronts of business, willing to take up the challenge and be crazy enough to get to those returns that they have talked about in their plan of things.

Twenty Questions Any Investor would like you to answer (Adapted from Indian Angel Network)

In order to help you prepare, outlined in the following are 20 questions that investors most frequently ask entrepreneurs. Following each, there is a brief explanation regarding what they might be trying to uncover. These questions are not necessarily in the order you will receive them, though the winnowing process was taken into consideration when creating this list.

1. *What is the market potential for your company's product or service offering(s)? What is the revenue potential for the industry, and what is its growth rate?*

Explanation: The investor wants to quickly ascertain whether the opportunity is large enough to pursue. What determines if the opportunity is large enough? Typically, it hinges on whether or not the investor will be able to achieve a healthy return within a designated timeframe (often three to five years). While all firms have different investment criteria, many investors are looking for an opportunity that will yield an ROI of 50 percent or more. To achieve that significant bogy, investors look for companies with considerable market potential for their products or services (often $500 million, $1 billion or more). All investors prefer growing markets to retrenching ones. Also, many investors focus on specific industries, so they will be trying to ascertain whether this deal is within their bailiwick.

2. *How did you calculate market potential? How do you determine industry sales and growth rate?*

Explanation: It is all too common for entrepreneurs to include very large market potential figures in their business plans and then indicate that they require only a miniscule fraction (e.g., one percent) of the market to achieve their revenue projections. These figures are often very suspect. If the company is capturing such a miniscule fraction of the market, then what is so special about it? What is its real value and position relative to the competition? Investors typically prefer companies that are trying to be the leader in a particular segment. Finally, market potential estimates should be supported by independent research as well as bottom-up or top-down calculations.

3. *What makes your business different or unique?*

Explanation: This question can have two wrong answers. That is because a business can be both too common and too unique for a particular investor. If it is too common, the investor will be concerned with the competition and the lifecycle of the business. If it is too unique, the investor will be concerned with the time required to achieve critical mass. Many truly revolutionary products require educating the marketplace, and that can be an uncertain and lengthy undertaking.

4. *Why would someone be 'compelled' to purchase your product or service? What specific needs does it address?*

Explanation: Investors look for businesses with products or services that address a demonstrable market need or demand. Is your product something the buyer needs? Or is it simply something that would just be nice to have? If it falls in the latter category, then it is critical to demonstrate how your product will gain traction, that is, how people will come to demand it based on market trends.

5. *How do you know that your business has high growth potential?*

Explanation: Investors want to know how you 'drew down' your revenue estimates from the market potential figures (which hopefully include estimates from external sources). Ultimately, they want to see a large growth opportunity that scales quickly, thereby allowing them to realise the payoff on their investment as soon as possible. Be prepared to explain in detail the process you used to estimate revenues from market potential.

6. *What is it about your management team that makes them uniquely capable of executing on this business plan?*

Explanation: You have probably heard that the three most important things in private equity investing are management, management and management. More specifically, Investors are typically looking for three things in management:

Experience in building a business, experience in the industry (or with the product) and strong character. What comprises the latter? Investors look for managers who demonstrate high energy or passion, resourcefulness, integrity, perseverance, risk-taking ability and mental horsepower. Also, a frequently overlooked quality is that of humility— for example, sometimes founders may need to step aside and let someone with more experience lead the company.

7. *What are the primary risks facing this opportunity?*

Explanation: Most people tend to think of 'the competition' when people ask them about risks facing their business opportunity. However, competition is only one risk. Other risks include changes or shifts in technology, governmental and regulatory policies, labour market conditions (availability to find qualified labour at a reasonable cost), business climate changes, product liability, computer crime, etc. And, do not forget financial risks. For example, what happens if your current capital doesn't allow you to reach breakeven or your next financing event? A business risk assessment of potential threats to your business can help you prepare for the scrutiny of investors.

8. *Who are your competitors?*

Explanation: You've heard the warning "never say never." When answering the above question, the warning might well be "never say none." There is more to this question than may first be evident. Certainly investors are interested in learning about the extent of competition your business will encounter and how you will distinguish your company. But, they also might be assessing your maturity as a businessperson. The answer "none" is typically incorrect because your business almost always has at least two competitors. Potential buyers could simply continue to function without your product (e.g., through the use a substitute, however less effective) or buyers could "do nothing" (e.g., choose not to utilise the product or service). Furthermore, if the investor is aware of competitors that you have not considered (as many have researched particular segments independently), he/she will lose faith in your business assessment skills— so be prepared.

9. *What gives your company a competitive advantage?*

Explanation: Investors want to know how you plan to outmaneuver the competition -- and this doesn't just pertain to existing competitors. They want to see that you've given thought to future market entrants and how you will stave them off. "First-mover advantage" is rarely a sufficient response to this question. A more effective answer usually depicts intellectual property barriers or the ability to reach the target market in a manner that is more effective than the competition. What is unique about your company that gives it an edge?

10. *Does the company have proprietary intellectual property in the form of patents, trademarks, copyrights, etc.?*

Explanation: What do you own? What can you protect? These are two critical questions. In some industries (e.g., biotech), patents play a critical role in protecting the research and development investments of the company and in helping to ensure that there is a window of opportunity (usually before competitor offerings arrive) for the company to realise a significant share of revenues for a particular category. Trademarks and copyrights are critical to protecting the company's intellectual assets and its "brand." Also, at some point, Investors will also want to ensure that you have taken the proper steps (through non-disclosure agreements, non-competes and/or employment agreements) to ensure that the company is protecting its intellectual capital.

11.   *When will your company break even in terms of profitability and cash flow?*

Explanation: Remember when you first became financially independent of your parents? Your income exceeded your expenses, and you no longer required their support. Hopefully, they didn't have to worry about you as much. The concept here is similar. Once you're financially independent, you are also less of a liability to an investor. Of course, the ultimate goal is to reach an exit scenario quickly. Profitable businesses are more attractive to potential buyers and the public markets.

12.   *How do you plan to acquire customers?*

Explanation: A well-developed business plan includes marketing strategies that demonstrate an understanding of market realities and customer behavior. Investors are looking for much more than a list of your marketing initiatives. You can anticipate questions, such as what are your company's customer acquisition costs? Have you calculated average and target revenue per customer? Do you know how many customers are required to break even? Do you know the product sales cycle?

13.   *How do you plan to keep customers?*

Explanation: The most successful companies seem to have a plan for keeping customers -- even before they acquire them. It is said that it costs five times as much to generate business from new customers as it does from existing customers. Customer retention is critical to the long-term success of most enterprises.

14.   *What drives customer satisfaction for this industry and for the product? Ana, how do you know?*

Explanation: Have you conducted research in order to assess what is truly important to your customers? Do you know what product features are critical vs. those that are ancillary? Once you've acquired customers, you'll need processes to ensure their ongoing satisfaction and your understanding of their changing needs. Have you considered how you're going to support the product and the expenses associated with such support? Will existing customers purchase your product or service again? Will they recommend it to others? Regular and consistent customer feedback is essential in order to obtain the answers to these types of questions.

15. *Who is the end user of the product or service offering?*

Explanation: Is this a consumer-based business, or will you sell your product or service to other businesses? What do you know about the demand for your product or service in that target market? What do you know about the buying habits of your target market? Do you anticipate any roadblocks? For example, will you have to educate the buyer? Also, think about how you can leverage partners or resellers to reach your target markets. Knowing the answers to these questions will be critical when you speak to an investor about your opportunity.

16. *What alliances or partnerships have you entered (e.g., joint ventures, marketing alliances, licensing arrangements, selling/distribution agreements, channel partnerships, software agreements, etc.)?*

Explanation: It is important to remember that alliances can be assets and liabilities. Investors will want to know if any of your alliance agreements have comprised your intellectual property claims and if the company has any outstanding obligations to third parties. On the positive side, you will want to demonstrate how alliances may have helped your company lock-up certain distribution or sales channels for your products and services. Do any of your alliances give you a competitive advantage? Do they create barriers to entry? Do they help you reach customers more efficiently?

17. *What is the anticipated lifecycle of your product or service offering? What are your current and future plans for R&D investments?*

Explanation: All great things come to an end. Products mature, competitors offer substitutes and customers demand change. Have you anticipated when the earnings power of your product will run its course— for first-time buyers as well as for follow-on sales to existing customers (e.g., upgrades)? What are your plans for R&D investments and how will you continue to generate revenues when existing products run their course?

18. *How do you plan to expand your labour force?*

Explanation: While the precise conditions of labour markets change, it is always a challenge to find the best people. Investors will not only be interested in the composition of your existing workforce, but also in how you plan to fill key positions now and in the future. Have you used an executive search firm? Do you have qualified candidates currently under review? How will you compensate people, so as attract, motivate and retain employees while keeping labour costs under control?

19. *What are the probable exit scenarios?*

Explanation: In a successful investment, the two most common exit scenarios are acquisition or IPO, and recently there has been significantly less activity in both of these areas. Investors need to know how they're going to monetise their investment, hopefully at an ROI of 50 percent or more -- so the exit strategy is quite important. As an entrepreneur, you should spend some time thinking about who could acquire your business down the road. Be both realistic (particularly on timing and valuation) and creative regarding M&A possibilities.

20.   *What is the planned "Use of Proceeds"?*

Explanation: Investors want to know that their money is being put to good use in order to directly accelerate the business opportunity, so that they will receive their ROI in a timely fashion. One "no no" is using investments to service existing debt obligations. Be prepared to present a timeline of milestones. Include a breakdown of how the money will be spent and what it will allow you to accomplish.

If you have answers to these 20 questions, you can be confident that you are ready for starting your venture.

16.7 Locating Venture Capitalists

The spread of VC firms in India is not confirmed to one specific location but are located mostly in large metropolitan type of locations. At the same time, there are global firms in this league that operate in India also. A composite list of some of the prominent VC firms in India along with their investment limits and industry focus is presented below in Table 16.2.

Table 16.2 Venture capital Firms in India

Member	Total Fund Size	Types of Financing	Investment Preference	Industry Focus
2i Capital (India) Pvt. Ltd.	NA	1. Early/Stage/Growth 2. Development/ Expansion	1. Less than 10 million	1. IT 2. Computer Software 3. Computer Hardware 4. IT-Enabled Services 5. Biotech
Acer Technology Ventures Advisory (India) Pvt. Ltd.	₹ 260 million	1. Early Stage / Growth 2. Development / Expansion	1. Less than 10 million	1. IT 2. Computer Software 3. Computer Hardware
Baring Private Equity Partners (India) Limited	₹ 2000 million	1. Development/ Expansion 2. MBO	1. Above 200 million	1. IT 2. Computer Hardware 3. Computer Software 4. IT-Enabled Services

Member	Total Fund Size	Types of Financing	Investment Preference	Industry Focus
Canbank Venture Capital Fund Ltd.	I - ₹164.25 million II - ₹105 million III - ₹ 300 million	1. Start Up 2. Early Stage/Growth 3. Development/ Expansion	1. 10–25 million 2. 25–50 million	1. IT 2. Computer Hardware 3. Computer Software 4. IT-Enabled Services 5. Biotech 6. Industries with promising growth potential
Chrys Capital Fund II, LLC	₹ 126.7 million	1. Start Up 2. Early Stage/Growth 3. Development/Expansion 4. Mezzanine	1. 2–5 million 2. 5–10 million	1. Biotech 2. Computer Hardware 3. Computer Software 4. IT 5. IT-Enabled Outsourcing Services
Chrys Capital Fund I, LLC	₹ 63.9 million	1. Development/ Expansion	1. 2–5 million 2. 5–10 million	1. Computer Hardware 2. Computer Software 3. IT 4. IT-Enabled Outsourcing Services
Frontline Ventures	₹ 50 million	1. Early Stage/Growth 2. Development/Expansion 3. Mezzanine	1. 50–100 million 2. 100–200 million	1. Computer Hardware 2. Computer Software 3. IT 4. IT-Enabled Services 5. Media/Retail
HSBC Pvt. Equity Management Ltd. India Liaison Off.	US $ 59.60 million			
ICF Ventures	₹ 750 million	1. Start Up 2. Early Stage/Growth 3. Development/Expansion	1. 50–100 million	1. IT 2. Computer Hardware 3. Computer Software 4. Biotech 5. Consumer 6. Media

Member	Total Fund Size	Types of Financing	Investment Preference	Industry Focus
IFCI Venture Capital Funds Ltd.	₹ 80 million	1. Seed 2. Start Up 3. Early Stage/Growth 4. Development/Expansion 5. Mezzanine	1. 10–25 million	1. IT 2. Computer Hardware 3. Computer Software 4. IT-Enabled Services 5. Biotech 6. Pharma
iLabs Venture Capital Fund	18 crore	Equity	NA	Technology
IL&FS Venture Corporation Ltd.	₹ 2270 million	1. Seed 2. Start Up 3. Early Stage/Growth 4. Development/Expansion 5. Mezzanine 6. MBO	1. 50–100 million	1. IT 2. Computer Hardware 3. Computer Software 4. IT-Enabled Services 5. Telecommunications 6. Biotech 7. Life Sciences 8. Retail 9. Auto Ancillary 10. Engineering
IndAsia Fund Advisors Pvt. Ltd.	₹ 534 million	1. Start Up 2. Early Stage/Growth 3. Development/Expansion 4. MBO	1. 100–200 million 2. Above 200 million	1. IT 2. Computer Hardware 3. Computer Software 4. IT-Enabled Services 5. Biotech 6. Media/Entertainment 7. Distribution/Logistics 8. Communications 9. Life Sciences (including Pharmaceuticals) 10. Companies changing their business paradigm
Industrial Venture Capital Ltd.	7 CR (USD)	1. Seed 2. Start Up 3. Mezzanine	10–25 (USD)	1. IT/Software/Hardware 2. Hi-Tech Printing 3. Construction 4. Textile

Member	Total Fund Size	Types of Financing	Investment Preference	Industry Focus
Infinity Technology Investments Pvt. Ltd.	₹1500 million	1. Seed 2. Start Up 3. Early Stage/Growth	1. Less than 10 million	1. IT 2. Computer Software 3. Computer Hardware 4. ITES
Jump startup Fund Advisors Pvt. Ltd.	₹ 2000 million	1. Start Up 2. Early Stage/Growth	1. 10–25 million	1. IT 2. Computer Hardware 3. Computer Software 4. IT-Enabled Services
Karnataka Information Technology Venture Capital Fund	15 CR (USD)	1. Development/ Expansion 2. Mezzanine	25–150 lakh (USD)	1. IT/ Software /Hardware
Kerala Venture Capital Fund	20 CR (USD)	1. Start Up 2. Early State/Growth 3. Development/ Expansion	25–150 lakh (USD)	1. IT/Software/ Hardware 2. ITES 3. Biotech 4. Tourism
Rajasthan Assest Management Co. Pvt. Ltd.	16 CR (USD)	1. Early Stage/Growth 2. Development/ Expansion	10–25 (USD)	1. IT/Software/ Hardware 2. ITES
Sicom Capital Management Ltd.	₹ 240 million	1. Early Stage/Growth	1. 10–25 million	1. Computer Hardware 2. Computer Software 3. IT
SIDBI Venture Capital Limited	₹ 1000 million	1. Early Stage/Growth 2. Development/ Expansion	1. 50–100 million	1. IT 2. Computer Hardware 3. Computer Software 4. IT-Enabled Services
Walden International	₹ 2100 million	1. Seed 2. Start Up 3. Early Stage/Growth 4. Development/ Expansion	1. Above 200 million	1. IT 2. Computer Hardware 3. Computer Software 4. IT-Enabled Services 5. Biotech

Member	Total Fund Size	Types of Financing	Investment Preference	Industry Focus
Waygate Capital		1. Mezzanine 2. MBO	1. 100–200 million	1. IT 2. Computer Hardware 3. Computer Software 4. IT-Enabled Services 5. Media/Entertainment

❏❏❏

At a Glance

1. USA is the birth place of Venture Capital Industry.

2. Specialised investment firms were later called Venture Capital Firms.

3. Concept of venture capital is relatively new to the Indian economy.

4. Venture Capital is one of the many ways in which growth oriented venture can obtain funds in exchange for certain equity in the venture. Venture capital funding is for supporting innovative ideas and concepts that are new to the context in which they are being presented. Further a venture capital fund is available to those sectors where there is high growth potential.

5. Research and Development Cess Act 1986 introduced in the fiscal budget for the year 1986-87, is the precursor of the concept of venture capital as a new financial service in India.

6. IDBI (Industrial Development Bank of India) has become the first to introduce venture capital fund scheme for financing ventures seeking development of indigenous technologies/adaptation of foreign technology to wider domestic application. Thereafter, Industrial Credit and Investment Corporation of India (ICICI) started financing technology oriented companies.

7. The different possible routes for exit form venture investment or disinvestment or divestments are in the following:
   • IPO
   • Trade Sale
   • Promoter buy back
   • Company buy back
   • Management buy out

8. Informal investors who invest because of interest in a sector or an offering are known as Angel Investors.

Multiple Choice Questions

1. The Network has invested in multiple sectors as follows:
   (a) Only Information Techonogy
   (b) Internet etc.
   (c) Hospitality, Mobile Internet, Education, Intellectual Property
   (d) All the above

2. Angels are interested in a diverse range of sectors including:
   (a) Media and Entertainment
   (b) BPO/KPO, IT product and services
   (c) Retail, Biotechnology and Pharmaceuticals
   (d) All of the above

3. A General characteristic sought by a Venture Capitalist before funding is:
   (a) Team of entrepreneurs- Willingness, Preparedness, Vision
   (b) Only team having vision
   (c) Information technology
   (d) All of the above

Ans. 1. c, 2. d, 3. a

Review Questions

3. Who is an Angel Investor? What are various types of Angel Investors?
4. Angle Network has invested in different sectors- which are these sectors?
5. Name the different range of sectors that Angles are interested in.
6. How venture Capitalists evaluate businesses?
7. Enlist as many questions that any investor would like you to answer.

Bibliography

- Entrepreneurship: A Contemporary Approach, Donald F. Kuratko and Richard Hodgetts, Harcourt College Publication
- New Venture Creation: Entrepreneurship for the 21st Century by J.Timmons and S. Spinelli. Irwin-McgrawHill publications.
- Factors Influencing Women Entrepreneurs of NGOs in India *Femida Handy, MeenazKassam, Shree Ranade*. Departmental Papers (School of Social Policy and Practice, University of Pennsylvania, 2003.
- http://www.123eng.com/forum on Problems of Women Entrepreneurs in India.
- Working Paper Series No. 2005-08-07, Aug 2005, IIM-Ahmedabad: A Reflection of the Indian Women in Entrepreneurial World *Bharti Kollan and Indira J. Parikh*
- N. Roozenburg and E. Eekels (1995) Product Design: Fundamentals and Methods, Lemma, Utrecht.
- M. Tassoul (2006) Creative Facilitation: a Delft Approach, VSSD, Delft.
- W. Gordon (1976) Synectics, The Development of Creative Capacity, Collier, New York.
- G. Wallas (1926, 1970) The art of thought, In: P.E. Vernon (eds.) Creativity, Penguin, Harmondsworth.
- Johnson, David (2001), What is Innovation and Entrepreneurship? Lessons for Larger Organisations, Industrial and Commercial Training. Volume 33. Number 4, pp 135-140
- Choi, David and Valikangas (2001), Pattern of Strategy Innovation, European Management Journal, Vol. 19, No.4, August 2001, pp424-428
- Chatterjee, S. (1998) Delivering Desired Outcomes Efficiency: The Creative Key to Competitive Strategy, California Management Review, Volume 40, Number 2, Winter 1998, pp 78-95
- Govindrajan, V and Gupta, Anil K (2001), Strategic Innovation: A conceptual Road Map: Business Horizons. July-August, 2001, pp3-10
- Venkatararnam and Saravasthy,: Strategy and Entrepreneurship: Outline of Untold Story, in MA HITT, ET, (EDS); Handbook of Strategic Management, Blackwell Business 2001, pp 650-668
- Hitt, M and Ireland, RD, The Inter Saras D, Cross-section of Entrepreneurship and Strategic Management Research, in Donald L. Saxton AND Haans Landstrom (eds): Handbook of Entrepreneurship, Blackwell Business, 2000, pp 45-63

- Mayer, D.G. and Happard, K.A. Entrepreneurial Strategies: The Dominant Logic of Entrepreneurship, in Meyer, G.D. and Heppard KA (editors), Entrepreneurship As Strategy: Competing on the Entrepreneurial Edge. Sage Publications, New Delhi, 2000, pp 1-22

- Eisenhardt, K.A., et al, Competing on the Entrepreneurial Age, in Meyer, G.D. and Heppard . K.A. (editors), Entrepreneurship Management As Strategy: Competing on the Entrepreneurial Edge, Sage Publications, New Delhi, 20000, pp 49-62.

- Amit, R.H. et al, Entrepreneurial Management as Strategy: Competing on the Entrepreneurial Edge. Sage Publications, New Delhi, 2000, pp 83-100

- Drucker, Peter (1998) The Discipline of Innovation, HBR Classic, November-December, 1998, pp 1-9

- Quinn, J.B., (1985), Managing Innovation: Controlled Chaos, HBR, May-June 1985, pp 73-83

- Nonaka, I. and Yamanouchi, T. (1989), Managing Innovation As a Self Renewing Process, Journal of Business Venturing, Vol 4, 1989, pp 299-315

- Bilton, Chris, Strategy as Creativity; in Stephen Cummings and David Wilson (eds) Images of Strategy, Blackwell Publishing, 2003, pp 197-227

- Nemeth, C.J. (1997), Managing Innovation: When Less is More, California Management Review Vol 40, No. 1 Fall, 1997, pp59-74

- Bettis, R.A. and Hitt, M.A. (1995). The New Competitive Landscape, Strategic Management Journal., Vol 16, 1995, pp 7-19

- Frohman, A.L. (1982), Technology as a Competitive Weapon, HBR, January-February, 1982, pp 97-105

- Madan mohan, T.R. (2000), Failures and Coping Strategies in Indigenous Technology Capability Process, Technology Analysis & Strategic Management, Vol. 12, No.2, 2000, pp 179-192

- Abetti, P.A. (2000), Critical Success Factors for Radical Technological Innovation A Five Case Stud, Creativity And Innovation Management, Vol 9, November 4-December 2000, pp 208-211

- Hamel, Gary (1999), *Bringing Silicon Valley Inside*, HBR, September-October, 1999, pp 71-84.

- Bernett Jr., F.W., and Berland, T.P., (1999), *Strategic Thinking on the Frontline*, The McKinsey Quarterly, Number 2, 1999, pp 118-124

- Miles, G.et al (2000), *Entrepreneurial Strategies: The Critical Role of Top Management*, in Meyer, G.D. and Heppard K.A. (editors), Entrepreneurship As Strategy: Competing on the Entrepreneurial Edge, Sage Publications, New Delhi, 20000, pp 101-114

- Raynor, M.E. and Bower, J.L. (2001)., *Lead From The Centre*, HBR May 2001, pp 93-100

- Ghosal, S, et al (2000), "Building an Entrepreneurial Organisation", Managing Radical Change, Chapter 11, Viking, 2000 pp 237-282.

- Hogg, George (1998), *Models and Concepts of Organisational Creativity*, in Peter Cook (ed), Best Practice Creativity, Gower, 1998, pp 61-81

- Kanter, R M (1997) *Restoring People to the Heart of the Organisation of the Future*, in Hasselbein, F., et al (eds), Organisation of the Future, Drucker Foundation Future Series, Josseu-Bass Publishers, san Francisco, 1997, pp 139-150

- Pinchot, Gifford, "Improving Your Climate for innovation" Intrapreneuring in Action, Berret-Koehler, 1999, pp 117-143

- Day, J.D. et al, *The Innovative Organisation*, McKinsey Quarterly, No.2, 2001, pp 21-21

- Cohen, W.S. and Levinthal, D.A., *Absorption Capacity: A new Perspective on Learning and Innovation*, Administrative Science Quarterly, Vol. 35, 1990, pp 128-152

- Websites of the following organisations
  - Ministry of SSI, Government of India
  - www.Entrepreneurs.com
  - NENonline.org
  - State bank of India
  - ICICI bank
  - NSIC
  - IDBI
  - SIDBI
  - http://everydayentrepreneurs.blogspot.com

Subject Index